Rescuing Beefsteak

"You better weigh your own faults before you measure those of others."

Beefsteak Harrison, newspaper interview in 1905

Rescuing Beefsteak

§

The Story of a Pragmatic Pioneer Idealist

2018

Myron Crandall Harrison
PO Box 2758
Jackson, WY, 83001
307.713.0050
myron48@mac.com

ISBN 978-1-7320326-0-6 (hardback)
978-1-7320326-1-3 (paperback)

Contents

INTRODUCTION

Rescuing Beefsteak is a historical biography of an ordinary man, George Harrison, who in 1841 was born to a poor Mormon family in Manchester, England. The Harrison family emigrated to Utah in 1856 as part of the Martin Handcart Company, which suffered greatly from food shortages and exposure to winter weather. George was additionally weakened by malaria, contracted near the Missouri River. About a hundred miles west of Fort Laramie, the fifteen-year-old sneaked away from the failing handcart company in search of food. He spent a winter with an Oglala Sioux family who saved him from starvation.

George Harrison subsequently experienced a number of entertaining pioneer adventures, including as a cook for US Army officers and later at an Overland Stage and Pony Express station. After settling in Springville, Utah, Harrison profited from two decades of freighting and trading. At age forty-two he was able to build a restaurant and hotel. His cooking, augmented by story telling and singing, made him a favorite among "drummers," the traveling salesmen who marketed to retail merchants. Because of the quality of Harrison's porterhouse steaks, the drummers nicknamed him "Beefsteak." His reputation as a cook and entertainer spread beyond Utah.

Harrison's unsolicited celebrity led to a more highly documented life than is typical of men who are not historically significant. Most importantly, Howard R. Driggs, a prominent writer, educator, and western trails activist, took an interest in Beefsteak. Driggs captured Harrison's early adventures in several stories targeted at young readers. George Harrison's later life is pieced together from family histories and contemporaneous news coverage after he attained celebrity.

I try to provide enough information about nineteenth century Utah to give context to Beefsteak's biography. As much as possible, I tell the story from the perspective of Springville. Above all, *Rescuing Beefsteak* seeks to be an entertaining account of one immigrant pioneer's life.

ACKNOWLEDGMENTS

Rescuing Beefsteak is largely an accident. In 2011, about a year after retirement, I came across a yellowed photocopy of a story about my great-great-grandfather, George "Beefsteak" Harrison. My father sent the article thirty years before, at which time I gave it only a cursory read. The story was written by Mae Harrison Smith and Ada Bissell Harrison and published by the Daughters of Utah Pioneers (DUP) in 1953. I assumed the authors were descendants of George Harrison, but knew no more about them.

Recalling only that George Harrison lived with Indians as a boy and was eventually known for his restaurant in Springville, Utah, I started to reread the biography. I was reintroduced to long forgotten subjects including glass blowing, the Mormon "Gathering," handcarts, and the Utah War. Out of curiosity, I went in search of George "Beefsteak" Harrison on the Internet.

Within several months, I accumulated a hodgepodge of newspaper articles and other documents with information about my ancestor. Among them was a Google e-book, *George The Handcart Boy*, authored by Howard R. Driggs. Though shorter, the story was very much like the DUP version that my father sent. Searching on Howard Driggs I learned that he was a prominent writer and educator who first interviewed Harrison in 1909 when the pioneer was almost seventy. The two met and communicated many times thereafter. In 1944-45, twenty-three years after Harrison's death, Driggs published his first account of the pioneer's story as seven installments in a children's magazine.

An early search on George Harrison's brother Aaron Harrison yielded an intriguing story. An article written by historian Curtis R. Allen mentioned Aaron only in two footnotes. The first stated that Aaron was one of four men who abandoned the Martin Handcart Company to join the US Army at Fort Laramie in 1856. Allen pointed out that the following year, Aaron and one other Mormon enlistee deserted the US Army. In another footnote Allen states, "It is a popular belief among many interested parties that Aaron Harrison did not desert but came into the Salt Lake Valley with 'Johnston's Army.'" This minor controversy helped to stoke my interest in Beefsteak and how his descendants captured that history.

Late in 2011, Internet searches were yielding little new information. I travelled to Springville, Utah, the longtime home of George Harrison. At the Pioneer Museum, I found useful histories of the town's early years and genealogies of the Harrison family. Museum staff gave me the name and phone number of Jan Storrs, a great-grandson of Harrison. Jan was both knowledgeable and extremely helpful. He provided DUP biographies of George Harrison's father, mother and wife. Jan also gave me a copy of Driggs' original story, "Handcart Boy," which I had not previously discovered. He introduced me to a highly informative history of the Harrison Hotel. None of these documents were discoverable on the Internet. Jan

Storrs referred me to other descendants of Beefsteak who invariably added stories that I could use.

Among these cousins, George Harrison's great-granddaughter, Barbara Bird Lee, was particularly well informed. A leather suitcase left by Rosella—George's wife—in the attic of the house that Beefsteak built in 1877 passed through the family and was inherited by Barbara in 1970. The suitcase contained a treasure of letters, histories, photos and other memorabilia. Barbara continued to add to the family history. Besides sharing these resources, she served as a dependable sounding board regarding George Harrison and his family.

About the time of my Springville visit, an online search on "Beefsteak Harrison" turned up the Howard R. Driggs Special Collection at the Sherratt Library at Southern Utah University. I learned from director Janet Seegmiller that extensive materials related to Driggs' "Beefsteak" stories were in the collection. I was able to obtain copies of documents that included Driggs' handwritten notes from his first interview of George Harrison, Driggs' first draft of "Handcart Boy," and handwritten letters from George Harrison to Howard Driggs.

Slowly, I began to recognize a wide gulf between the information that I gathered on Beefsteak Harrison and existing biographies of the pioneer—all of which were derived from the account that Howard Driggs wrote for children. By late 2012, I envisioned another history of George Harrison that targeted adult readers, captured Harrison's entire life, and included more historical context. A chance meeting with Ron Barney, then Executive Director of the Mormon History Association, was instrumental. Though fully aware that I had no experience researching or writing history, he encouraged me to write my ancestor's story.

In early 2013, the yield from research was diminishing and I knew I needed to start writing. I decided to force the issue by registering for the Jackson Hole Writers' Conference, which offered the opportunity to submit text for professional critiques. Two months of hard work produced some rudimentary prose, but I benefitted greatly from the evaluations. I returned for three succeeding years, with an increasingly better work product. John Byrne Cook, Jeremy Schmidt, Mark Hummel and Mary Beth Baptiste were especially good teachers.

Individuals in Utah who offered significant comments on *Rescuing Beefsteak* included Sandy Allison, Roger Nielson, Barbara Lee, Daryl Tucker, Janet Seegmiller, Bertrand Kent Harrison, Glenn Bird and Lyndia MacDowell Carter. Lyndia did more than anyone in her detailed attention to my grammar, writing style and historical accuracy. Multiple members of Springville's Historical Society encouraged my efforts. Staffs at the Springville Pioneer Museum, The Springville Library, The Springville Museum of Art, and Springville's Family Search Center assisted my research. The Teton County Library in Jackson, Wyoming, helped with interlibrary loans and provided a comfortable setting for most of my writing.

As an amateur historian, I need to mention the great extent to which Utah's history is made accessible to the untrained. The Utah Historical Society, the Church History Library, and the Daughters of Utah Pioneers libraries and museums are notable. Likewise, Brigham Young University, Southern Utah University, Utah

State University and University of Utah make their library resources available by many different routes, increasingly digitized and online.

Finally, I learned that converting a manuscript into a form required for publishing is a significant chore. I was very fortunate to encounter Bryan Buchanan who helped me through the process.

1

Glass Blowing and the "Gathering"

ven under the best circumstances, a child born in Manchester, England, in the 1840s had no better than a fifty percent chance of living to age five.[1] George Harrison's odds were lessened by an unceremonious entry into the world. His mother, Hannah, who previously lost an infant son, was alone when she began to experience pain. She went to a neighbor's house for help. Nature did not wait, and before Hannah could get back home, George was born on the cobblestone walk.[2] His birth in August 1841 presaged later perilous adventures.

Five years earlier, George Harrison's parents married and moved from the small town of Warrington to Manchester. William Harrison and Hannah Ellis were seeking a better life in the world's most dynamic city in terms of manufacturing, commerce, and social change.[3] William was able to secure a job as a glass blower, a craft he learned in his youth.[4] The large majority of Manchester's population performed manual labor. Many in this "working class" experienced a drop in their standard of living as machines eliminated jobs.[5] Even skilled artisans such as William Harrison lived largely hand-to-mouth.

The quality of life for the working class in Manchester was shown most clearly in the living conditions. Worker housing was small and poorly constructed. Because there was no public transportation, the units were built near factories that burned coal continuously.[6] In *Hard Times*, Charles Dickens wrote that "Coketown," a fictional city based upon Manchester, lay shrouded in haze that appeared impervious to the sun's rays—"You only knew the town was there, because you knew there could have been no such sulky blotch upon the prospect without a town."[7] Nor was there any public sanitation in the smoke-choked city. All forms of waste were found in the narrow streets. "In the most wretched slums a single communal privy might serve as many as forty multi-family dwellings," wrote Richard Altick.[8] He

1. Richard D. Altick, *Victorian People and Ideas* (New York: W. W. Norton & Company, 1973), 44.

2. Myrl Storrs Stewart, "Biography of Hannah Ellis Harrison," July 1957, Daughters of the Utah Pioneers Camp 49, South Company, Weber County. Stewart was a great granddaughter of Hannah Harrison. History obtained from Jan Storrs, Spanish Fork, Utah.

3. Jan G. Harris, "Mormons in Victorian Manchester," *BYU Studies* 27, no. 1, 49.

4. Stewart, "Biography of Hannah Ellis Harrison."

5. E. P. Thompson, *The Making of the English Working Class* (New York: Vintage Books, 1966), 445.

6. Harris, "Mormons in Victorian Manchester," 49.

7. Charles Dickens, *Hard Times*, (New York: Signet Classics, 2008), 17.

8. Altick, *Victorian People and Ideas*, 43.

added that cesspools, where they existed, constantly overflowed. Infectious diseases, including tuberculosis, cholera and typhoid fever, were prevalent in the overcrowded conditions.

Though the Harrisons were working class and poor, they were not in desperate straits. The family's address in the 1851 census was 14 Garrick Street.[9] According to Manchester historian and archaeologist Peter Bone, the area was solidly respectable working class. The conditions were much better than the city's worst slums.[10] Hannah was able to stay home to cook, clean and take care of children, which made the family's life relatively comfortable and nurturing. Years later, George Harrison told Howard Driggs that his father would come home tired from the glass factory, "but he always found good cheer there."[11] He added that his mother worked hard to keep things tidy and clean and always had some good food for him and his siblings. George's recollections of his young life may be somewhat romanticized. Nonetheless, an often-invoked stereotype of Victorian working class life as crippling poverty is not representative of his childhood.

Active participation in church was an important part of the family's life. William and Hannah were probably raised as Anglicans. After moving to Manchester they attended meetings held by missionaries for the Church of Jesus Christ of Latter-day Saints. Hannah was baptized in the Mormon Church in December 1840. William was more measured about conversion to a new religion, but followed in February 1842.[12] The Harrison children gained exposure to reading and music through participation in the Mormon congregation. They also received some formal education. In the 1851 census both Mary Ann and Alice, ages seven and five, are designated as "scholars," a term reserved to children attending school.[13]

George Harrison's father worked at a "smoky old factory" near the family home.[14] George described William dipping his blower into the hot glass and, with puffed cheeks, blowing glass bubbles that he shaped into tumblers, goblets and flasks.[15] By the 1830s the craft of blowing glassware was reserved to expensive leaded crystal, also known as "flint glass." When William took a job in 1836, there were only two flint glass factories in Manchester, one of which was the Manchester Flint

---

9. 1851 England Census, Lancashire, Manchester, Ancoats, district 1jj, p. 25. Available online at https://www.ancestry.com/interactive/8860/30859_A008127-00229#?imageId=30859_A008127-00261 (subscription required). The document shows that William, George and his older brother Aaron were employed at a glassworks.

10. E-mail from Peter Bone, 2012.

11. Howard R. Driggs, *George The Handcart Boy*, Southern Utah University Press, Reproduction of 1952 publication by Aladdin Books, New York. Howard Driggs was a prominent writer who interviewed George Harrison often beginning in 1909.

12. Myrl Storrs Stewart, "Biography of William Harrison," July 1957, Daughters of the Utah Pioneers Camp 49, South Company, Weber County. History obtained from Jan Storrs, Spanish Fork, Utah.

13. 1851 England Census.

14. Driggs, *George The Handcart Boy*, 1.

15. Howard R. Driggs, "Handcart Boy," *The Children's Friend*, Jul 1944, 292. The story was published as seven installments in the children's magazine from July 1944 through January 1945.

The Manchester Flint Glass Works, where George Harrison worked, was similar to this 1850 image of the Falcon Glass House in London.
Courtesy antiqueprints.com

Glass Works on Kirby Street.[16] Contemporary maps show that the Harrisons' home was only a tenth of a mile from the glass works on Kirby.[17]

Labor historian Takao Matsumura, wrote that flint glass artisans worked in teams of four.[18] The most skilled was a "workman" who shaped glass while sitting on a special chair before the furnace. Two assistants helped the blowing and shaping. The fourth member of the team was a boy called a "taker-in." Each weekend a new load of silica and other metals was mixed and heated. On Monday morning liquid glass was ready to be blown and molded. The four-person team, known as a "chair," began the workweek at seven in the morning and shaped glass until one pm. Another chair relieved them and worked until seven in the evening. The first chair returned for another six-hour shift, and at one in the morning the second chair came back. This chaotic "relay" schedule precluded a full night's sleep and mandated living close to the factory. The extreme heat of the glass factories made the six-hour shifts a centuries-old tradition.[19]

16. Peter Bone, "The Glass Industry in Manchester & Salford," *The Journal of the Glass Association* 8, Appendix, "Manchester Glassworks 1800 to 1967" (table), 28. The table shows only two flint glass works in Manchester before 1840.

17. Manchester maps; The neighborhood in which the Harrisons lived and worked is mapped on two "Old Ordnance Survey Maps"—the Ancoats (North) map published in 1848, and the Ancoats map published in 1849. Reproductions of these maps are published by Alan Godfrey Maps, Leadgate, Consett, DH8 7PW, alangodfreymaps.co.uk.

18. Takao Matsumura, *The Labour Aristocracy Revisited; The Victorian Flint Glass Makers, 1850-1880* (Manchester, UK: Manchester University Press, 1984), 33.

19. Ibid., 34.

A Victorian glass house was essentially a dark, high-ceilinged cave in the middle of which was a pit that contained a twenty-ton pile of burning coal. A brick platform over this "furnace" supported eight or ten clay pots containing molten glass at over 2000° F. Openings in the brick structure allowed the workers to access the pots with their blowing tools. The air temperature in front of these openings was measured at 172° F.[20] A number of journalists toured the glass houses in the 1850s. Charles Dickens wrote, "We were aroused by a sensation like the sudden application of a hot mask to the countenance. As we instinctively placed a hand over our face to ascertain how much of the skin was peeling off."[21] In reviewing the journalists' observations, Isobel Armstrong was struck that the writers were reticent to condemn the conditions. She wrote, "*Is this hell?* – is the unasked question. It is never spoken, perhaps because such blasphemy would be too easy and too difficult, genuinely exposing the problem that these furnaces are man-made."[22]

Despite suffocating heat and a disruptive sleep schedule, glass blowing was an elite occupation. An 1849 observer wrote, "Perhaps there is no employment so dependent upon steadiness of nerve, self-possession, and skillful manipulation, as Glass-making."[23] The total number of flint glass blowers in England was about one thousand in 1851, and they maintained an unusually strong union, the Flint Glass Makers Friendly Society. Matsumura points out that the guild controlled entry through an apprentice system and tried to prevent adoption of technology that threatened jobs.

During the 1850s, leaded crystal was a luxury. Demand and production volumes were low, while quality and price were high.[24] However, no one doubted that mechanization would displace artisans in flint glass manufacturing as occurred years before in cheaper "pressed glass" production. Even with his profession still protected, William Harrison's financial situation was frustrating. The average wage of a glass blower in the 1850s was forty-five shillings per week—equivalent to about one hundred and ten pounds British Sterling annually.[25] At least three hundred pounds yearly was considered necessary to gain the security, educational opportunities and social status of the middle class.[26] A good indicator of the Harrison family's precarious finances is that the children were employed in full-time jobs at early ages. Their situation was not unusual. In 1850, sixty percent of ten-year-old working class boys in England were in the labor force, as were many girls.[27]

20. Ibid., 40. Matsumura quotes from the *Children's Employment Commission, Second Report,* 1843

21. Isobel Armstrong, *Victorian Glassworlds* (New York: Oxford University Press, 2008), 27.

22. Ibid.

23. Matsumura, *Labour Aristocracy Revisited,* 70.

24. Bone, "Glass Industry," 27.

25. Matsumura, *Labour Aristocracy Revisited,* 51. Twenty shillings equaled one pound.

26. Susan L. Fales, "Artisans, Millhands, and Laborers: The Mormons of Leeds and Their Nonconformist Neighbors," in Richard L. Jensen and Malcolm R. Thorp, eds., *Mormons in Early Victorian Britain,* (Salt Lake City: University of Utah Press, 1989), 164.

27. David Keys, "Revealed: Industrial Revolution was powered by child slaves," *The Independent,* Aug. 1, 2010. Available online at http://www.independent.co.uk/news/uk/home-news/revealed-

George Harrison was eight years old when he entered the work world as a taker-in at the glass works.[28] At the time in England, many jobs performed by children were characterized as cruel. The taker-in was certainly part of that conversation. The young boys had the same workday as the men—twelve hours divided into two shifts.[29] Their primary job was to carry the goblets and bottles crafted by the workmen to big ovens where the glass was placed to cool off slowly. The takers-in were exposed to the same searing heat as the glass blowers.[30] Matsumura wrote that a taker-in could walk more than thirty miles a day within a glass works, often with as much as three pounds of glass held at the end of an iron stick. Harrison recalled to Howard Driggs that the factory supervisor "boxed his ears" if he dropped a glass on the way to the annealing oven.[31] A contemporary glass maker said, "a man could not do a taker-in's work; it would kill him."[32]

One of young George's responsibilities was a nightly trip on behalf of the plant supervisor, whom he described as "a big burly fellow who was a hard drinker."[33] At about ten pm, George ran to the Brown Cow Inn to pick up a drink order for his boss.[34] The inn was located about a third of a mile from the worksite.[35] The "old keeper" filled a pitcher with porter beer and added lemon and sweetening. He then stuck a red-hot poker into the mix to heat the drink almost to boiling. Harrison ran back to the glassworks with the "Fettled Porter." He told Driggs that if the drink was not just right the boss cracked him on the head.[36] An occasional slap on the head was probably worth the nightly escape from the heat of the glass works.

A taker-in was paid four shillings for the workweek—about ten pounds British Sterling annually.[37] The amount was approximately ten percent of his father's annual earnings. George told Howard Driggs that his family needed the money. He added that becoming a "blower" was a possible future for him.[38] Fortunately, something dramatic changed George's bleak prospects.

---

industrial-revolution-was-powered-by-child-slaves-2041227.html. Keys is quoting historian Janet Humphries.

28. Driggs, "Handcart Boy," Jul 1944, 292.

29. Howard R. Driggs, "Handwritten notes of interview with George (Beefsteak) Harrison," Howard R. Driggs collection, box 17, folder 9, Gerald Sherratt Library, Southern Utah University.

30. Matsumura, *Labour Aristocracy Revisited*, 40, Matsumura quotes from the *Children's Employment Commission, Second Report*, 1843.

31. Driggs, *George The Handcart Boy*, 8.

32. Matsumura, *Labour Aristocracy Revisited*, 40.

33. Howard R. Driggs, "Handcart Boy (First Draft)," box 17, folder 9, p. 4, Howard R. Driggs collection, Gerald R. Sherratt Library, Southern Utah University. This original typed document with extensive handwritten editing has an attached note that reads "First Draft ?"

34. The Brown Cow Inn, located at the corner of Butler St. and Woodward St., was originally licensed in the 1820s and operated until demolition in 1960. Pubs of Manchester: Past & Present. http://pubs-of-manchester.blogspot.com/2013/07/brown-cow-woodward-street.html (accessed 2014).

35. Manchester maps.

36. Driggs "Handcart Boy (First Draft)," 4.

37. Matsumura, *Labour Aristocracy Revisited*, 53.

38. Driggs, "Handcart Boy," Jul 1944, 292.

Hannah and William Harrison and seven children emigrated from Manchester, England, to
Springville, Utah, in the Martin Handcart Company of 1856. Ca. late 1860s/early 1870s.
Copies given to author by Shirley Smith.

In 1856, William and Hannah Harrison decided to emigrate to the United
States as part of the Mormon "Gathering."[39] The LDS Church stated that the
primary purpose for emigration was to satisfy a "first principle" of their faith – the
obligation for the pure of heart "to gather" to Zion (then in Utah) in order to
build the Kingdom of God.[40] Leaders stressed that the second coming of Christ
was imminent and that Gentiles, meaning non-Mormons, would be destroyed.[41]
Only those Saints (as LDS Church members called themselves) living in Zion
were assured of escaping God's wrath.[42] George Harrison later recalled that all the
Saints could talk about in 1856 was getting to Zion. In addition to encouragement
from the pulpit, missionaries frequently visited the Harrison home. George told
Howard Driggs that he always knew when they were coming because his mother
would bake a mincemeat pie.[43]

Besides religious motivation, promoters of the Gathering made exuberant
economic appeals. Every Saint was promised his own land to farm, and the

39. Ibid.

40. Leonard J. Arrington, *Great Basin Kingdom: An Economic History of the Latter-Day Saints,
1830-1900* (Urbana: University of Illinois Press, 2005), 24.

41. Leroy R. Hafen and Ann W. Hafen, *Handcarts to Zion* (Lincoln, NE: Bison Books, 1992),
26.

42. Throughout this book "Utah" is used to refer to both Utah Territory and to the state of
Utah. The territory was created in 1850 from land purchased by the United States from Mexico in
1848. Utah achieved statehood in 1896.

43. Driggs, "Handcart Boy." Jul 1944, 292.

hardships of frontier life were underplayed. "Here, too, we are all rich – there is no real poverty," apostle Parley Pratt wrote from Utah in 1849.[44] During the previous year a substantial number of colonists were suffering hunger pains. Pratt was among those who complained of hunger and claimed to have no milk, meat or butter.[45] The reality was that most of those who gathered to Utah experienced decades of subsistence living due to both the harsh environment and a Church-controlled, communal economy.

Mormon recruiters in England were most misleading when confronted with reports that the LDS Church practiced polygamy in the United States. "The missionaries from America had consistently and vehemently denied polygamy, even when some of them, such as Parley P. Pratt, had more than one wife," wrote historian Polly Aird.[46] At the time that Pratt's denial of polygamy was published in England, he was married to five women. In 1852, at a conference in Salt Lake City, the Mormon Church announced and defended its twenty-year practice of polygamy, which was referred to as "plural marriage" or "celestial marriage." Brigham Young maintained that polygamy was a "domestic issue," relegated by the US Constitution to the governance of state and territorial officials. This "popular sovereignty" argument was identical to the American South's defense of slavery. In stating what seemed to be impossible in 1852, Young wrote, "As for congress, they might as well abolish slavery in the South as plurality in Utah."[47]

A year later, the admission regarding polygamy was printed in the Church's European newspaper, the *Millennial Star*. A Scottish convert wrote that the revelation "fell like a thunderbolt upon the Saints, and fearfully shattered the mission."[48] Church membership in the British Mission plummeted from nearly 33,000 in 1851 to 13,000 in 1859.[49] Most who left were unwilling to embrace polygamy. Many Saints were also offended that their leaders lied to them for decades. Whatever William and Hannah Harrison thought about polygamy, their faith and the desire to emigrate to Zion were more important.

Few English Saints could afford the cost of emigration to Utah. In 1852, a Church program called the Perpetual Emigration Fund (PEF) was made available to Mormons in Europe. The fund offered financial assistance to emigrants who pledged to reimburse the Church when their circumstances allowed. From 1852 through 1855, the PEF delivered increasing numbers of the poor to Zion, while

---

44.　Philip A. M. Taylor, "Why Did British Mormons Emigrate," *Utah Historical Quarterly* 22, no. 3, 257.

45.　D. Robert Carter, *Founding Fort Utah, Provo's Native Inhabitants, Early Explorers, and First Year of Settlement* (Provo: Provo City Corporation, 2003), 53.

46.　Polly Aird, *Mormon Convert, Mormon Defector: Scottish Immigrant in the American West, 1848-1861* (Norman: The Arthur H. Clark Company, 2009), 88.

47.　John G. Turner, *Brigham Young, Pioneer Prophet*, (The Belknap Press of the Harvard University Press, 2012), 204.

48.　Aird, *Mormon Convert*, 88.

49.　Robert L. Lively, Jr., "Some Sociological Reflections on the Nineteenth-Century British Mission," in Richard L. Jensen and Malcolm R. Thorp, eds., *Mormons in Early Victorian Britain* (Salt Lake City: University of Utah Press, 1989), 25.

incurring large debts.[50] Severe drought and cricket plagues in Utah in 1855 caused sharp decreases in food supplies, which led to reductions in tithing and donations to the PEF. Lacking money, many in the Church hierarchy recommended a temporary halt to the PEF's emigration efforts.

Church President Brigham Young was unwilling to interrupt the flow of Saints to Zion. Though the Gathering was promoted as a theological principle, Leonard Arrington pointed out that it was also a program for supplying the laborers needed to build the Kingdom.[51] Young decided that the emigrants could push handcarts rather than use expensive wagons and oxen to carry the food necessary to cross the western plains of America. A well-built handcart cost Church agents in the United States about $20 compared to $220 for a wagon and two yoke of oxen.[52] Many in the PEF leadership questioned the safety of an untested program. Apostle John Taylor, in charge of receiving emigrants in New York City and Boston, was the most outspoken. He wrote, "it looked too much like hard work for men to perform labor that has hitherto only been considered proper for beasts of draught and burden."[53] Taylor eventually gave qualified support to the plan with caveats regarding food, essential supplies, number of ox-driven wagons, and the need for resupply en route. He was particularly concerned about the danger of shoddy workmanship in handcart construction and warned Young, "If the wheels should break down on the road, the company would be ruined."[54]

Young appointed Apostle Franklin Richards, President of the Church's European Mission, to manage the novel experiment. Richards, like his leader, promoted the plan as divinely inspired. In the *Millennial Star*, the apostle prophesied, "When ancient Israel fled from bondage into the Wilderness, they had not even the privilege of taking provisions for their journey, but had to trust to the good hand of the Lord for their daily bread ... The Lord can rain manna [bread] on the plains of America just as easily as He did on the deserts of Arabia."[55] John Jaques, a Church elder from London, wrote for the *Millennial Star* and was equally fervent in his support of God's plan.[56] To his credit, Jaques "ate his own cooking" when he and his family chose to emigrate to Utah by handcart.[57]

Historian Philip A. M. Taylor wrote that motives for emigration differed, but they included personal, family, economic, political, and religious considerations. He

50. Arrington, *Great Basin Kingdom*, 102.

51. Ibid., 97.

52. William G. Hartley, "The Place of Mormon Handcart Companies in America's Westward Migration Story," *The Annals of Iowa* 65, nos. 2 & 3, 109.

53. John Taylor, "*The Mormon* on Handcart Emigration, John Taylor, December 1, 1855" in Sandra Ailey Petree, ed., *Recollections of Past Days; The Autobiography of Patience Loader Rozsa Archer* (Logan: Utah State University Press, 2006), 177.

54. Will Bagley, "One Long Funeral March: A Revisionist's View of the Mormon Handcart Disasters," *Journal of Mormon History* 35, no. 1, 66.

55. Hafen and Hafen, *Handcarts to Zion*, 35.

56. Ibid., 41.

57. Jaques was a member of the Martin Handcart Company. Two of his daughters died during the journey. He wrote the first account of the company's struggles, which was published in installments in the *Salt Lake Daily Herald* in 1878-79.

added that there was also an element of attraction to a new country and repulsion from an old.[58] Forty-one-year-old William Harrison had to consider the challenges of learning to farm in Utah and the risk of an untested handcart plan. He ultimately chose what Wallace Stegner described as "the irresistible double promise of a new start on earth and a guaranteed Hereafter."[59] While the Harrisons hoped for better economic prospects, there is little doubt that the desire to gather in anticipation of the Millennium was very important. Years later, George remembered, "we were willing to stand the jibes and persecution for the sake of what we felt was truth. We were willing even to give up all we possessed, together with our jobs, for the gospel's sake."[60]

Most of the Harrison family was excited when William decided to emigrate to Utah. Only George's brother Aaron voiced concern. His independence is not surprising as he was nineteen and no longer living with the family.[61] George recalled that Aaron was eager to leave his poorly paid job in an iron foundry, but he worried about the difficulty of pushing handcarts across the plains and mountains.[62] After consulting one of the missionaries, George's brother remained skeptical. Reluctantly, Aaron told the family that he would do his part.

Aaron raised another critical issue—the family would spend all their savings for transportation to Iowa City, Iowa, plus the handcart and supplies needed to cross the plains.[63] In 1856 the Perpetual Emigration Fund charged nine pounds per person for the handcart journey to Utah. The Harrisons' total cost, including infant Sarah Ellen at a reduced rate, amounted to seventy-five pounds, well over half of what the family earned in a year.[64] Whether they saved enough to cover the cost of the trip as Aaron suggested, Church records show that William Harrison received PEF assistance.[65] George's father was probably unwilling to lead his family on the uncertain experiment without contingency funds.

British Saints who continuously wished to emigrate oversubscribed the resources of the PEF. In 1856 Brigham Young instructed Church leaders in England, "In your elections of the Saints who shall be aided by the Fund, those who have proven themselves by long continuance in the Church shall be helped first."[66] William and Hannah were on that list. The Harrisons received a letter assigning them passage to America on the ship, *Horizon*, scheduled to depart Liverpool in

---

58. Taylor, "Why Did British Mormons," 253.

59. Wallace Stegner, *The Gathering of Zion: The Story of the Mormon Trail* (Lincoln, NE: University of Nebraska Press, 1992), 222.

60. Driggs, "Handcart Boy," Jul 1944, 292.

61. Aaron's address, 4 Grimes Square, was captured on June 17th, 1855 when he was ordained as a priest. Aaron Harrison, "Membership of The Church of Jesus Christ of Latter-day Saints, 1830-1848," Ancestry database. Available online at http://ancstry.me/2mnmGd0 (subscription required).

62. Driggs, *George The Handcart Boy*, 10.

63. Ibid., 13.

64. Seventy-five British pounds equaled 375 US dollars.

65. Perpetual Emigration Fund (PEF) records of passengers on the *Horizon* show the Harrison family and lists them as PEF sponsored. Mormon Migration database. Available online at https://mormonmigration.lib.byu.edu/.

66. Hafen and Hafen, *Handcarts to Zion*, 31.

late May. George and his family expected an arduous five thousand-mile trip by ship, train and handcart. The mismanaged and deadly journey that followed was probably inconceivable to the most hardened critics of the handcart experiment.

2

Boats, Trains and the Twin Relics

On the evening of their last day in Manchester, the William Harrison family joined a large group of emigrating Saints and friends for a farewell celebration. Church elders gave speeches, which were followed by recitations and singing late into the evening.[1] The Harrisons' journey began the next morning, probably with a walk to Victoria Railway Station, only a mile from their home. The station was filled to overflowing when they arrived. An agent of the Perpetual Emigration Fund (PEF) was present to make sure that all went smoothly. The train's conductor allowed time for a last hymn, after which a cheer went up, and a long blast of the engine whistle signaled departure.[2] Fourteen-year-old George Harrison was probably fascinated by the thirty-five-mile train ride—possibly his first. Another young emigrant who made the same trip in 1850 described the view as the train emerged from a long tunnel that went underneath the city of Liverpool. She recalled, "The sight that met my eyes was wonderful to me, as I had never seen a ship nor the sea; but there I saw the ships for miles along the harbor, and the broad ocean spreading out before me; what a wonder!"[3]

As the Saints detrained, they were shepherded onto a steamer that took them to a Mormon-chartered ship in the harbor. The Church's agents ensured that no one was subjected to the numerous con men and pickpockets who preyed upon naive emigrants. As soon as all were on board, Edward Martin was presented to the Saints for a sustaining vote of approval as president of the emigrant company.[4] Martin's first duty was to divide the ship into eight wards, each overseen by a Church elder. The elders instructed the passengers about expectations for the voyage—up early, prayer meetings twice a day, clean the ship twice a day, and early to bed.

At a time when 250,000 people were emigrating from Great Britain annually, the tiny Mormon fraction became notable for orderliness and good behavior aboard their ships.[5] Charles Dickens wanted to learn first hand whether this reputation was warranted. In 1863, after visiting a ship that was preparing for departure, he praised the Mormons' conduct and aptitude for organization. Dickens wrote that

---

1. John William Southwell, "Autobiography of John William Southwell," in *Liverpool to Boston* (aboard the *Horizon*), Mormon Migration database. Available online at https://mormonmigration. lib.byu.edu.

2. Ibid.

3. Dean L. May, "Rites of Passage: The Gathering as Cultural Credo," *Journal of Mormon History* 29, no. 1, 12.

4. Gustive O. Larson, *Prelude to the Kingdom*, (Boston: Marshall Jones Company, 1947), 130.

5. Ibid.

he boarded the ship "to bear testimony against them . . . to my great astonishment they did not deserve it."[6]

One of the few things that could be described as "lucky" in the six-month history of the Martin company's journey to Utah was their draw of the ship, *Horizon.* The massive vessel was 230 feet long with three masts and three full decks.[7] By measure of its capacity of 1775 tons, the sailing ship was the largest used in the history of Mormon emigration.[8] The *Horizon* was so impressive that its construction in an Ellsworth, Maine, shipyard served as the inspiration for parts of Henry Wadsworth Longfellow's patriotic poem, *The Building of the Ship.*[9] A total of 836 Saints plus crew packed the large ship to the limits.[10] The crowded conditions below deck were typical of "steerage," the least expensive ocean passage.

A day after the emigrants boarded, the *Horizon* sailed a short distance out of Liverpool's harbor into the main stream of the Mersey River. On the morning of May 25, 1856, a local pilot with knowledge of the river's strong currents came on board, as did Apostle Franklin Richards. The *Horizon* was towed twenty miles out to open sea, and the apostle made a final speech before he and the pilot departed on a steamer.[11] The sails were raised, and, within a day, almost every passenger was stricken with seasickness. Most of the ill eventually acclimated to the rolling waves.

Children especially appreciated the open water, the birds that followed the ship out to sea, and the marine life. There were multiple sightings of dolphins and porpoises. George Harrison recalled a whale that came along side and spouted a shower of water.[12] Equally memorable, especially to the young boys, was the *Horizon's* encounter with a large "man-eating" shark described by John Southwell.[13] One of the ship's mates had a Sharps rifle, and a single shot incapacitated "the monster." Another sailor harpooned the shark, which was hoisted onboard. An old whaler estimated its weight at 2,500 pounds. The carcass was cut up and deposited in a large barrel in the ship's hold where chemicals were added to extract valuable "whale oil."

The boys were allowed to explore the large ship from the top deck down to the hold. Harrison told Howard Driggs that they became friends with many of

---

6. Richard J. Dunn, "Dickens and the Mormons," *BYU Studies* 8, no. 3, 7.

7. The *Horizon* is described in an article about the ship building industry in Ellsworth, Maine, in the nineteenth century. Mark E. Honey, "A Dockside View of Ellsworth, When Lumber was King," *The Ellsworth American.* Accessed 2012, No longer available online.

8. "Mormon Emigrant Companies." Available online at http://user.xmission.com/~nelsonb/ship_list.htm. This site gives the size and carrying capacity of all ships that were used for Mormon emigration.

9. Honey, "Dockside View."

10. *Horizon* ship register, roster of Edward Martin Company, 188. *Liverpool to Boston* (aboard the *Horizon*). Mormon Migration database. Available online at https://mormonmigration.lib.byu.edu.

11. John Jaques, "Life History of John Jaques," *Liverpool to Boston* (aboard the *Horizon*). Mormon Migration database. Available online at https://mormonmigration.lib.byu.edu.

12. Driggs, *George The Handcart Boy,* 14-15.

13. Southwell, "Autobiography of John William Southwell."

the crew, who did not mind the lively youths so long as they kept out of the way.[14] Perhaps no one enjoyed the open water and sense of freedom more than George Harrison, who for the previous six years spent most of his waking hours in a glass factory. The sailors fascinated George and his friends as they scrambled up and down the masts and tended the sails. Sadly, the riggings were the source of tragedy for a seven-year-old boy who grabbed a loose hanging rope, somehow swung out over the edge of the ship, and was never seen again.[15] Captain Reed was distraught and wept bitterly.

All meals were prepared in a single large cooking galley on the top deck of the *Horizon*. A young Scot named Henry Hamilton negotiated to be the company's main cook in return for his passage.[16] The PEF assigned three men to assist Hamilton in feeding the more than eight hundred Mormons on board. John Southwell wrote that the food was typically salt beef, salt pork, vegetables, sea biscuits, and often pudding as a side dish.[17] He added that many emigrants had a "goodly supply" of their own more palatable fare.

During one of his tours of the ship, George Harrison ventured alone into the kitchen where he watched "a big mulatto" making pancakes.[18] Pancakes were not on the menu for passengers in steerage, and George probably encountered the man who served the ship's captain and crew. His name was possibly "Jackson," who was listed in the ship's register as a cook and member of the crew.[19] After watching the cook pour out batter and flip the cakes, George asked if he could try. Though it was not easy at first, he learned the trick of watching the batter until it bubbled before turning the pancakes. George later told Howard Driggs that he got his first desire to be a cook while on board the ship.[20]

Ship passengers mentioned one particularly bad storm when the vessel seemed close to capsizing. John Southwell recalled the event as "near being fatal," and some of the old and feeble were felled and remained helpless for several days.[21] On the whole, many Saints characterized the trip as agreeable. Josiah Rogerson wrote that the passage was a beautiful voyage.[22] He added that there was plenty of food and water, and the captain was a fine man who treated the passengers well. The company's head cook wrote, "There was little sickness amongst us. There was 2 marriages, 4 or 5 deaths & 3 or 4 births while on the voyage."[23]

14. Driggs, *George The Handcart Boy*, 14.
15. Southwell, "Autobiography of John William Southwell."
16. *Horizon* ship register.
17. Southwell, "Autobiography of John William Southwell."
18. Driggs, "Handcart Boy," Jul 1944, 292.
19. *Horizon* ship register.
20. Driggs "Handcart Boy," Jul 1944, 292.
21. Southwell, "Autobiography of John William Southwell."
22. Josiah Rogerson, "Autobiographical Sketch of Josiah Rogerson," *Liverpool to Boston* (aboard the *Horizon*), Mormon Migration database. Available online at https://mormonmigration. lib.byu.edu.
23. Henry Hamilton, "Journal of Henry Hamilton," *Liverpool to Boston* (aboard the *Horizon*), Mormon Migration database. Available online at https://mormonmigration.lib.byu.edu.

The thirty-five-day voyage accomplished more than simply transporting George Harrison and his family across the Atlantic Ocean. The organization and discipline on an LDS Church ship made these passages a crash course in "practical Mormonism," according to historian Dean May.[24] He wrote that the trips were agents of cultural change during which Saints came to understand that their survival depended on learning to recognize authority, obey counsel, deny self, and exercise faith in God's care. For the poor and inexperienced city dwellers, surrendering individualism and personal freedom to gain the Church's protection was not a difficult choice.

When the *Horizon* dropped anchor in Boston Harbor on June 30, 1856, the Saints stayed on board for a day while custom officials and medical inspectors fulfilled their duties. Once the ship was docked at Constitution Wharf, the passengers were given the "privilege of going where we was a mind to," according to Heber Robert McBride. He added that all the boys had a good time running all over the town getting into all kinds of mischief.[25] George Harrison was likely in the mix, but all he recalled about Boston was its narrow, crooked streets, filled with hurrying people.[26]

After a day or two, a train of cattle cars was brought up next to the pier for the first leg of rail travel. One Saint speculated that the Mormons were being punished because they were held in low regard.[27] In fact, the PEF negotiated the lowest fare of $10 for adults and $5 for children to travel by rail to Iowa City.[28] The Saints, sitting on their baggage, rode to Greenbush, New York, on the east bank of the Hudson River. They crossed the river by steamboat to reach Albany where another train awaited.[29] The emigrants were upgraded to "third class accommodations"— boxcars with benches that were two-inch wide planks without a seat back. "In this miserable way we were conveyed to Cleveland, Ohio at a very slow pace," wrote Southwell.[30] The pace was slow enough that young men jumped off the train to fill their pockets with fruit from the many orchards along the track.

Cleveland was the scene of parades, firecrackers and artillery—a July 4 celebration that few of the English immigrants understood.[31] A steady rain began, and the Saints huddled in a large barn for the night. A mob showed up and spent hours throwing stones at the barn and yelling anti-Mormon insults. Henry

---

24. May, "Rites of Passage," 40.

25. Heber Robert McBride, "Autobiography of Heber Robert McBride," *Liverpool to Boston* (aboard the *Horizon*), Mormon LDS Migration database. Available online at https://mormonmigration.lib.byu.edu.

26. Driggs, "Handcart Boy," July 1944, 292.

27. Louisa Mellor Clark, "Autobiography of Louisa Mellor Clark," *Liverpool to Boston* (aboard the *Horizon*), Mormon Migration database. Available online at https://mormonmigration.lib.byu.edu.

28. Don H. Smith, "Leadership, Planning and Management of the 1856 Mormon Handcart Emigration," *The Annals of Iowa* 65, nos. 2 & 3, 140.

29. Samuel Openshaw, "Autobiography of Samuel Openshaw," *Liverpool to Boston* (aboard the *Horizon*), Mormon Migration database. Available online at https://mormonmigration.lib.byu.edu.

30. Southwell, "Autobiography of John William Southwell."

31. Ibid.

Hamilton was outside on guard duty and recalled, "men came along & inquired about the number of Saints & talking about polygamy & their hearts as black as hell."[32] The immigrants, including the Harrison family, did not anticipate the unprovoked antagonism. Unknowingly, they arrived in the middle of an unusually vitriolic political campaign during which both leading parties derided Mormons.

The newly formed Republican Party was running its first presidential campaign. The party's platform was based in part upon opposition to slavery, which Democrats continued to support.[33] The trouble for the Saints arose from the Mormon leadership's practice of polygamy—a behavior that most Americans viscerally opposed. The new party cleverly adopted a resolution that "it is both the right and the duty of Congress to prohibit in the Territories those twin relics of barbarism – polygamy and slavery."The "twin relics of barbarism"became the dominant narrative of the 1856 election.[34] In laboring to separate from an association with polygamy, Democrats tried to outdo the Republicans in vilifying Mormons. An example of the rhetoric came from a leading Democrat who described practices in Utah as, "a state of things at which morality, decency, [and] shame revolts." Newspapers were less restrained. The influential *New York Herald* called upon federal troops to "exterminate the Mormons."[35]

Despite their hostile reception in the New World, the Harrison family had more consequential worries. As they departed from Cleveland, the emigrants were thinking about a difficult 1300-mile march while pushing untested handcarts. The Saints also knew that they were behind the conventional schedule for a safe departure to cross the plains. George Harrison recalled his brother Aaron's increasing skepticism about the handcart company's ability to complete the journey in 1856.[36]

The Martin company was delayed an entire day upon reaching the Mississippi River at Rock Island, Illinois. Two months earlier, travelers enjoyed a swift and easy train ride across the river. In the interim, a steamboat pilot intentionally rammed the first bridge to span the Mississippi, causing a fire that destroyed the wooden structure.[37] The Saints took a day to detrain, transport baggage to a steamboat and cross to Davenport, Iowa. The local newspaper captured the passage of the company of pioneers in a pejorative article that typified the country's prevailing stereotype. The reporter wrote, "Eight hundred more of the deluded followers of Mormonism

32. Hamilton, "Journal of Henry Hamilton."

33. Ronald W. Walker, "Buchanan, Popular Sovereignty, and the Mormons: The Election of 1856," *Utah Historical Quarterly* 81, no. 2, 108.

34. Ibid., 120.

35. Ibid., 126.

36. Driggs, *George The Handcart Boy*, 17.

37. David A. Pfeiffer, "Bridging the Mississippi: The Railroads and Steamboats Clash at the Rock Island Bridge," *Prologue Magazine* 36, no. 2. Available online at http://www.archives.gov/publications/prologue/2004/summer/bridge.html.

passed through our city yesterday . . . composed of a class of persons more illiterate, than it seems to us could be scraped together in any portion of this country."[38]

The final train ride, only sixty miles from Davenport to Iowa City, was the worst. George Harrison told Driggs that the newly laid track in Iowa was so bad that it seemed that the Saints were riding on ties. He also recalled that the train had a jerky engine so that women and children were often sent tumbling.[39] By all accounts, the succession of uncomfortable train rides was much less enjoyable than the ocean voyage. Late in the day on July 8, the Saints reached Iowa City, the farthest western extension of rail in the United States. Their campground was three miles west, along the edge of today's University of Iowa campus.[40] Rain began to fall as the Harrisons started walking. They spent the night in soggy bedding.[41] Though anxious about a late start, George and his family eagerly looked forward to pushing handcarts in a few days.

38. Fred Woods, "Iowa City Bound: Mormon Migration by Sail and Rail, 1856-1857," *The Annals of Iowa* 65, nos. 2 & 3, 181. Woods is quoting from an article in the July 9, 1856 edition of the *Davenport Daily Gazette.*

39. Driggs, "Handcart Boy," Jul 1944, 292.

40. William G. Hartley, "Mormons and Early Iowa History (1838 to 1858): Eight Distinct Connections," *The Annals of Iowa* 59, no. 3, 253n85.

41. McBride, "Autobiography of Heber Robert McBride."

3

Handcarts and Prophecies

Daylight at the Iowa City campground revealed a jarring reality—only a few handcarts were available for the emigrants from the *Horizon*. According to Don H. Smith, in 1856 the Perpetual Emigration Fund paid qualified craftsmen in St. Louis and Iowa City to build two hundred handcarts.[1] By the time the Martin company arrived in Iowa City, the first three of the year's six handcart companies were departed with 158 vehicles— nearly all built by skilled wheelwrights.[2] The unskilled emigrants in the last three handcart companies (Willie, Martin and Haven) were forced to build most of their vehicles.

The Mormon handcart was straightforward in design. A shallow box, five feet long and three feet wide, sat on a single axle. At the ends of the axle, five feet diameter wheels were spaced apart the same width as wheels on wagons that travelled the overland trails. Staves that attached to the sides of the box extended about four feet in front with a connecting crossbar that a person or two could push. Depending upon materials, the carts weighed fifty to seventy-five pounds.[3] Out of necessity, the Saints stepped forward and, under the direction of missionary and wheelwright, Chauncey Webb, were soon busy felling trees, planing lumber, and building carts.[4] One pioneer wrote, "If a brother comes in camp and don't catch hold of an axe and cut down a tree for to make hand carts, or break in a pair of oxen, or make himself useful in some way, he is but little respected."[5] Amazingly, the pioneers in the last two companies built their handcarts in only seventeen days. Despite their best efforts, the vehicles were veritable time bombs. Smith wrote that the spokes and wheel rims were probably purchased, but the critical wheel hubs were made on site of green wood.[6] Chauncey Webb complained bitterly that the construction was "penny wise and a pound foolish."[7]

George Harrison recalled the delay in Iowa City as a terribly trying time for his family.[8] A series of rainstorms tested their camping skills. One particularly bad outburst at night nearly washed the family away. Water poured into their light

1. Smith, "Leadership, Planning, and Management," 148.

2. Ibid., 150-52.

3. Josiah Rogerson, "Martin's Handcart Company, 1856 [No. 3]," *Salt Lake Herald*, 27 Oct 1907.

4. Hafen and Hafen, *Handcarts to Zion*, 81n2.

5. James Reese, "James Reese to Bro. Taylor, 29 July 1856," Company Unknown (1856), Mormon Pioneer Overland Travel database. Available online at https://history.lds.org/overlandtravel/sources/8716/.

6. Smith, "Leadership, Planning, and Management," 156.

7. Southwell, "Autobiography of John William Southwell."

8. Driggs, "Handcart Boy," Jul 1944, 292.

EMIGRANTS CROSSING THE PLAINS.

The artist drew this picture of a Mormon handcart company near Fort Des Moines, Iowa in 1856. At that point the pioneers were about 120 miles west of the Iowa City campground. The drawing was printed in *Ballou's Pictorial*, Boston on September 20, 1856. The publisher commented that the striking scene could be relied upon for its fidelity.
Used by permission, Utah State Historical Society.

tent, and George's father and mother worked hard to keep six-month-old Sarah Ellen from drowning.[9] They could not keep a candle burning, and the only way to tell that the infant was alive was by lightning flashes.[10] The family probably placed their tent in a low spot, a mistake that highlighted many skills, small and large, that they were yet to learn. Wallace Stegner wrote of these city folk turned handcart pioneers, "Most of them . . . dumped here at the brink of the West, had never pitched a tent, slept on the ground, cooked outdoors, built a campfire. They had not even the rudimentary skills that make frontiersmen."[11]

In addition to the usual responsibilities of cooking and childcare, the company's women finished sewing large tents that held as many as twenty people. One of the sad activities for some Saints was the need to comply with a limit of seventeen pounds per person of bedding, clothes, and other baggage on the handcarts. After carrying valued possessions from England, many families had to sell them "for a song." The boys in the company, true to form, became acquainted with the nearby countryside, and swimming was the order of the day.[12] George Harrison was probably having fun, though he was worried about the delayed departure.

9. Ibid.
10. Driggs, "Handwritten notes," 4.
11. Stegner, *Gathering of Zion*, 221.
12. McBride, "Autobiography of Heber Robert McBride."

Finally, the day came when the Saints were ordered to pack bedding and food on to the handcarts and "take up the march."[13] Daniel Spencer had authority at the campground and sent the last three handcart companies westward. He knew that the inexperienced pioneers were too late in the year to travel safely to Utah and that the poorly built vehicles created additional danger. Spencer's reckless decision is difficult to understand. Perhaps he assumed that the emigrants would be held at the Missouri River.

The first contingent from the *Horizon* to depart the Iowa City campground was known as the "sixth" handcart company. Jesse Haven, a cousin of Brigham Young, captained the group. Haven's group was smaller than Edward Martin's "fifth" handcart company, which probably allowed them to complete preparations a week earlier. Late in the day on July 22, Haven's company was rushed onto the trail and traveled one mile before making camp. The emigrants sat for a day and moved a few miles on July 24. Captain Haven went back to the main camp in Iowa City the next day, still trying to get all things ready for the journey.[14] When the Haven handcarters moved three miles on July 26, a wagon that held their tents was mistakenly left behind. Rain began to fall, and families sat in a downpour all night. In the morning the emigrants let their captain know what they thought of his leadership. Haven was appalled that he was blamed. He warned the Saints to stop grumbling—otherwise, "sickness would get into their midst and they would die off like rotten sheep."[15] The Haven company's chaotic first week on the trail was not typical of the PEF's usual efficiency.

The Harrison family first pushed their handcart on July 25. Albert Jones and his brother Samuel were at the head of the column. Albert later wrote about his youthful strength and pointed out that he was never sick for the entire journey.[16] However, the Jones brothers were atypical of the Martin company. Josiah Rogerson wrote that they were "the 'cleanings up' of that year's emigration, and comprised the halt, lame, feeble, and from the babe in the arms to the East Indian veteran, Father Wood, aged 86."[17]

The purpose of the Martin party's first day of travel was to allow the Saints to learn to manage the carts. George Harrison later told Howard Driggs that pushing handcarts was not as easy as expected. More than a few toppled over that day, which scattered bedding, foodstuff, pots and pans all about.[18] After supper the pioneers assembled for counsel. Captain Martin repeated the rules learned on the *Horizon*—be up at daybreak; say your prayers; get breakfast over and be moving

13. Driggs, "Handcart Boy," Jul 1944, 292.

14. Jesse Haven, "Journals, 1852-1892, vols. 4-5.," excerpts in Edward Martin Company (1856), Mormon Pioneer Overland Travel database. Available online at https://history.lds.org/overlandtravel/sources/5319/.

15. Ibid.

16. Albert Jones, "Address, 4 Oct. 1906, in Handcart Veterans Association, Scrapbook, 1906-1914," excerpts in Edward Martin Company (1856), Mormon Pioneer Overland Travel database. Available online at https://history.lds.org/overlandtravel/sources/20745/.

17. Josiah Rogerson, "Martin's Handcart Company, 1856 [No. 4]," *Salt Lake Herald*, 3 Nov 1907.

18. Driggs, "Handcart Boy," Aug 1944, 344.

with the caravan by six; be cheerful and helpful; obey your leaders; keep together
for protection; and at night, say your prayers and go to sleep. The next morning the
bugle blew at five, as it would every day thereafter, and the company was on the trail
as the sun came over the hills.

The Harrison family of nine had one handcart, which probably weighed about
fifty pounds. They were limited to seventeen pounds per person of clothing, bedding,
utensils and belongings for adults and half of that for the three youngest children.
Infant, Sarah Ellen, and two-year-old Hannah certainly rode on the cart. The cart's
loaded weight departing the Iowa campground was over two hundred pounds. With
two strong men, William and Aaron, to push the family handcart, the Harrisons
were in a relatively favorable position. Hannah was able to concentrate on her
five daughters. Her youngest son, fourteen-year-old George, was still growing into
manhood and occasionally helped push. On most days he was helping herd the
company's fifty cattle, which, next to flour, were the emigrants' largest source of
food. Herding was a dusty job, but as George told Howard Driggs, "to get a pony to
ride made every boy willing to stand the dust."[19] He added that Bobby Loader was
usually his companion at this cowboy work. Historian Lyndia Carter is not aware
of the mention of ponies by other company members and believes the herding was
likely done on foot.[20] Perhaps Howard Driggs added the ponies to make the story
more attractive to young readers.

The Martin party's first significant day of travel came on July 31 when they
travelled five to seven miles.[21] The going was slow as the novice pioneers received
a rough introduction to frontier life. Carter wrote, "Bare feet would become
toughened, exposed skin would turn leathery with sunburn, and bodies would grow
accustomed to the relentless heat, the choking dust, the sudden thunderstorms, the
cruel humidity, and the strains of uphill tugging and downhill braking."[22] The "trial
run" across Iowa, as Carter refers to the thirty-day trek, was tough enough if the
PEF gave the Saints sufficient food. In fact, the daily food allotment was, at best,
meager. Emigrants in all the handcart parties reported being constantly hungry.
The daily ration—ten to twelve ounces of flour, occasionally supplemented with
small amounts of beef, rice, sugar, coffee and bacon—struck one member of the
Willie Handcart Company as "scarcely worth mentioning."[23]

Some Saints benefitted from the ability to buy food in the small towns and
farms that dotted the trail in Iowa. George Harrison recalled that his father
purchased some extra food in Iowa City and traded for venison near Des Moines.[24]
It is likely that William Harrison made many similar transactions with the money
the family saved in Manchester. Lyndia Carter wrote that Saints without resources

19. Ibid.
20. Personal communication from Lyndia Carter, Springville, Utah, 2014.
21. Lyndia McDowell Carter, "Handcarts Across Iowa: Trial Runs for the Willie, Haven, and
Martin Handcart Companies," *The Annals of Iowa* 65, nos. 2 & 3, 214.
22. Ibid., 191.
23. John Chislett, "Narrative," in T. B. H. Stenhouse, *The Rocky Mountain Saints: A Full and
Complete History of the Mormons* (New York: D. Appleton and Company, 1873), 313-32.
24. Driggs, "Handcart Boy," Aug 1944, 344.

resorted to begging or stealing in order to maintain the strength needed to push handcarts.[25]

Occasionally the Mormon emigrants received the same jeering from Iowans that they experienced during their train ride. Just a week on the trail, the Martin company was greeted with two wagonloads of rough characters looking to start a fight. John Jaques described a stream of western profanity rolling from their tongues, but the visitors failed to provoke the Saints.[26] Another member of the company recalled young hoodlums who went ahead to the next river or creek to ridicule women when they raised their dresses to wade the streams.[27]

As often as the Saints were derided, the handcart companies were treated well by other Iowans, who often sold them food. Elizabeth Sermon wrote, "Some farmer[s] who lived between Iowa [City] and Florence, Neb. would take up the children that had to walk and bring them along for a few miles. Some of the farmers kindly gave the children food to eat."[28] The handcart pioneers also received advice against trying to cross the wilderness west of the Missouri River so late in the year. Samuel Jones recalled that in Newton, a community of farmers, the handcarters were "earnestly entreated" to stay until the next spring, and jobs were offered to the able-bodied.[29] The same message was received when the Saints reached Council Bluffs. A community leader suggested that the Saints stay in Iowa and find work with farmers who needed help harvesting their crops.[30] George recalled that his brother and Samuel Jones were among those who wanted to stay for the winter.[31]

On August 22, 1856, the Martin handcarters were ferried across the Missouri River, a dozen handcarts at a time. The company camped on the outskirts of Florence, now part of Omaha, Nebraska. Many who pushed carts were already exhausted from the 260 miles of relatively good road. In fact, historian Steven F. Faux wrote that the benign Iowa road was the pioneer's last contact with civilization. He added, "Iowans must have viewed handcart Mormons leaving Iowa as also leaving their senses."[32]

The Saints spent a busy two days acquiring flour, cattle and other supplies, as well as trying to repair handcarts. George told Howard Driggs that the wheels, built hurriedly of green timber, were becoming wobbly. Some emigrants tried to soak them with water at night and others tied them with wet rawhide. George added that the wheels only grew worse and caused great delay for the pioneers.[33]

25. Carter, "Handcarts Across Iowa," 196.

26. John Jaques, "Some Reminiscences," *Salt Lake Daily Herald*, 1 Dec 1878

27. Carter, "Handcarts Across Iowa," 215.

28. Elizabeth Whittear [Sermon] Camm, "Reminiscence," in Edward Martin Company (1856), Mormon Pioneer Overland Travel database. Available online at https://history.lds.org/overlandtravel/sources/7526/.

29. Driggs, "Handwritten notes."

30. Driggs, "Handcart Boy," Aug 1944, 344.

31. Driggs, *George The Handcart Boy*, 27.

32. Steven F. Faux, "Faint Footsteps of 1856-57 Retraced: The Location of the Iowa Mormon Handcart Route," *The Annals of Iowa*, Vol. 65, No. 2, 2006, p. 233.

33. Driggs, "Handcart Boy," Aug 1944, 344.

Jesse Haven's "sixth" handcart company crossed the Missouri three days ahead of the Martin company and was prepared to depart Florence on August 23. Apostle Franklin Richards arrived and unexpectedly combined the fifth and sixth handcart companies under the leadership of Captain Martin. Years later, two Saints recalled the reason for the reorganization of the companies. William Binder wrote, "Elder Martin's company now consisted of his own and Captain Haveri [Haven], he having refused to conduct the emigrants any further without he had issued a certain amount of provisions which he deemed necessary for the journey."[34] Another company member said, "It was reported a Brother Leslie [Jesse] Haven declined to obey his [Richards'] command on account of the hardships of the women and children."[35]

The Martin company also learned that two LDS Church wagon trains, the Hunt and Hodgetts companies, would leave Florence after all the handcarters departed. John Jaques wrote that the PEF instructed the ninety ox-driven wagons to stay close to the last handcart party during the overland expedition.[36] This wise decision, which ultimately saved many lives, was a rare demonstration of PEF concern for the safety of the inexperienced handcart emigrants.

The same precaution was not applied to the critical issue of a late departure. Historian Howard Christy wrote that Church leaders warned for years that a May departure from the Missouri River was needed to ensure arrival in Utah before winter storms.[37] Questions about the lateness of the season continued to circulate among the Saints. Franklin Richards called a meeting for the evening of August 24.[38] Four hundred emigrants who made up the Hunt and Hodgetts wagon trains joined more than six hundred members of the enlarged Martin company for the event. Apostle Richards was one of the Church's highest-ranking officials and an enthusiastic architect of the handcart experiment. He had the authority to postpone the reckless departure until spring, but he chose differently. According to Hodgetts company member John Bond, Richards acknowledged that some Saints were fearful of snowstorms in the Rocky Mountains. He then prophesied, in the name of Israel's God, that the handcart company would be protected from all storms, that God would keep the way open, and that they would arrive in Zion safely.[39] Howard Christy observed that everyone in charge of managing the handcart emigration

34. William Lawrence Spicer Binder, "Biography and journal," excerpts in Edward Martin Company (1856), Mormon Pioneer Overland Travel database. Available online at https://history.lds.org/overlandtravel/sources/44069.

35. Camm, "Reminiscence."

36. John Jaques, "Some Reminiscences."

37. Howard A. Christy, "Weather, Disaster, and Responsibility: An Essay on the Willie and Martin Handcart Story," *BYU Studies* 37, no. 1, 11-13.

38. Rogerson, "Martin's Handcart Company, 1856 [No. 3]."

39. John Bond, "Handcarts West in '56," excerpts in William B. Hodgetts Company, Mormon Pioneer Overland Travel database. Available online at https://history.lds.org/overlandtravel/sources/5317.

seemed to accept the comforting idea that "God would 'overrule' the elements sufficiently to assure success irrespective of the degree of risk."[40]

In fact, John Bond recalled two exceptions to the leadership's wishful thinking. Joseph A. Young, Brigham's eldest son, warned that the Martin company would not be able to cross the Rocky Mountains safely because of the freezing weather, higher altitudes and the shortness of food. He continued, "Such would cause untold agonies, sickness and much loss of life . . . my father's agents have lost too much time in starting the Saints to arrive in the valley safely."[41] Chauncey Webb, who oversaw construction of the handcarts at Iowa City, also urged the Saints to winter along the Missouri.[42]

Understandably, Apostle Richards' prophecies were not vigorously contested and most of the emigrants agreed to keep going. Margaret Griffiths captured the prevailing spirit that day, "It never occurred to my young mind being but sixteen years of age, that we should experience ought but joy and happiness on our long pilgrimage to that promised land."[43] George Harrison who turned fifteen on the last day in Florence probably felt similarly. The next morning, August 25, 1856, more than two months after any rationally safe departure from the Missouri, PEF officials sent the naïve and vulnerable Martin Handcart Company into the wilderness.

40. Christy, "Weather, Disaster, and Responsibility," 73.
41. Bond, "Handcarts West in '56,"
42. Rogerson, "Martin's Handcart Company, 1856 [No. 3]."
43. Margaret A. Clegg, "Margaret A. Clegg's Statement," in Edward Martin Company, Mormon Pioneer Overland Travel database. Available online at https://history.lds.org/overlandtravel/sources/15815.

4

"A Killing Business"

Two or three days after departing the Missouri, George Harrison became ill.[1] Nonspecific weakness was probably his only complaint at first, but soon he was burning up, followed by shaking chills. George developed classic symptoms of "intermittent fever," which decades later became widely known as malaria. His parents knew immediately how their son acquired the feverish disease. George, Aaron, and several other boys went swimming one evening during their brief stay in Florence, Nebraska.[2] The boys first considered the Missouri River, but were told that it was too dangerous. Instead, they found a greenish-looking pond near a sawmill. George and his friends splashed around, while putting up with mosquitoes that stung them badly. Everyone cooled off and felt better when they went to bed.

George's fellow swimmer, Tom Wilkins [actually, Wilkinson], developed the same illness.[3] As George and Tom weakened, they were carried in the company's "invalid wagon." Harrison recalled that he was in the wagon for about ten days before he started walking again and he periodically returned.[4] The form of malaria acquired by the boys was likely *Plasmodium vivax*, which was endemic throughout America and rarely fatal.[5] Harrison suffered severe weight loss, probably because of dysentery and diarrhea that often accompanied the sickness. His family was very fortunate that Aaron escaped the illness and was able to continue pushing the handcart.[6] If Aaron was also incapacitated, the Harrisons probably would have encountered disaster. The family was also lucky that the single invalid wagon was not yet overcrowded. A few weeks later, William and Aaron would be required to carry George on the handcart.

Pushing handcarts across Nebraska was considerably more difficult than the "trial run" in Iowa. The emigrant trail along the Platte River was often covered with deep sand. The handcarts were heavier because the PEF distributed 14,000 pounds of flour among the Martin Company's 146 handcarts in Florence. The company's six ox-drawn wagons carried 18,000 pounds.[7] The total of 32,000 pounds of flour

---

1. Driggs, "Handcart Boy," Aug 1944, 345.

2. Ibid.

3. Joseph Thomas Wilkinson, in Edward Martin Company, Mormon Pioneer Overland Travel database. Available online at https://history.lds.org/overlandtravel/pioneers/51081.

4. Driggs, *George The Handcart Boy*, 30.

5. Andrew McIlwaine Bell, *Mosquito Soldiers, Malaria, Yellow Fever, and the Course of the American Civil War* (Baton Rouge: Louisiana State University Press, 2010), 11. A much more lethal form of malaria, *Plasmodium falciparum*, was found only in the Deep South.

6. Driggs, "Handcart Boy," Aug 1944, 345.

7. John Chislett, "Narrative," in T. B. H. Stenhouse, *The Rocky Mountain Saints: A Full and Complete History of the Mormons* (New York: D. Appleton and Company, 1873), 313-32. Chislett

was intended to last sixty days. Most families received a ninety-eight-pound bag of flour on their handcart, though Josiah Rogerson wrote that an additional bag was added to carts pushed by "two able bodied men."[8] William and Aaron Harrison probably qualified for that distinction, which increased their load to over four hundred pounds. A further challenge arose because both wolf and Indian attacks upon the cattle herd were legitimate threats west of the Missouri. Able-bodied men were forced to forego needed sleep to perform guard duty every other night.[9]

However, the most significant change compared with Iowa was the almost complete absence of additional food in the unsettled wilderness. Despite the dramatic increase in work, the company's leaders continued to distribute an inadequate daily allotment of one pound of flour per adult. A pound of flour provides 1600 calories of energy, equal to what an average-sized male at complete bed rest burns in twenty-four hours. The flour was sometimes supplemented with a half pound of beef, which contains about four hundred calories. A man pushing a heavily loaded handcart for ten hours, plus making and breaking camp, could expend four or five times the calories in the PEF's daily ration. Without access to other sources of food, the handcarters catabolized their bodies at a rate of one to two pounds a day. Initially, body fat, which stores 3500 calories per pound, disappeared.[10] Once fat was gone, skeletal muscle and critical organs such as heart and brain were consumed.

Though PEF organizers had no knowledge of calories, common sense dictated that the pioneers would require huge amounts of food to do work historically performed by oxen. Perhaps some of the organizers believed that bread would truly fall from heaven as promised by Franklin Richards. Others may have thought that the inexperienced city dwellers would somehow "live off the land." Some emigrant parties were able to supplement food supplies by shooting buffalo. Josiah Rogerson wrote that Captain Martin and his company's other "shots" occasionally hunted, but without success.[11]

After the Martin Company departed from Florence, Franklin Richards put the Hodgetts and Hunt wagon trains on the trail before he and thirteen missionaries left on September 3, 1856. The "Swiftsure Company" overtook the Martin handcart party four days later.[12] Richards' group rode in four carriages, each pulled by four mules, as were the three wagons that carried provisions and supplies for the missionaries.[13] After a brief visit, the apostle wrote in his report to Brigham Young that the Martin company had "the greater proportion of the feeble

wrote that wagons leaving Florence were loaded with about three thousand pounds of flour.

8. Rogerson, "Martin's Handcart Company, 1856 [No. 4]."

9. Ibid.

10. All figures on calories expended by work, calorie content of food, and calories stored in human tissue are found in standard physiology and nutritional textbooks.

11. Rogerson, "Martin's Handcart Company, 1856 [No. 4]."

12. Franklin D. Richards and Daniel Spencer, "Journey from Florence to G. S. L. City," in Edward Martin Company, Mormon Pioneer Overland Travel database. Available online at https://history.lds.org/overlandtravel/sources/8762.

13. Christy, "Weather, Disaster, and Responsibility," 62n37.

emigrants." He added that they were in excellent spirits and good health.[14] Many of the handcarters were worn out even before leaving Florence. Perhaps, Richards wrote what he believed his leader wanted to read.

Five days later, John Chislett saw the "grand outfit of carriages and light wagons" come into the Willie company camp.[15] The Swiftsure Company stayed the night. In the morning, Richards "gave us plenty of counsel to be faithful, prayerful, obedient to our leaders, etc." wrote Chislett. The apostle repeated his prophecy that God would open the way through any storms and promised that the emigrants would be resupplied with provisions and bedding at Fort Laramie. Before departing, Captain Willie, at the request of the missionaries, killed the company's fattest calf for Richards' party. Chislett later wrote, "I am ashamed for humanity's sake to say they took it. While we, four hundred in number, traveling so slowly . . . with our mixed company of men, women, children, aged, sick, and infirm people, had no provisions to spare . . . these 'servants of God,' took from us what we ourselves so greatly needed and went on in style with their splendid outfit."[16]

Years later when John Jaques wrote the first account of the Martin Handcart Company, he stated that drawing a heavily-loaded handcart was "a killing business."[17] That reality was already clear by the time the company reached Fort Laramie on October 8. Jesse Haven, who drove a wagon for the Hodgetts company after his demotion in Florence, saw the handcarters for the first time in six weeks. He wrote to Brigham Young, "In Bro- Martin's handcart Comp—that is now camped near us there has been between 20 and 30 deaths since they left Florence and are now dying daily. I understood 3 or 4 died yesterday. They are truly a poor and afflicted people, my heart bleeds for them."[18]

In a cruel replay of the Church's failure to provide dependable handcarts in Iowa City, no food awaited the starving Saints at Fort Laramie. Families such as the Harrisons who had money or goods to trade were able to obtain some provisions at high prices. John Jaques sold his watch for thirteen dollars and bought biscuits, rice, bacon and other supplies at the fort's sutler store.[19] Some of the emigrants tried to trade with nearby Indians, but the natives had no food to spare. Albert Jones found a willing trading partner—"I sold an extra over-coat at Laramie to one of the cooks for some dried Peaches, apples and a little bacon and some flour."[20]

While the Martin company was camped near Fort Laramie, Josiah Rogerson was among a party of men who went to the fort with ten handcarts to pick up

14. Richards and Spencer, "Journey from Florence to G. S. L. City."

15. Chislett, "Narrative." 319.

16. Ibid.

17. John Jaques, "Some Reminiscences," *Salt Lake Daily Herald*, 19 Jan 1879

18. Jesse Haven, "Haven, Jesse, to Brigham Young, October 9, 1856, Fort Laramie," in Edward Martin Company, Mormon Pioneer Overland database. Available online at https://history.lds.org/overlandtravel/sources/86089.

19. John Jaques, "[Diary]," excerpts in Edward Martin Company, Mormon Pioneer Overland Travel database. Available online at https://history.lds.org/overlandtravel/sources/7540.

20. Albert Jones, "Autobiography," excerpts in Edward Martin Company, Mormon Pioneer Overland Travel database. Available online at https://history.lds.org/overlandtravel/sources/7543.

buffalo robes.[21] When Franklin Richards visited the fort two weeks earlier, he purchased one hundred robes for "the P. E. Fund passengers in the rear."[22] Rogerson wrote that the robes were distributed the next morning "judiciously and with general satisfaction."[23] Robert Loader told Howard Driggs that his family might have frozen if his folks did not buy two robes at Fort Laramie. George Harrison remembered that his father did the same.[24] George and Robert probably did not realize that Richards paid for the robes. The important point in their recollections was how critical the bedding was to their families' welfare. Rogerson agreed when he wrote that the robes saved many lives.[25]

The three companies of the US Army's 6th Infantry stationed at Fort Laramie were well below full strength in 1856. Rogerson wrote, "Inducements and persuasions were offered and made to numbers of our young men to enlist . . . The comfortable adobe quarters, and the snug and warm log rooms were quite tempting for a winter's rest, with plenty to eat."[26] The Martin company travelled seventeen miles on October 10, and that night, four men, including Aaron Harrison, walked back to Fort Laramie to enlist in the army.[27] Aaron's decision is not surprising given his early and ongoing skepticism concerning the handcart experiment. Though his lack of trust in those managing the handcart emigration was justified, the abandonment of his family placed them in a perilous situation. George told Howard Driggs that his brother's decision shocked the family. Hannah pleaded with Aaron not to leave.[28] In *George The Handcart Boy*, Driggs introduced a description of Aaron's departure, in which he portrays the decision as inconsequential.[29]

As the Martin company continued west of Fort Laramie, the difficulty of pushing handcarts increased dramatically. The roads were broken, rocky, and difficult to travel, according to Elizabeth Kingsford.[30] Carts were breaking and causing great delay. Mary Ann and Alice Harrison, twelve and ten years old, were helping William push the family's handcart. George could only stagger along. Howard Driggs later wrote that Patience Loader volunteered to take Aaron's place at pushing the Harrisons' cart.[31] In fact, Patience was the strongest member of the Loader family and was fully employed with their problems. Sandra K. Petree, who edited Patience Loader's autobiography, states that the idea that she took

21. Josiah Rogerson, "Martin's Handcart Company, 1856 [No. 5]," *Salt Lake Herald*, 10 Nov 1907.

22. Richards and Spencer, "Journey from Florence to G. S. L. City."

23. Rogerson, "Martin's Handcart Company, 1856 [No. 5]."

24. Driggs, "Handcart Boy," Aug 1944, 345.

25. Rogerson, "Martin's Handcart Company, 1856 [No. 5]."

26. Rogerson, "Martin's Handcart Company, 1856 [No. 4]."

27. Ibid.

28. Driggs, "Handcart Boy," Aug 1944, 380.

29. Driggs, *George The Handcart Boy*, 36. Driggs' portrayal of Aaron's regrettable decision was probably the result of pressure from George Harrison's descendants.

30. Elizabeth Horrocks Jackson Kingford, "[Reminiscences]," excerpts in Edward Martin Company, Mormon Pioneer Overland Travel database. Available online at https://history.lds.org/overlandtravel/sources/7550.

31. Driggs, *George The Handcart Boy*, 36.

over for Aaron is implausible.[32] Possibly, Loader and others occasionally helped the Harrison family over particularly difficult parts of the trail.

Several days west of Fort Laramie, John Bond observed from the Hodgetts wagon train that many of the Saints were walking barefooted and in clothing that was badly worn.[33] George was among the many hiking without footwear. He told Howard Driggs that his father purchased enough shoes for the family's journey, but had nothing to grease the leather. The shoes became dry and "galled the feet." Harrison finally threw his last pair away and went in stockings that soon wore out.[34] George recalled that it was sometime after Fort Laramie that his sickness finally left—"It had nothing left to live on, I guess."[35] He added, "I could hold my hands up to the sun and see the bones through my skin."

As the work increased, the daily rations were cut. "First, the pound of flour was reduced to three-fourths of a pound, then to a half pound, and afterwards to still less per day," wrote Elizabeth Jackson.[36] George remembered that his daily ration was two ounces of flour—enough for a small biscuit.[37] Many of the Saints stopped trying to bake the scant flour and ate it as a gruel or dry powder.[38] Deaths accelerated, and wolves began "following the trains making their monotonous howlings in all directions a hideous sound to the ears," wrote Bond.[39]

The Martin Handcart Company reached Deer Creek, near present-day Glenrock, Wyoming, on October 17. The next morning, Captain Martin called a meeting and said that the company needed to travel faster as winter was near. He directed the Saints to discard every piece of unnecessary luggage—including extra clothing and bedding.[40] John Jaques recalled that good blankets and other bedding and clothing were burned, though needed more than ever as four hundred miles of wilderness remained.[41]

While the fire burned on the morning of October 18, George Harrison made a decision that undoubtedly saved his life. He slipped away from his family to hide in the willows that bordered Deer Creek.[42] George did not discuss the plan with his family—probably because he feared they would talk him out of it. Distracted by the fire and the rush to break camp, no one noticed the young man's absence. George staggered east while thinking he might get to his brother at Fort Laramie. He was able to walk no farther than an Indian camp about a mile back on the trail.

---

32. Personal communication from Sandra K. Petree, Jan 2012.

33. Bond, "Handcarts West in '56."

34. Driggs, "Handcart Boy," Sep 1944, 390.

35. Driggs, "Handcart Boy (First Draft)," 7.

36. Kingford, "[Reminiscences]."

37. Driggs, "Handcart Boy," Sep 1944, 390.

38. Elizabeth Wright Andrews, "Reminiscences," excerpts in Edward Martin Company, Mormon Pioneer Overland Travel database. Available online at https://history.lds.org/overlandtravel/sources/13352772994137629278.

39. Bond, "Handcarts West in '56."

40. Driggs, "Handcart Boy," Sep 1944, 390.

41. Jaques, "[Diary]."

42. Driggs, "Handcart Boy," Sep 1944, 390.

Harrison later recalled that he went to the nearest tepee where an Indian boy about his size was standing in front.[43] He started speaking in English, forgetting that the boy would be unable to understand. The puzzled Indian paused a moment before running into the tepee. George followed and found an Indian mother and half a dozen children staring in astonishment. In the middle of the tent was a kettle in which something was cooking. George pointed and asked for food. The Indian woman looked at him pityingly and heaped up a plate of boiled buffalo meat. Harrison finished the first plate and reached for more. The squaw heaped his plate a second time, and the starving boy quickly devoured the food. George wanted more, but the Indian mother motioned for him to go. As Harrison turned to leave, he passed out and fell into a pile of buffalo robes where he remained for the night.

The next morning there was word of a "white skeleton" in camp.[44] Every Indian mother came with something to feed George. He remembered that they had mostly meat—antelope meat, buffalo meat and even dog meat, which the Indians thought was the most delicious. As Harrison continued to gorge himself, a French trapper arrived. He was the husband of the squaw who first fed the starving boy. Upon seeing George's emaciated condition and the amount of meat he was consuming, the trapper yelled at him to stop eating or George would kill himself. Harrison later admitted to Howard Driggs that it was a wonder that he lived to tell about it.[45]

The Martin handcarters travelled almost twenty miles the day they departed Deer Creek.[46] Only after the Harrisons made camp did they realize that George was missing. Hannah became frantic. Possibly that night, but likely the next morning, William left to backtrack and look for his son.[47] On the morning of October 20, he walked into the Indian camp and wanted to take his son back to the handcart company.[48] George recalled his difficulty standing up. William wanted to carry his son, but the trader addressed him as "old man," and said that he could hardly carry himself. The Frenchman told William to leave his son for the winter, and that the Indians would treat him well. His father agreed that George was in no condition to continue travelling.[49] George's father was able to buy a few supplies, including some jerked buffalo, from the trader. After giving his blessing to George, he started back west to rejoin his wife and daughters.

Without William, Hannah and the girls continued with the handcart party on October 19, 1856, which was remembered as the worst day in the Martin company's history. The emigrants arrived in mid-afternoon at a crossing on the North Platte

43. Ibid.

44. Ibid.

45. Driggs, "Handcart Boy," Sep 1944, 391.

46. This assumes that the company covered about same distance that the Willie company did when they departed Deer Creek on October 9. Paul D. Lyman, *The Willie Handcart Company* (Provo: BYU Studies, 2006), 139 and map 62.

47. Ibid.

48. Ibid.

49. Ibid.

Winter storms that struck the Martin Handcart Company were brutal, but in no way early or unseasonal.
Used by permission, Utah State Historical Society

River near where the restored Fort Caspar now stands. The Saints watched the Hodgetts wagon train finish fording to the north bank. John Bond was able to look back and see the handcart emigrants from his wagon. He wrote that rain and sleet started just as the Saints arrived at the opposite bank. Many of them were exhausted and reluctant to cross so late in the day. Captain Tyler, astride his mule, told everyone to have faith in God, and they would not take cold.[50]

The width of the ice-filled North Platte River was over two hundred yards. Weaker Saints were carried off their feet by the strong current. A number of men made multiple trips carrying helpless emigrants across the river. Mary Ann and Alice were perhaps able to ford without assistance, but someone else must have pushed the Harrison family's handcart through the treacherous current. Patience Loader and her sisters experienced a near tragedy. Loader wrote, "we started to cross the river and pull our own cart the water was deep and very cold and we was drifted out of the regular crossing and we came near being drowned the water came up to our arm pits poor Mother was standing on the bank screaming . . . several of the brethren came down the bank of the river and pulled our cart up for us."[51]

The storm intensified into a blizzard as the soaked Martin company emerged from the river. The Saints stopped briefly for supper and then pushed their handcarts another one or two miles looking for a better campsite.[52] Historian Howard Christy estimates that the wind chill was fifty to seventy degrees below

---

50. Bond, "Handcarts West in '56."
51. Petree, ed., *Recollections of Past Days*, 73.
52. Rogerson, "Martin's Handcart Company, 1856 [No. 5]."

zero.[53] The pioneers' wet clothing froze. As night fell, the frozen tents could not be raised. The Saints crawled under the stiff, icy material to gain some protection from the wind.[54] Many lacked adequate bedding because it was discarded and burned at Deer Creek. Presumably Hannah and her daughters still had the family's two buffalo robes. A dozen people died that night. Over the next four days the Martin company struggled to travel eight miles. Deaths continued, and the victims increasingly included men who were strong and healthy when they left Florence, Nebraska. Elizabeth Kingsford's thirty-two-year-old husband was typical. He demonstrated the classic signs of starvation before dying. She wrote, "his ambition was gone, all attempts to arouse him to energy or much active exertion were futile."[55]

Children also died from the work of pushing handcarts. Samuel Jones told Howard Driggs about the death of a fourteen-year-old boy a day or two after the last crossing of the Platte. "During the blizzard in the uplands, Charley Twelves, a fine young man, was struggling to pull his cart . . . I saw him drop between the shafts and called to his father and mother . . . All we could do for our loved Charley was to make a grave in the snowdrift . . . It was just cold storage for the wolves."[56]

The Martin company was probably camped near Red Buttes by the time William Harrison rejoined his family. He was able to tell Hannah that he found George and believed that their son was in good hands with an Indian family. As William and Hannah Harrison looked over the snowbound camp, they probably feared for their five daughters. Louisa Mellor remembered, "We all gathered around and held a meeting, praying God to help us, as we knew it was him alone who could deliver us from death."[57]

The handcart company's exhausted pioneers could only chip out shallow graves in the frozen ground. John Bond recalled, "Loved ones in the early morn [would] see them scratched up by large gray wolves and eaten, a skull bone here, a leg, hip, and arm bone on the hills in a bloody condition in the snow."[58] The Saints did not fail for lack of faith or courage. Grueling work and lack of food defeated them. The final insult to many of the handcarters was hypothermia. However, well before the first encounter with winter storms on October 19 while crossing the Platte River, the Martin company was an inhumane manmade disaster. As described by company member Samuel Jones, the expedition was "one long funeral march."[59]

53. Christy, "Weather, Disaster, and Responsibility," 41.

54. Petree, ed., *Recollections of Past Days*, 74

55. Kingford, "[Reminiscences]."

56. Howard R. Driggs, "Theirs Was the Handcart Way to Zion," *The Instructor* 91 (July 1956), 203.

57. Louisa Mellor Clark, "History of Louisa Mellor Clark," excerpts in Edward Martin Company, Mormon Pioneer Overland Travel database. Available online at https://history.lds.org/overlandtravel/sources/18557.

58. Bond, "Handcarts West in '56."

59. David L. Bigler, *The Forgotten Kingdom; The Mormon Theocracy in the American West, 1847–1896* (Spokane: The Arthur H. Clark Company, 2005), 113. Bigler references Orson F. Whitney, *History of Utah* (George Q. Cannon and Sons, 1904), 4:297.

5

Rescued and Forgotten

Franklin Richards led his well-fed and comfortable entourage into Salt Lake City on October 4, 1856, twenty-nine days after departing the Missouri. The first three handcart companies arrived ahead of Richards. The early companies experienced no winter weather, were not burdened by faulty handcarts, and benefitted from resupply of food on multiple occasions. Though exhausted and hungry, they suffered no unusual mortality. The Church reported, "The companies with handcarts have been wonderfully successful thus far ... One fact is established—that the Saints can cross the Plains almost without means."[1] Richards surprised everyone in Salt Lake City with the unwelcome news that the experiment was not complete. He announced that the Willie and Martin handcart companies were somewhere west of the Missouri. The next day, the Church President changed the agenda of a previously scheduled semi-annual Church conference to a single topic, "many of our brethren and sisters are on the plains with handcarts ... the subject matter for this community is to send for them and bring them in before winter sets in."[2]

Brigham Young called upon the Church's bishops to immediately assemble mule teams, wagons and twelve tons of flour. He asked for volunteers to drive the wagons, and asked the women for blankets, stockings, shoes and clothing. "Otherwise," Young told the 12,000 Saints in attendance, "your faith will be in vain ... and you will sink to Hell."[3] The response to Young's call was overwhelming. Over the next two months nearly three hundred rescuers drove east into the mountains with hundreds of wagons full of supplies collected from every community in Utah. The contribution from the small town of Springville was typical. "Every available team in our village was called into requisition; freighted with warm blankets, plentiful supplies, and rushed by forced drives to rescue the unfortunates," wrote historian Don Carlos Johnson.[4]

At the front of the volunteer army was the "advance rescue party," made up of twenty-seven men charged to make contact with the Willie and Martin handcart companies. They were a seasoned group, which included first-rate scouts and frontiersmen. Historian Rebecca Cornwall wrote, "Some were considered rather rough company by local citizens—they drank, swore, and occasionally wrestled in the streets—but in the rescue effort they would justify their place in pioneer Utah society."[5] The lead party, under the command of George D. Grant, departed from

1. Hafen and Hafen, *Handcarts to Zion*, 90.
2. Ibid., 120.
3. Ibid., 121.
4. Don Carlos Johnson, *History of Springville* (Springville: Art City Publishing, 2003), 39.
5. Rebecca Cornwall and Leonard J. Arrington, *Rescue of the 1856 Handcart Companies*

Salt Lake City on October 7, with sixteen wagonloads of food and supplies. Five hundred miles to the east, the exhausted and starving Martin Handcart Company neared Fort Laramie.

The advance rescuers, on dry roads with wagons pulled by horses rather than oxen, traveled quickly. On the fifth day they camped at Fort Bridger, where some expected to find the Willie company. Three days farther east, Daniel W. Jones wrote, "Our hearts began to ache when we reached the Green River and yet no word of them."[6] When the company reached the Big Sandy River without contact, some rescuers believed that the handcart companies stopped somewhere for the winter.[7] Grant proceeded, and on the east side of South Pass his company was overtaken by a severe winter storm—the same one that struck the Martin company a day later as they crossed the North Platte. For their own safety, the rescuers were forced to go into a sheltered camp.[8]

On the evening of October 20, James Willie, captain of the fourth handcart company, rode into Grant's camp. He was a day or more ahead of his party—a last effort to find help. The next day the advance rescuers covered twenty-six miles of snow-packed trail and found what looked like an Eskimo village.[9] What they encountered "would stir the feelings of the hardest heart," wrote Daniel W. Jones.[10] He continued, "Babies and children were crying from hunger, while their parents were gaunt and apathetic. Some were obviously dying and others had limbs that were frozen black and rotting."[11]

Grant left a few rescuers and six wagons of food with the Willie company and continued east in search of the year's last handcart company. Six days of bitter cold and snow-covered trail brought the rescuers to Devil's Gate. Finding no sign of the Martin company, Grant sent an express of three riders eastward with instructions to "not return until the immigrants were found."[12] Joseph A. Young, Abel Garr and Daniel W. Jones rode the company's best saddle horses and led a pack mule. Mid-afternoon of the second day the express riders found the Martin company camped on the North Platte River near Red Buttes. John Bond, in the nearby Hodgetts wagon train camp, described the approaching riders, "three men on horses driving another slowly in the deep crusted snow, and the wolves were howling in all directions."[13] Cheers, laughter and tears spread throughout the camp. While the horsemen brought no food or blankets to distribute, they brought hope to the Saints, including William, Hannah and their daughters.

(Provo: Charles Redd Center for Western Studies), 10.

    6. Daniel W. Jones, *40 Years Among the Indians* (Springville: Council Press, 2004), 42.

    7. Howard K. Bangerter and Cory W. Bangerter, *Tragedy and Triumph; Guide to the Rescue of the 1856 Willie and Martin Handcart Companies* (Provo: MC Printing, 2006), 27.

    8. Jones, *40 Years Among the Indians*, 42.

    9. Cornwall and Arrington, *Rescue of the 1856 Handcart Companies*, 13.

    10. Jones, *40 Years Among the Indians*, 43.

    11. Cornwall and Arrington, *Rescue of the 1856 Handcart Companies*, 13.

    12. Ibid., 17.

    13. Bond, "Handcarts West in '56."

The rescuers went through the camp telling the Saints that supplies were three days to the west. Patience Loader wrote, "they came to our fire seeing us out there, br. Young ask how many is dead or how many is alive. I told him I could not tell, with tears streaming down his face he ask where is your captains tent."[14] After conferring with Edward Martin, Young ordered that the flour ration be increased to one pound, and that the few remaining cattle be killed and eaten. Loader wrote, "we felt quite encouraged we got our flour and beef before night came on and we was all busy cooking and we felt to thank God and our kind brothers."[15]

Reenergized by a good meal and the promise of a resupply of food ahead, the company moved their camp the next morning. William, Mary Ann and Alice were pushing the family's handcart. The train was strung out for more than three miles on a steep and muddy trail. Daniel Jones was using his horse to help pull the laggards.[16] After two difficult days, the Saints reached Willow Creek. Deaths continued, but no one had the energy to keep track. Patience Loader later captured William Whittaker's last night. His death exhibited the neurological destruction that characterized terminal starvation. Loader wrote, "there was a young woman sleeping and she was awoke by poor Br. Whiticar [Whittaker] eating her fingers. He was dying with hunger and cold, he also ate the flesh of his own fingers that night."[17]

Captain Grant reached the Martin company on October 31 at Greasewood Creek.[18] The rescuers did not have enough food to increase the Saints' rations, but they were able to give many of them either a blanket, a pair of shoes, socks, or a coat. Twenty-four days after departing from Salt Lake City, the advance rescue company turned westward.[19] Though the youngest children and sickest emigrants were carried in wagons, most of the exhausted pioneers were still pushing handcarts. Hannah was along side the Harrisons' cart, checking frequently on her three youngest daughters. Possibly, she was one of the fortunate recipients of shoes from Grant's inadequate supplies. If not, she was still leaving bloody footprints in the snow, as later recounted by her great-granddaughter.[20]

At Devil's Gate, frigid winds kept the Saints from moving for two days. Food supplies were dangerously low, and the rescuers were in as much peril as those they came to save. Daniel W. Jones recalled, "We were at a loss to know why others had not come on to our assistance."[21] Grant asked Joseph A. Young to carry a letter to his father, Brigham, in Salt Lake City. He wrote, "You can imagine between five and six hundred men, women and children, worn down by drawing hand carts through

14. Petree, ed., *Recollections of Past Days*, 76.
15. Ibid., 77.
16. Jones, *40 Years Among the Indians*, 46.
17. Petree, ed., *Recollections of Past Days*, 79.
18. Hafen and Hafen, *Handcarts to Zion*, 228.
19. Cornwall and Arrington, *Rescue of the 1856 Handcart Companies*, 21.
20. Stewart, "Biography of Hannah Ellis Harrison."
21. Jones, *40 Years Among the Indians*, 47.

snow and mud; fainting by the way side; falling, chilled by the cold; children crying ... I think that not over one-third of br. Martin's company is able to walk."[22]

To escape the wind at Devil's Gate, the rescuers decided to move the handcart company to a sheltered location in a nearby range of granite hills. The day is remembered as the second most difficult in the Martin company's history. Historian Chad Orton wrote that for much of the morning of November 4, the wind-chill factor was well below zero.[23] About noon, a lull in the gale enabled the handcart company to travel two miles to a crossing on the Sweetwater River. The river was only two feet deep and forty yards wide but was choked with sharp-edged ice. Recalling their disastrous crossing of the North Platte, most of the Saints lacked the will to proceed.[24] Even Patience Loader, as psychologically strong as any Utah pioneer, did not want to enter the water. She wrote, "when I saw this Stream of water we had to go through I felt weak and I could not keep my tears back, I felt ashamed to let those brethren [rescuers] see me shedding tears."[25] Orton wrote that at least eighteen of the advance rescue team assisted the Saints in crossing the river.[26] One brother took the Loader family's cart across, and others carried the girls. When Patience tried to thank one of the "mountain boys" he said, "Oh damn that ... We have come to help you." Patience and her mother decided that they were all kind-hearted, good men, but "rather rough in their manners."[27]

Able Saints were still expected to wade and push carts as hundreds of the pioneers needed help while daylight was disappearing.[28] The strong team of Samuel and Albert Jones was an example of the difficulty of the crossing. William Binder recalled, "After I had crossed I again went in the stream and assisted Bros. S. S. and Albert Jones out of the water they being fast in the bed of the River and perfectly discouraged so that they could not pull an ounce."[29] William Harrison and his daughters undoubtedly needed help to push their handcart across the Sweetwater.

The camp was in a sheltered hollow—a location now known as Martin's Cove. The handcart party remained there for five days with the flour ration back down to four ounces a day. A rescuer wrote on November 6, "Colder than ever. Thermometer 11 degrees below zero."[30] One night almost every tent was blown down. Starvation and hypothermia continued to claim lives. Eight-year-old John Kirkman later recalled. "Upon awakening one morning, I found my father James Curtman [Robert Lomax Kurtman], and my infant brother with fifteen others frozen to death. Little Jimmy, my two year old brother, had his feet frozen so badly

---

22. Hafen and Hafen, *Handcarts to Zion*, 258.
23. Chad M. Orton, "The Martin Handcart Company at the Sweetwater: Another Look," *BYU Studies* 45, no. 3, 16.
24. Ibid., 5.
25. Petree, ed., *Recollections of Past Days*, 83.
26. Orton, "Martin Handcart Company," 12.
27. Petree, ed., *Recollections of Past Days*, 83
28. "Orton, "Martin Handcart Company," 15.
29. Binder, "Biography and Journal."
30. Hafen and Hafen, *Handcarts to Zion*, 22.

that one half of each came off."[31] Thirty-four-year-old Robert Kirkman was one of many previously healthy young men who died of starvation.

Captain Grant made a difficult decision that saved the lives of many Saints. "Upon awakening He ordered the Hodgetts and Hunt wagon trains, camped nearby at Devil's Gate, to unload all nonessential freight. Many of the eighty-seven wagons were freed to carry fatigued and frostbitten handcarters, as well as their tents, bedding, and other essentials. On November 9, the weather improved enough that the advance rescuers led survivors westward.[32] All but a few pioneers left their handcarts at Martin's Cove. William and his two oldest daughters were still walking, while Hannah Harrison was probably in a wagon with her youngest daughters. The food supply was essentially gone. Men who pushed heavy carts for months while eating the PEF's insufficient food rations, continued to die. John Jaques observed their neurological degeneration, "the manliness of tall, healthy, strong men would gradually disappear, until they would grow fretful, peevish, childish, and puerile, acting sometimes as if they were scarcely accountable beings."[33]

No one in the Martin company seemed less likely to die from exhaustion and starvation than forty-six-year-old David Blair. He was a branch president of the LDS Church in London. More impressive to the young boys, Blair was a member of the elite, mounted Life Guard assigned to protect Queen Victoria.[34] Albert Jones wrote, his "grand physique and gigantic frame was the admiration of us boys of the London branch, whenever he attended meetings in his regimentals."[35] Blair pulled three children and the family's supplies on his cart, with occasional help from his wife.[36] Jones recalled that he dwindled down to a wreck, and that his wife drove him around camp with a willow to make him fetch wood or water.[37] When the once proud soldier finally dropped, he was probably wearing his regimental coat. Forty years later, his wife still possessed the coat as well as the sword given to him by his captain in the Queen's Guard.[38]

Two days west of Martin's Cove, a lone rider, Ephraim Hanks, came into the company's camp leading two mules packed with freshly killed buffalo meat. More importantly, he brought news that five or six wagons of flour were waiting near South Pass.[39] Grant sent a group of rescuers to bring the wagons east. On November 12, seventy-nine days after departing the Missouri, the Martin company experienced

31. Mary Chase Finley, *A History of Springville*, Art City Publishing, Springville, Utah, Third Printing, 1992, p. 25

32. Cornwall and Arrington, *Rescue of the 1856 Handcart Companies*, 24.

33. Jaques, "Some Reminiscences," *Salt Lake Daily Herald*, 5 Jan 1879,

34. Lynne Watkins Jorgenson, "The Mormon Handcart Disaster: The London Participants," *Journal of Mormon History* 21, no. 2, 178-79.

35. Jones, "[Reminiscences]."

36. Petree, ed., *Recollections of Past Days*, 77.

37. Jones, "[Reminiscences]."

38. 1891 *History of Harrison County Iowa*, Find a Grave website, Deborah Jane Bushnell Blair Chapman available online at https://www.findagrave.com/cgi-bin/fg.cgi?page=gr&GRid=873 64164.

39. Cornwall and Arrington, *Rescue of the 1856 Handcart Companies*, 25.

its first significant resupply of food.[40] Hanks also told Grant that additional rescue teams were delayed by nearly impassable trails. In fact, believing that the emigrants in the Willie and Martin companies as well as Captain Grant's company probably perished, most of the rescue parties decided to return to Salt Lake City.[41]

Hanks did not yet know that Brigham Young, having learned of the disgraceful retreat, sent a group led by Hosea Stout to turn around the rescue wagons.[42] With that accomplished, Stout's party continued eastward, picking up a few companies that stayed the course. When Stout, leading thirty wagons, met Grant's rescue company at South Pass, all of the Martin company survivors were able to ride in wagons.[43] One of the rescue parties included Joseph Tickle Ellis, Hannah Harrison's younger brother.[44] Ellis was searching for Hannah at a camp when she went up to him saying, "Don't thee know thy sister?" Hannah was too emaciated to be recognizable.[45]

With all of the emigrants stowed in horse-drawn wagons, the rescue party was able to travel twenty-five miles or more in a day. "There was no appreciable mitigation of the piercing cold, but its intensity rather increased," recalled John Jaques.[46] Light wagons used as ambulances hurried ahead of the rescue train carrying critically ill patients, mostly small children. Rebecca Cornwall wrote, "Of the remainder of the company, two or three more died each day while the survivors, except for a sturdy few, could no longer act for themselves."[47]

The burden of taking care of Saints who were suffering from starvation and frostbite injuries was daunting. Sometimes the duty fell to a family member, as in the case of Elizabeth Sermon, who earlier buried her husband near Devil's Gate. Soon after, she was trying to salvage the frostbitten feet of her six-year-old son. "I had to take a portion of Robert's feet off – portions that were decaying. I severed the leaders [tendons] with some scissors I carried by my side. Little did I think when I bought them in old England, they were bought for such a purpose. Every day some portion was decaying and had to be removed, until the poor boy's feet were nearly all gone."[48] Ephraim Hanks performed the same horrible duty for many victims. He washed damaged tissue with water and castile soap until the frozen parts would fall off and then severed shreds of flesh from the remaining limbs with his scissors.[49]

According to John Jaques, the coldest night came on the Big Sandy River on November 20. He described the experience as "a most searchingly cold night . . .

40. Hafen and Hafen, *Handcarts to Zion*, 225.
41. Cornwall and Arrington, *Rescue of the 1856 Handcart Companies*, 25.
42. Ibid., 29.
43. Hafen and Hafen, *Handcarts to Zion*, 226.
44. Bangerter and Bangerter, *Tragedy and Triumph*, 91.
45. Stewart, "Biography of Hannah Ellis Harrison."
46. John Jaques, "Some Reminiscences," *Salt Lake Daily Herald*, 22 Dec 1878.
47. Cornwall and Arrington, *Rescue of the 1856 Handcart Companies*, 31.
48. Camm, "Letter."
49. Ephraim Hanks, "Ephraim K. Hanks' Narrative." Edward Martin Company, Mormon Pioneer Overland Travel database. Available online at https://history.lds.org/overlandtravel/sources/97569.

impossible to get warm sleeping in a wagon."[50] A few days later, storms dumped four feet of snow on the Wasatch Mountains, creating drifts as deep as twenty feet across the trail.[51] Brigham Young sent his son, Joseph A. Young, to lead a party to open the trails. The frontiersmen spent days driving ox-teams and wagons back and forth to pack the snow and, when necessary, used shovels to clear the drifts.

The Church President was in the Salt Lake Tabernacle on Sunday, November 30, as the survivors of the Martin company were brought down Emigration Canyon. Young told the assembled Saints to go home and prepare to give the new arrivals something to eat, and wash them and nurse them up. "You know that I would give more for a dish of pudding and milk, or a baked potato and salt, were I in the situation of those persons who have just come in, than I would for all your prayers."[52] Six months after departing Liverpool, the wasted company arrived on the east side of the temple grounds. If the rescue directed by Young was delayed a week, few in either of the last two handcart companies would have survived.[53] Willie Handcart Company survivor, John Chislett, wrote in 1873, "Brigham Young did all that man could to save the remnant and relieve the sufferers. Never in his whole career did he shine so gloriously in the eyes of the people."[54]

Nonetheless, many of the survivors were in terrible condition. John Jaques recalled that there was no joy among those who were there to meet the Martin company, and, "Some were so affected that they could scarcely speak."[55] A reporter for a New York newspaper was present and wrote, "When they reached here there were not 50 in the train who could help themselves; the rest were stowed in the bottoms of the wagons which had been sent for them, ragged and filthy beyond conception; helpless and despairing they could or would not get out of the wagons to attend to the calls of nature, and if the weather had not been intensely cold it would have bred a pestilence."[56] A young girl in the Martin company watched the scene from inside her wagon. Years later she wrote, "President Young met us, and when he saw us he was so melted down with grief at sight of our condition he had to go home sick."[57]

A month before the Martin company survivors arrived in Salt Lake City, news of the suffering of the handcart companies was filtering back to the valley. The Saints were murmuring that Brigham Young and his counselors were to blame. Young

---

50. Jaques, "Some Reminiscences," 22 Dec 1878.

51. Cornwall and Arrington, *Rescue of the 1856 Handcart Companies*, 32-33.

52. "Remarks," *Deseret News* [Weekly], 10 Dec. 1856, in Edward Martin Company, Mormon Pioneer Overland Travel database. Available online at https://history.lds.org/overlandtravel/sources/8543.

53. Christy, "Weather, Disaster, and Responsibility," 52.

54. Josiah Rogerson, "Martin's Handcart Company, 1856 [No. 10]," *Salt Lake Daily Herald*, 8 Dec 1907.

55. John Jaques, "Some Reminiscences" 22 Dec 1878.

56. "Latest from Utah. Death of an Eminent Mormon Saint. Hand-Cart Trains in a Wretched Condition," *New York Semi Weekly Tribune*, 27 Feb. 1857, in Edward Martin Company, Mormon Pioneer Overland Travel database. Available online at https://history.lds.org/overlandtravel/sources/15915.

57. Clark, "History of Louisa Mellor Clark."

initiated an aggressive campaign of damage control before he knew the location or condition of the year's last handcart party.[58] On November 2, the Church's three highest officials went before the congregation in the Tabernacle. First counselor Heber Kimball impugned the character of anyone who questioned the Church's leadership. Young followed and ascribed responsibility for the disaster to Franklin Richards and Daniel Spencer, who quietly accepted their scapegoat roles. Second counselor Jedediah Grant delivered a white-hot sermon in which he blamed the victims.[59] Historian Gene Sessions wrote that for Grant, "the death and suffering of the hapless handcart Saints resulted from the same disobedience and sinfulness that had induced spiritual sleepiness among the people already in Zion."[60]

As the full scope of the tragedy emerged, the Church promoted the idea that reports were exaggerated. *The Deseret News* reported, "as was to be expected they [the Willie and Martin companies] have suffered considerably from storms and inclement weather, and several have had their feet and hands more or less frosted."[61] Starvation was not mentioned and severe frostbite injuries including amputations were dismissed. In a letter to a number of national newspapers, Brigham Young wrote "the relief so promptly, freely, liberally, and timely sent from here was so blest in rescuing them, that but few comparatively, have suffered."[62]

At least on the surface, the Church's effort to downplay the handcart tragedies worked well. Lyndia Carter wrote that a shroud of silence came down for many years.[63] A local Saint, George Hicks, wrote, "I remember well our leaders telling us that we were to say nothing about the handcart failure for if we did, God would curse us."[64] As importantly, many of the handcart pioneers were inclined to move on. John Jaques wrote that the affair was "one of those disagreeable things that people tacitly agree to forget."[65] William Harrison was certainly disillusioned with the mismanagement of the handcart journey, but there was little reason to dwell on the experience. His energy was best spent learning to make a living from the soil.

No accurate count of the deaths in the Martin company is possible as records are poor. Lyndia McDowell Carter references estimates of deaths that vary

58. Jedediah M. Grant, "Discourse," *Deseret News* [Weekly], 12 Nov. 1856, in Edward Martin Company, Mormon Pioneer Overland Travel database. Available online at https://history.lds.org/overlandtravel/sources/8827.

59. Ibid.

60. Gene A. Sessions, *Mormon Thunder: A Documentary History of Jedediah Morgan Grant*, 2nd ed. (Salt Lake City: Greg Kofford Books, 2008), 299.

61. "Arrival," in Edward Martin Company, Mormon Pioneer Overland Travel database. Available online at https://history.lds.org/overlandtravel/sources/8748.

62. "Arrival of the Hand-Carts at Great Salt Lake City," in Edward Martin Company, Mormon Pioneer Overland Travel database. Available online at https://history.lds.org/overlandtravel/sources/8884.

63. Lyndia McDowell Carter, "The Mormon Handcart Companies," *Overland Journal* 13, no. 1, 14.

64. Polly Aird, Jeff Nichols and Will Bagley (eds.) *Playing with Shadows, Voices of Dissent in the Mormon West* (Norman, OK: The Arthur H. Clark Company), 157.

65. John Jaques, "Some Reminiscences," *Salt Lake Daily Herald*, 19 Jan 1879, 1

George Harrison with Patience Loader at her home in Pleasant Grove, Utah, in 1918. Photo taken by Howard Driggs. The two pioneers first met as members of the Martin Handcart Company and probably crossed paths at Camp Floyd.
Courtesy Gerald R. Sherratt Library, Southern Utah University

from 135 to 200.[66] Perceptions of those who survived the catastrophe may be as illuminating as the actual numbers. Louisa Mellor remembered, "a goodly number died; some were frozen to death and others were with frozen hands and feet. Only about one-half of our company survived to reach Salt Lake Valley."[67] Patience Loader recalled, "our provisions would not have lasted as long as they did had all our brethren and sisters lived, but nearly half the company died and caused our provisions to hold out longer."[68] Little is known about the extent of amputations and other frostbite injuries, but journals and autobiographies indicate that they were numerous. Probably, two-thirds of the more than six hundred emigrants in the Martin company either died or suffered permanent injury. By anyone's estimate, the disaster caused the greatest loss of life suffered by an emigrant company in the country's history of overland travel.

Understandably, the courage of the handcarters and the heroism of the rescue, including Young's leadership, are enduring narratives of the Martin Handcart Company. However, the PEF's decision to allow the inexperienced Saints to cross the wilderness late in the year, and the failure to provide adequate food and well-built handcarts should not be ignored. Young's successor as President of the

66. Carter, "Mormon Handcart Companies," 13.
67. Louisa Mellor Clark, "A Record Given at Spring Lake," excerpts in Edward Martin Company, Mormon Pioneer Overland Travel database. Available online at https://history.lds.org/overlandtravel/sources/1855.
68. Petree, ed., *Recollections of Past Days*, 77.

Church, John Taylor, wrote, "I knew of the weakness and infirmity of many women, children and aged persons that were calculated to go, [but] I did not consider that a few dollars were to be put in competition with the lives of human beings."[69] Years later, the always-faithful John Jaques described the bitter experience as "cruel to a degree far beyond the power of language to express, and the more so for the reason that the worst parts of the experience were entirely unnecessary, because avoidable by timely measure and more sagacious management."[70]

---

69. Hafen and Hafen, *Handcarts to Zion*, 90.
70. Jaques, "Some Reminiscences," 19 Jan 1879.

6

Springville and the Timpanogos

Few of the Martin company survivors were able to care for themselves when the rescue company arrived at Temple Square. In some cases, relatives were present to meet immigrants and take them to their homes. For others, Brigham Young alerted bishops to send teams to transport pioneers to the territory's communities. Within an hour, members of the handcart company were claimed by or assigned to someone.[1] The Harrisons were carried fifty miles south to Springville, a town they probably never heard of when they left Manchester.

Springville historian Don Carlos Johnson, who was nine years old at the time, recalled that the Harrisons were among those who recovered on the first floor of Bishop Aaron Johnson's home.[2] Johnson wrote, "All during the winter of 1856-57 the large rooms in the Johnson home were filled with the weary toilers, who had pushed and pulled the handcarts with their scanty fare, from the Missouri river ... how wretched was the appearance of the remnant of that company, as they rested their gaunt frames upon the floors of the Johnson home."[3]

Hannah Harrison did not fully recover from frostbite to her feet. She experienced difficulty and pain with walking the rest of her life.[4] Sarah Ellen Harrison was a victim of Hannah's malnutrition—"When her baby nursed, instead of getting milk it would get blood."[5] The infant lived for a few months after arriving in Springville and was buried in the town's "Historic Cemetery."[6] William Harrison and the other daughters suffered no permanent physical injury. The family's relative good fortune was certainly enabled by William's ability to buy food during their handcart ordeal. However, the funds, which they would have used to get started in the New World, were largely gone. The Harrisons were able to move out of the bishop's home and into the community about the beginning of April 1857. Hannah delivered her last child, Martha, in 1858, when as she later recalled, the family did not have a chair to sit on.[7]

---

1. Cornwall and Arrington, *Rescue of the 1856 Handcart Companies*, 35.
2. Johnson, *History of Springville*, 16.
3. Ibid., 39.
4. Stewart, "Biography of Hannah Ellis Harrison."
5. Ibid.
6. Driggs, "Handwritten notes," 28. Springville's original cemetery was established in 1851 at 300 West on 400 South and is known as the "Historic Cemetery." There is no record of the location of Sarah Ellen's burial within the cemetery. The Harrisons were extremely poor in 1857, and likely buried their daughter in the equivalent of a "potter's field." In 2012, a headstone recognizing Sarah Ellen was placed near the graves of her parents, William and Hannah, in the original Springville cemetery.
7. Ada Bissell Harrison, "Biography of Hannah Ellis Harrison," Camp Aaron Johnson, Daughters of the Utah Pioneers of Utah County, Springville, Utah.

Photo of Aaron Johnson's home in Springville, Utah, ca. 1858. The large space on the first floor was used for meetings, dances, and some religious functions. Handcart survivors, including William Harrison's family recovered on the first floor during the winter of 1857-58. Multiple wives stand in front of the home.
Courtesy, Springville/Mapleton Daughters of Utah Pioneers

If any of the Harrisons were well enough to sit up when their rescue wagon approached Springville, their first impression was of a large earthen wall that surrounded the village. The fort was the result of years of hostilities with the indigenous Indians. Those conflicts were the most salient feature of life for early settlers in what came to be known as Utah Valley. The contested ground was a valley defined by the largest natural fresh-water lake west of the Mississippi River. The lake was the source of fish that were a large percentage of the natives' food supply. The Indians who were resisting the intrusion of Mormon settlers called themselves Fish-Eaters or Timpanogos, after the name of the river and lake where they fished.[8] Many trappers and explorers, including Kit Carson, Jim Bridger and John Frémont, knew the area well, and spoke of the fertile soil, abundant game and a rich yield of fish. In 1847, as Brigham Young led the original pioneer party to the Great Basin, he considered the location for his first settlement.[9] About thirty miles west of South Pass, Wyoming, Young's company encountered Jim Bridger who gave a highly favorable description of the Timpanogos Valley coupled with a warning regarding the valley's bellicose Indians. A month later Young wrote to

---

8. Jared Farmer, *On Zion's Mount; Mormons, Indians, and the American Landscape* (Cambridge: Harvard University Press, 2008), 1.

9. Carter, *Founding Fort Utah*, 32.

an advance party to avoid the Indians "for the present" and settle in the Salt Lake Valley.[10]

Leonard Arrington described Mormon colonization as a carefully planned process, rather than the result of decisions by individuals.[11] In the case of the Timpanogos Valley, impatient Saints started migrating without direction from Brigham Young. Playing catch-up in 1849, the Church hastily assembled and sent a colonizing party to a location that became Fort Utah and, eventually, Provo, Utah.[12] Over the next nine months the Mormon settlers were busy plowing fields, planting and harvesting crops, and building log cabins. The pioneers turned the cabins into an enclosed fort by filling the gaps with pickets. Historian Robert Carter wrote, "The Timpanogos saw the colonists shooting their game, catching their fish, squatting on one of their traditional camping grounds, using their berries, wood, and water, and turning their pastures into farmland."[13] The Indians, commonly known by white men as Utahs or Utes, reasoned that it was fair to steal cattle as compensation, and confrontation was unavoidable.

An unexpected influx of forty-niners, who were taking the southern route to California, postponed the fight. Both the Timpanogos and the settlers benefitted from providing shelter, provisions, clothes and horses to the emigrant prospectors. By October the forty-niners moved on to California. One of the colonists wrote that the Indians became very bold and troublesome, and open war seemed inevitable.[14]

War with the Utes presented a dilemma for the LDS Church. Mormon scripture stated that Indians, called Lamanites, were a chosen people who would be a part of the Kingdom following the Millennium.[15] Within days of settling in the Salt Lake Valley, Brigham Young naively preached that the Saints would take Indian squaws, wash and dress them, teach them English, teach them how to work, and convert them to the Mormon religion.[16] Moreover, the Mormons would "raise up children" by the Indian women. Through this process the Church president said that the Utes would "become a white & delightsome people."[17] Not surprisingly, the Indians were not interested in Young's vision of their future. Richard Holzapfel wrote that the pioneers were forced, once they arrived in the region, to reconcile their plans for the Native Americans.[18]

The reconciliation coalesced at a meeting of Church leadership on January 31, 1850. Willard Richards, the third highest-ranking official, said, "My voice is for War [and] exterminate them." Brigham Young concurred and added that the women and

10. Ibid., 35.

11. Arrington, *Great Basin Kingdom*, 89.

12. Carter, *Founding Fort Utah*, 75.

13. Ibid., 141.

14. Ibid., 152.

15. LDS Church, "Peace and Violence among 19th-Cenutry Latter-day Saints," Gospel Topics Essays, available online at www.lds.org/topics/peace-and-violence-among-19th-century-latter-day-saints.

16. Bigler, *Forgotton Kingdom*, 40.

17. Ibid.

18. Richard Neitzel Holzapfel, *A History of Utah County* (Salt Lake City: Utah State Historical Society, 1999), 40.

children should live "if they will behave themselves."[19] In future years, Young often urged the Saints to feed the Utes rather than fight them. However, when Indians caused too much trouble the Mormon settlers, in keeping with two hundred years of European and American colonization, killed them indiscriminately.

On February 8, 1850, a hundred of the Church's militia, the Nauvoo Legion, surrounded a large Indian village along the Provo River. The soldiers poured bullets "more or less blindly" into the Indian camp, and their foe returned a hail of bullets through the dense foliage.[20] The Mormons also pulverized the village with a cannon whose muzzle was "as wide as a stove lid," and loaded "with scrap iron, bits of chain, rocks, etc." The battle made a mockery of platitudes about sparing women and children. After two days of intense fighting, the Utes abandoned their village. The militia who entered the camp gave reports that varied from "a few of the Indians killed" to "The dead and wounded lay thick." Robert Carter wrote that as the Battle of Provo River ended, "the power of the Utes in Utah Valley was diminished and they were on the run."[21]

Brigham Young was dissatisfied that many Utes escaped the battle near Fort Utah. The Church president dispatched Nauvoo Legion Major General Daniel H. Wells to Utah Valley with an extermination order to not leave the valley until every Indian was out.[22] Wells led a hundred of the militia in a sweep of the southern part of the valley. No attempt was made to distinguish hostile from friendly Utes and many innocent people, including women and children, were killed in cold blood. The Mormons made their point that "they were prepared to meet specific depredations with general destruction," wrote Jared Farmer.[23]

The establishment of additional settlements in Utah Valley followed quickly upon the Battle of Provo River and the subsequent massacres. In September 1850, Aaron Johnson led a large wagon train of emigrants into Salt Lake City. Brigham Young asked his friend to establish a new settlement in an area previously identified by Mormon traders as "Hobble Creek."[24] On September 18, Johnson, with eight wagons and thirty-four pioneers, crossed a low area about five miles southeast of Fort Utah. The colonists encountered many small streams and named one of the largest "Spring Creek." The creek was memorable because the steep banks nearly capsized the lead wagon driven by nineteen-year-old Martin P. Crandall.[25] The settlers circled their wagons on a high spot on the north bank of Hobble Creek. The location at present-day 200 West and 200 North Streets was the site of the first Springville fort.[26]

19. Carter, *Founding Fort Utah*, 158.

20. Ibid., 173.

21. Ibid., 188.

22. Farmer, *On Zion's Mount*, 73-74.

23. Ibid., 76.

24. Alan P. Johnson, *Aaron Johnson, Faithful Steward* (Salt Lake City: Publisher's Press, 1991), 191.

25. Finley, *History of Springville*, 2.

26. Ibid.

Winter was not far away, and the Saints rushed to complete log houses and the walls of a fort that enclosed about one-and-a-half acres.[27] Additional settlers arrived to help, and the fort was completed before the first winter storm. When spring came, the colony's first order of business was to plant crops. Once the crops were in the ground, the water of Hobble Creek was turned out on both sides to flood the new farmland. The 1851 harvest exceeded expectations. "Many bushels of wheat, oats, and barley, with an abundance of melons, squash, and vegetable were raised," wrote Springville historian Mary Chase Finley.[28]

Later that fall, the Hobble Creek settlers were rattled to find two hundred Indians in black war paint camped nearby.[29] Chief Waccara, a prominent Ute who was well known to the Mormons, led the threatening party. He was also called "Walkara" and "Walker." The chief prospered for many years as a horse thief and slave trader. The slaves that Waccara traded to Mexican buyers were children that his well-trained cavalry stole from weaker bands of Indians in the Great Basin.[30] Waccara was politically astute and solicited favor with Brigham Young. Earlier in 1851, Young ordained the previously baptized chief as a high priest in the Mormon Church.[31]

Several of the settlers ventured out of the Hobble Creek Fort to talk with Waccara. Apparently, the chief's only purpose was a show of force, as he and his warriors rode away without making demands. A few weeks passed before a smaller group of Waccara's followers, accompanied by squaws, again camped near the fort.[32] The Utes performed a dance ceremony that culminated in a request for flour, bread and melons. Finley wrote, "The settlers generously donated until the Indians were well supplied, and satisfied."[33] Having enjoyed an abundant harvest, the Hobble Creek pioneers were in the desirable position of being able to feed rather than fight the Indians.

Eventually, the conflict between two irreconcilable ways of life ended the peace. Richard Holzapfel wrote, "Tensions over pioneer expansion, a decline in Indian population resulting from disease, the continued decrease of natural food sources, and LDS leaders' efforts to stop slave trading exploded in July [1853] at Spring Creek near Springville."[34] A settler got into the middle of a dispute between a Ute and his wife. The Indian suffered a head injury and later died. The Utes demanded relatively insignificant compensation, but the Springville bishop refused to pay.

---

27. Kent D. Johnson and Nelson W. Knight, "Historic Resources of Springville City," National Register of Historic Places, Multiple Property Documentation Form, National Park Service, 1997, 1. Available online at https://npgallery.nps.gov/pdfhost/docs/NRHP/Text/64500673.pdf.
28. Finley, *History of Springville*, 8.
29. Ibid., 9.
30. Bigler, *Forgotten Kingdom*, 66.
31. Carter, *From Fort to Village; Provo. Utah, 1850-1854* (Provo: Provo City Corporation, 2003), 69.
32. Finley, *History of Springville*, 9.
33. Ibid.
34. Holzapfel, *History of Utah County*, 41.

Luke Gallop wrote that the hostilities were probably unavoidable in any case as some of the settlers and Indians "have long fostered a spirit of war."[35]

The ensuing "Walker War" was, according to David Bigler, "less a war in the customary sense than a series of atrocities by both sides, ambushes and mutilations by one and outright executions, sometimes billed as 'skirmishes' by the other."[36] For the first time, Mormons suffered significant casualties at the hands of the Utes. During the 1853-54 conflict, settlers in Utah Valley were on continuous alert. By then, Springville's initial 1850 fort was broken up by removal of houses to city lots and farms.[37] The village's one thousand citizens embarked upon an ambitious project—constructing an adobe wall to encompass a much larger area of Springville.

The new fort was a three-quarter-mile square formed by walls built on 400 North, East, South and West streets. Construction was accomplished by packing a set of movable wood forms with wet dirt. Men set the forms and shoveled the dirt, while boys carried water and packed the mud. The wall was four feet wide at its base, eight to twelve feet high, and three feet wide on top. Large gates were built where Main Street intersected the north and south walls and where Center Street intersected the east and west walls.[38] In addition to fort building, the men of Springville were busy with guard duty and carrying out intermittent expeditions against the Utes. Mary Chase Finley wrote, "the women were obliged to help on the farms and on the threshing floors."[39] In spite of the fear of unpredictable Indian attacks, the settlers were able to harvest good crops.

In November 1853, Chief Waccara indicated that he wanted to end the conflict.[40] Deadly skirmishes continued into the spring of 1854 while the chief continued to negotiate. Some of the Indians made their own peace during this period. The settlers at Springville were able to sit down with forty Utes led by Chief Sowiette for a banquet and a "big smoke" in Aaron Johnson's home.[41] Finally, Brigham Young and Waccara agreed to meet at Chicken Creek near Nephi. On May 11, Young and his entourage reached Waccara's camp to find the chief drunk and unwilling to talk. The Mormons left cattle, flour, shirts, guns and ammunition for the chief, and the next morning Waccara was receptive to a meeting. The white men and the Utes passed around a peace pipe while agreeing there would be no more war.[42] Scattered bands of Indians continued to steal cattle and kill Mormon settlers over the summer and fall of 1854. Brigham Young went to great lengths to keep angry Saints from committing reprisals. By the end of the year, hostilities

35. Carter, *From Fort to Village*, 165.
36. Bigler, *Forgotten Kingdom*, 74.
37. Finley, *History of Springville*, 17.
38. Ibid., 18-19.
39. Ibid., 13.
40. Carter, *From Fort to Village*, 195.
41. Finley, *History of Springville*, 13.
42. Carter, *From Fort to Village*, 205.

ceased.[43] Springville's impressive new fort was dedicated on New Year's Day, 1855.[44] The structure never served to protect settlers during the Walker War but played an instrumental role in later events in Springville.

Waccara died of natural causes in early 1855. He was buried in a manner commensurate with his status among the Utes, though certainly unique for a high priest in the LDS Church. A large burial pit was dug, and two Indian women and as many as twenty horses were killed and placed beside the corpse. Two living Indian children were tied to Waccara's body in order to guide the chief's spirit to its new home. As the corpse decomposed, the starving children pleaded with the natives, but no one intervened.[45]

A brief conflict in February 1856, known as the Tintic War marked the end of seven years of intermittent hostilities between Mormon settlers and the Utes. Severe food shortages afflicted the settlers, and the Indians were doing worse. Chief Tintic and his followers rustled Mormon cattle to feed their families. Acting on a federal warrant, a US Marshal tried to arrest Tintic at his camp near Fairfield. During a fight in which four Ute warriors and one squaw were killed, a Fairfield resident, George Carson, was speared and bled to death.[46] The next day Tintic followers killed his brother Washington.[47] Brigham Young directed Colonel Peter Conover to pursue Tintic with Utah Valley militia. Don Carlos Johnson wrote that a large party from Springville was included. They followed the Indians as far south as the Sevier River and suffered severely from the cold.[48] The soldiers recovered some cattle, though many of the animals froze to death. Tintic and his followers disappeared westward into unmapped mountains that were later named after the chief. Over the two-week duration of the war, there were seven fatalities among the settlers and no accounting of numerous Indian deaths.

Though the Utes did not concede their claim to live in Utah Valley, an extended period of peace followed the Tintic War. However, a decade later during the Black Hawk War, all Springville citizens experienced years of anxiety due to the constant threat of Indian attacks.

---

43. Ibid., 210.

44. Finley, *History of Springville*, 19.

45. Bigler, *Forgotten Kingdom*, 88.

46. Edward W. Tullidge, *Tullidge's Quarterly Magazine* 3 (1883), 246. Available online at https.//archive.org/details/tullidgc1.

47. The death of the Carson brothers in Feb. 1856 would later have a direct effect upon Aaron Harrison. See ch. 11.

48. Johnson, *History of Springville*, 37.

7

Theocracy and the
Mormon Reformation

When the Harrison family arrived in Springville in December of 1856, the town's citizens were enjoying a period of freedom from the threat of hostile Indians. However, a religious revival, which was more terrifying to some Saints than the Utes ever were, was gaining steam. The previous year, the Martin Handcart Company was only a few weeks west of the Missouri, when the Mormon Reformation began as a positive affirmation of religious principles. By early 1857, as handcart survivors continued to heal on the first floor of Aaron Johnson's home, the movement was also an intolerant and angry crusade against those who did not subscribe to the beliefs of the LDS Church.

Ten years earlier, the Mormons settled in the remote and desolate Great Basin of North America. Brigham Young's plan was to establish a sovereign nation on land that was owned and largely ignored by Mexico. Within days of arriving in the Salt Lake Valley, the Church President articulated a goal from which he never deviated—"We do not intend to have any trade or commerce with the gentile [non-Mormon] world . . . I am determined to cut every thread of this kind and live free and independent, untrammeled by any of their detestable customs and practices."[1]

Hopes of a sovereign kingdom disappeared in 1848 when the United States paid $20 million to purchase the "Mexican Cession."[2] The following year, Young petitioned the US Congress to establish the State of Deseret, a bold proposal that included much of the land acquired from Mexico. Instead of granting statehood, the Congress created Utah Territory, encompassing a large portion of the proposed State of Deseret.[3] As a US territory, Utah was in theory governed by federally appointed officials and judges. In fact, a form of dictatorship known as a theocracy was the true government of Utah for decades. Brigham Young's authority as ruler of the Mormon Theocracy was based upon the claim that he was God's sole spokesperson. The Church President held no interest in the laws and statutes of the United States. One of Young's biographers, John Turner, wrote that the leader

---

1. Arrington, *Great Basin Kingdom,* 47.
2. The transfer of land was part of the treaty that settled the Mexican-American War. The cession included all or part of ten eventual states –California, Nevada, Utah, New Mexico, Arizona, Kansas, Colorado, Wyoming, Oklahoma and Texas.
3. Bigler, *The Forgotten Kingdom,* 48.

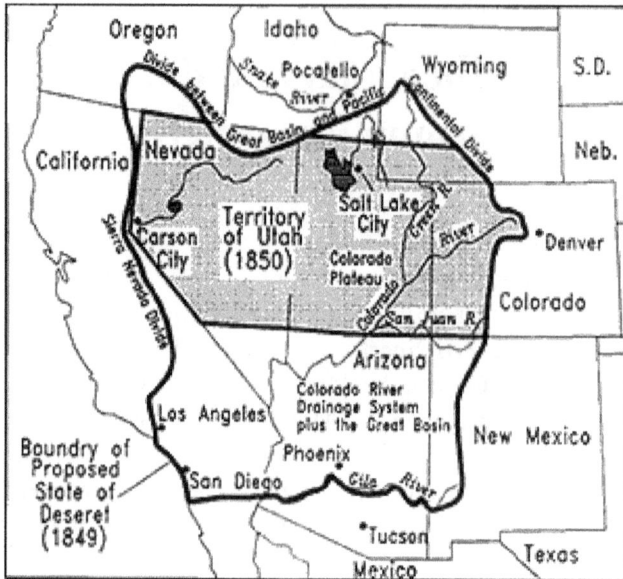

The map shows the 1849 proposed state of Deseret, which included Pacific coastline that extended from the Mexican border to north of Los Angeles. The smaller, though very large, original Utah Territory created by the US government in 1850 is also shown.

depended upon his "Council of Fifty," consisting of the Twelve Apostles and other trusted officials to govern.[4] Young maintained that his unelected priesthood was "a perfect system of code laws." Turner added that he dismissed any criticism of his absolute rule whether it came from his own flock, the few Gentiles in Utah, or federal officials.[5]

Wallace Stegner observed that Brigham Young's control of both church and state was "the most potent and absolute government any part of the United States ever saw."[6] The great majority of the Saints willingly accepted this autocratic rule. Many, including the Harrisons, were poor immigrants who understood that their survival in a hostile wilderness was dependent upon "practical Mormonism"—obey authority, organize for the collective good, and maintain faith in divine oversight and care. However, some Mormons voiced skepticism about their leader's direction. Historian Paul Peterson wrote, "Brigham Young observed in the fall of 1854 that while the majority of the population came intending to serve the Lord, some were

---

4. Turner, *Brigham Young*, 184.
5. Ibid.
6. Wallace Stegner, *Mormon Country* (Lincoln, NE: University of Nebraska Press, 2003), 93.

'actually trying to see how much evil they can commit and at the same time keep their standing among the Saints.'"[7]

Partly in response to disobedient Church members, Young attempted to implement the Mormon "Law of Consecration." This doctrine called upon the Saints to deed all their property and belongings to the Church.[8] The Church priesthood would then assign stewardship of property deemed to be "sufficient for him and family" to each head of household.[9] Surpluses would be distributed to the poor or used for programs such as the Perpetual Emigration Fund. Paul Peterson observed that the initiative in 1854 was not only about the social benefits of redistributing wealth. The effort included a component aimed at "checking the worldliness of some Saints."[10] Despite pressure from local bishops, no more than a third of Church members signed papers to consecrate their wealth.[11] In the end, no property transferred ownership.

Brigham Young was not happy with the Saints' pallid response to his call to centralize control of the Kingdom's wealth. Other events throughout 1855 and 1856 were even more troubling. Poor crop yields due to a truly biblical cricket plague and drought placed many in the territory on the brink of starvation. A severe winter that killed two thirds of the Church's cattle compounded the food shortages.[12] The experience in Springville mirrored the rest of Utah. Historian Don Carlos Johnson wrote that in the spring of 1856 many residents never tasted bread for months. Instead the Saints dug in the pastures for thistle roots, pigweeds, red root and sego bulbs in order to survive.[13] The Church hierarchy was also disturbed by the territory's fourth failed campaign to gain statehood. Animosity toward Mormons, as experienced by George Harrison's family when they crossed the country in 1856, was also on the rise. "Like old Testament prophets, they [the Church leaders] reasoned that modern Israel's problems were rooted in disobedience and unrighteousness," wrote Peterson.[14]

Brigham Young warned his followers, "The time is coming when justice will be laid to the line . . . and if you are not heartily on the Lord's side you will be hewn down."[15] Young's second counselor, Jedediah Grant, frustrated that his twenty-three years of preaching did not alter the Saints' behavior, raised the stakes.[16] In a sermon on September 14, 1856, Grant threatened to excommunicate anyone who did not submit to rebaptism and reconfirmation.[17] The next day he

7. Paul H. Peterson, "The Mormon Reformation of 1856-1857," *Journal of Mormon History* 15, 61.

8. Ibid.

9. James B. Allen and Glen Leonard, *The Story of the Latter-day Saints* (Salt Lake City: Deseret Book Company, 1976), 75.

10. Peterson, "Mormon Reformation," 61.

11. Gustive O. Larson, "The Mormon Reformation," *Utah Historical Quarterly* 26, no. 1, 59.

12. Peterson, "Mormon Reformation," 62-63.

13. Johnson, *History of Springville*, 32.

14. Peterson, "Mormon Reformation," 63.

15. Ibid., 64.

16. Sessions, *Mormon Thunder*, 261.

17. Ibid.

directed the immersion of approximately five hundred Saints. This innocuous event is cited as the beginning of the Mormon Reformation. Three weeks later, at a General Conference that primarily concentrated on the emerging Willie and Martin handcart disasters, Grant raged against the disobedience of the Saints in attendance. One of them wrote, "The people shrunk, shivered, wept, groaned like whipped children. They were told to get up in meeting and confess their sins. They did so till it was sickening, and brought disease."[18]

In early November, Young signaled his displeasure with Church members by withdrawing the sacrament.[19] Reformation leaders also decided that mass rebaptisms, though emotionally fulfilling, were not yielding results.[20] They replaced the revival-type meetings with a prescriptive approach that targeted specific failings in individuals. Brigham Young and Jedediah Grant developed a twenty-seven-question "catechism" that all Saints were required to answer. The subjects included murder, theft, adultery, lying and swearing, as well as failures to pray, tithe or bathe.[21] A cadre of young and earnest "home missionaries" was instructed to "wake up" the people.

Initially, the catechism was administered publicly, which caused embarrassment for many Mormons. Group confessions spawned enough discontent to cause the Reformation's leaders to move the inquiries from public exhortation to personal interviews in the Saints' homes. Young missionaries were often overzealous in their interrogations. One bishop knew of many instances when "teachers without wisdom or the spirit of God, have gone into families and raised a spirit of opposition and rebellion."[22] Church member James Allen Browning wrote of "scathing investigations" that were humiliating.[23]

In Springville, Bishop Johnson designated the south room on the first floor of his home as the location for personal interviews. "All Saints eight years of age and over were required to visit and divulge their inequities to a father confessor," wrote the bishop's son, Don Carlos Johnson.[24] Handcart survivors were still recovering at the other end of the house's first floor. William and Hannah Harrison likely observed the stream of penitents. Along with daughters, Mary Ann and Alice, they were probably asked to confess their sins. Neither George nor Aaron Harrison were yet in the Kingdom and never experienced the interrogations of the Reformation.

The home missionaries were allowed to question Saints on subjects that were not part of the catechism. Failure to enter into polygamy was the most frequently discussed form of disobedience.[25] "Celestial marriage" was strongly urged, and a

18. Ibid., 280.

19. Polly Aird, "You Nasty Apostates, Clear Out'; Reasons for Disaffection in the Late 1850s," *Journal of Mormon History* 30, no. 2, 165. The Latter-day Saints' sacrament is the ordinance of partaking of bread and water in remembrance of Christ's sacrifice. In doing so, Church members renew their baptismal covenants.

20. Peterson, "Mormon Reformation," 68.

21. Ibid., 70.

22. Larson, "Mormon Reformation," 54.

23. Peterson, "Mormon Reformation," 72.

24. Johnson, *History of Springville*, 45.

25. Peterson, "Mormon Reformation," 71.

great number of men took plural wives. George Hicks observed, "young women from 13 to 16 years of age were many of them sealed to men three times their own age. The girls were told that if any faithful man made them an offer of marriage, it was their imperative duty to accept the offer."[26] Another Saint, Charles Derry, wrote that he commonly saw "a blooming young girl adorning the shriveled and withered person of some old man."[27] The fifty-year-old bishop of Springville, Aaron Johnson, married his ninth, tenth and eleventh wives on March 1, 1857.[28] Fourteen-year-old Julia Johnson was the youngest and the fifth niece who Aaron Johnson married. The bishop found fifteen-year-old Sarah Maria James, a survivor of the Willie Handcart Company, nearby on the first floor of his home. Cecilia Sanford, also fifteen, was the daughter of Johnson's friend, Cyrus Sanford.

Paul Peterson wrote that despite the anxiety and shame that the interrogations caused among some Saints, Church leaders intended the Reformation "to be a time of mercy and forgiveness."[29] Many Saints benefited from repentance followed by rebaptism and reconfirmation of the Church's covenants. Historian Andrew Neff wrote, "the spiritual tone of the entire Mormon commonwealth was markedly raised."[30] Unfortunately, the compassionate and tolerant side of the Reformation was not how all Saints experienced the religious movement.

Brigham Young introduced "blood atonement" into the fabric of the Mormon Reformation when he said to his congregation, "There are sins that men commit for which they cannot receive forgiveness in this world." He continued that if they had their eyes open, "they would be perfectly willing to have their blood spilt upon the ground."[31] The Old Testament idea, that grievous sins can be expiated only by killing the transgressor, was not new to Young. John Turner wrote that Young believed in and discussed the doctrine for years prior to the Reformation.[32] Mormon Frederick Loba left Utah in 1857 because of the fanaticism that he witnessed. The following year he wrote, "murder was openly advised in the public meetings . . . and persons whose faith in Mormonism was suspected were searched in the hope of finding evidence against them."[33] Murderers, adulterers, and thieves were candidates for blood atonement, as were "apostates"—those who abandoned or criticized the Mormon religion.[34]

The LDS Church's website includes a discussion of the regrettable period during which "members participated in deplorable violence against people perceived to be their enemies."[35] Springville became particularly radicalized. Long-lived prominent and faithful church member, Noah Packard, became one of two counselors to the

---

26. Aird, et al., *Playing with Shadows*, 144.
27. Ibid., *Playing with Shadows*, 234.
28. Johnson, *Aaron Johnson*, 319-25.
29. Peterson, "Mormon Reformation," 74.
30. Larson, "Mormon Reformation," 63.
31. Peterson, "Mormon Reformation," 66.
32. Turner, *Brigham Young*, 258.
33. Aird, "'You Nasty Apostates,'" 163.
34. Aird, *Mormon Convert*, 159n10.
35. LDS Church, "Peace and Violence."

stake president soon after his arrival in Springville in 1851.[36] Don Carlos Johnson described Packard as "one of the eloquent preachers of the early '50s, a man of great piety and scriptural lore."[37] Packard became disenchanted with the extremism of the town's leadership and resigned after several years. He observed, "I have hardly had the liberty of conscience or speech since I have been living in Springville."[38] Following his resignation, "wicked men" stalked Packard hoping to catch him doing or saying something for which he could be cut off from the Church. Don Carlos Johnson similarly recalled the environment of fear and distrust. He wrote, "Some of the more impetuous became quite frantic in their religious fervor. 'All who are not for us, are against us,' and, 'It may be necessary to cleanse the platter,' were quotations frequently uttered by some whose zeal had run into fanaticism."[39]

The intolerance in Springville resulted in three infamous murders, which were preceded by a bungled assassination attempt in southern Utah. Historian Ardis Parshall wrote that in early 1857 Brigham Young sent letters to Church officials warning of two swindlers who were released from jail in Salt Lake City.[40] Young believed that Ambrose and Betts might steal Church-owned horses as they left Utah for California. If theft occurred, the Church President wanted to hear that the perpetrators were eliminated, and "we do not expect there would be any prosecutions or false imprisonment or tale bearers left for witnesses." Young added, "have a few men that can be trusted on hand, and make no noise about it and keep this letter safe. We write for your eye alone."[41]

Soon after sending the letters, the Church president delivered another sermon in which he advocated blood atonement. He included a frightening interpretation of the second commandment. Young preached that Christ believed that "love thy neighbor as thyself" means that to murder someone who committed a grievous sin was an act of love.[42] The novel interpretation of scripture was printed in the *Deseret News* for distribution throughout Utah. Young's sermons and letters left little doubt that Church officials were empowered to murder undesirables.

On February 17, unknown assailants attempted to kill four California-bound travelers who were bedded down for the night near the Santa Clara River.[43] More than fifty rounds were fired into the camp. As the intended victims scrambled away in the dark, three were hit by gunfire and one was seriously injured. They returned to the campsite the next morning and found evidence that their assailants were white men. Ardis Parshall makes a credible case that Church officials in southern Utah directed the attacks, believing that Ambrose and Betts were among the group.[44]

36. Ronald O. Barney, *One Side by Himself: The Life and Times of Lewis Barney 1808-1894* (Logan: Utah State University Press, 2001), 181.

37. Johnson, *History of Springville*, 121.

38. Barney, *One Side by Himself*, 181.

39. Johnson, *History of Springville*, 45.

40. Ardis E. Parshall, "'Pursue, Retake & Punish': The 1857 Santa Clara Ambush," *Utah Historical Quarterly* 73, no. 1, 72.

41. Ibid.

42. Aird, *Mormon Convert*, 175.

43. Parshall, "'Pursue, Retake & Punish,'" 64-65.

44. Ibid., 84.

Isaac Haight, stake president in nearby Cedar City, drew attention to himself with the preposterous claim that the attackers were Indians. However, as Parshall points out, no conclusive evidence of guilt ever emerged.

In contrast, the facts of the Parrish-Potter murders in Springville were thoroughly documented by contemporaries.[45] Aaron Johnson was among those who received Brigham Young's "Ambrose and Betts" letter advising extralegal violence. Johnson enjoyed sole jurisdiction over all affairs in Springville. He was reluctant to delegate authority except for the most mundane affairs and ruled every facet of the citizens' lives.[46] In early February the bishop shared the content of Young's letter with about fifteen followers at his home. On February 20, Johnson called another council meeting to specifically discuss William Rice Parrish. The forty-year-old Mormon moved to Springville from the eastern United States in 1856. Parrish suffered a loss of faith as he witnessed the workings of the Reformation. The doubter's unwelcome opinions were widely known, as he was "a bold outspoken man," according to Don Carlos Johnson.[47] Parrish talked openly about leaving the territory.

Bishop Johnson ordered Gardiner "Duff" Potter and Abraham Durfee to find out Parrish's plans. He also commented that "some of us would yet 'see the red stuff run.'"[48] John M. Stewart, justice of the peace, later wrote that Duff Potter asked for the privilege of killing Parrish. Aaron Johnson responded, "shed no blood in Springville," which Stewart interpreted to mean that blood would probably be shed, but do it outside of the town.[49]

Potter and Durfee started meeting with William Parrish daily and convinced him that they could no longer tolerate Mormonism and wished to leave Utah. Parrish's trust was gained in part because the conspirators claimed that they were out of favor with the Church. As chronicled by Springville's "village scribe," Luke Gallop, the two men were "disfellowshipped" (excommunicated) on March 5.[50] About the same time, Parrish experienced a series of unpleasant confrontations with Church officials regarding the theft of his horses. He was told that he would be killed if he continued to press the issue.[51] No doubt fearing for his life, Parrish made a plan to leave Springville on the night of March 15th. His sons, Beason, twenty-two, and Orrin, nineteen, planned to accompany him. Bishop Johnson's spies, the supposedly excommunicated Potter and Durfee, were also included.

45. Aird, "'You Nasty Apostates,'" 172-191. Readers who are interested in the Parrish-Potter murders should read Aird's full description of the event.

46. Lyndon W. Cook, ed., *Aaron Johnson Correspondence* (Orem: Center for Research of Mormon Origins, 1990), viii-x.

47. Johnson, *History of Springville*, 40.

48. Aird, "'You Nasty Apostates,'" 179.

49. Ibid., 180.

50. Luke William Gallup, "Luke William Gallup, Reminiscences and Diary 1842 May-1891 March," 196, MS 8402, Church History Library, Salt Lake City. Available online at https://dcmo.lds.org/delivery/DeliveryManagerServlet?dps_pid=IE1754642. Bishop Aaron Johnson designated Gallup as the "village scribe in 1852.

51. Aird, "'You Nasty Apostates,'" 182.

On the agreed day, William Parrish and Duff Potter went out the east gate of the wall that surrounded Springville. Abraham Durfee led Parrish's sons through the west gate. The two groups planned to meet after dark about a quarter of a mile south of the town's southern wall. Assassins were waiting at the rendezvous. Beason Parrish and Duff Potter were killed by gunfire—the latter accidentally. William Parrish was also murdered, but from knife wounds, including deep cuts to his neck.[52]

Multiple shots were fired at Orrin Potter as he accomplished an unlikely escape. Aided by darkness, the young man was able to run back to Springville's south wall, climb the eight-foot to ten-foot adobe structure, and separate from his pursuers. Orrin was injured when he fell from the wall on the Springville side, though he was able to run to his uncle's house.

Luke Gallop was attending a meeting on the evening of the assassinations. He wrote that just before closing, H. H. Kearns [Carnes], the Captain of Police, and some of his men were called out of the meeting because a "row was up somewhere."[53] Gallup continues that men who started to "run away" were killed about a mile south of the town. The murders were "said to be by Indians." The police chief left the meeting to search for Orrin Parrish. After visiting the house of William Parrish, Carnes and a posse went to the home of Orrin's uncle. The police chief arrived, saying he wanted Orrin Parrish dead or alive. He tried to enter to take Orrin.[54] Orrin's aunt heroically stood up to Carnes who relented and placed guards outside the home.

About 10 pm, Carnes led a company of men to retrieve the bodies. John M. Stewart, the town's Justice of the Peace, was awakened and told to accompany the group. The men, handpicked by those who planned the murders, were told to hold an inquest at the scene of the crimes. Stewart acted as coroner for a sham investigation conducted in a dark field. The charade continued the next morning when, as Polly Aird wrote, "a farce of a 'court of inquiry' was held."[55] Stewart first questioned Abraham Durfee, who later said that Bishop Johnson threatened him that he would be "sent the same way" if he described the murder. Durfee had no information for the justice. Orrin Parrish was brought into the inquiry, but only after his uncle warned that the officials would kill him if he knew anything about the murders. Orrin said no more than Durfee. The jury quickly found that the victims "came to their deaths by the hands of an assassin, or assassins, to the jury unknown." Bishop Johnson ordered Justice Stewart not to report the proceedings to the county court as required by law. Several years later, after Stewart fled the territory, he wrote that if he disobeyed Johnson his fate would be the same as the Parrishes.[56]

---

52. Ibid., 183-84.
53. Gallup, "Luke William Gallup," 196-97.
54. Aird, "'You Nasty Apostates,'" 185.
55. Ibid., 186.
56. Ibid., 187.

The Parrish-Potter murders were quickly known throughout Utah and the nation. There was little doubt about what happened. A Saint in the Big Cottonwood Ward wrote in his diary, "Went to the evening meeting I heard some good preaching and was glad to hear that the law of God has been put in force in Springville on some men who deserved it." George Hicks tied the violence to the preaching of the Reformation and wrote, "My wife and myself both saw the blood of the Parrishes at Springville two days after the murder. Those were truly perilous times as such as only fanatics know how to bring on a country."[57] There is no reason to believe that Brigham Young knew anything of the Parrishes before they were murdered. Nonetheless, his oratory and letters condoning the murder of sinners, including apostates, were inflammatory and explicit. Young's failure to investigate either the attempted murders at the Santa Clara River or the Parrish-Potter murders was viewed as an endorsement of the acts.

Polly Aird wrote that following the Parrish-Potter murders Brigham Young possibly realized that matters were spiraling beyond his control.[58] Some aspects of the Reformation such as the catechism, rebaptism and reconfirmation started to wind down. Saints in good standing were once again allowed to take the sacrament. Unfortunately, Young did not tone down rhetoric meant to demonize Gentiles. About six months after the Parrish-Potter murders a wagon train of "strong well-equipped emigrants" from Missouri passed through Springville on their way to California by the Southern Route. Springville historian Mary Chase Finley wrote that the travelers camped where Spring Creek crossed North Main Street close to a large stack of wild hay.[59] The emigrants removed a fence and turned their animals into the hay. When confronted, the strangers were insolent and indifferent. Finley continued, "This same defiant, insulting attitude was manifest in their entire journey through the settlements which culminated in serious trouble and tragedy in southern Utah." That serious trouble is known as the Mountain Meadows Massacre. Church officials in Cedar City and Parowan directed the murder of all but a few of one hundred and thirty emigrants, most of whom were women and children.[60] Though the outsiders were arrogant, the grievous sin that warranted murder in Zion in 1857 was that they were Gentiles.

If the Parrish murders happened as planned by Bishop Johnson, the bodies would be buried, and little more than speculation would follow. Orrin's improbable escape, which was assisted by Springville's wall, created numerous witnesses and a messy attempt at a cover-up. William and Hannah Harrison, still living on the first floor of Aaron Johnson's house, likely observed a hectic two days as Johnson orchestrated the debacle. The recent immigrants certainly were struck by the differences between the humble, peace-loving congregation they left in Manchester and the Church's absolute control of both religious and secular behavior in Zion.

---

57. Ibid., 198n214.
58. Aird, *Mormon Convert*, 180.
59. Finley, *History of Springville*, 29.
60. See Juanita Brooks, *The Mountain Meadows Massacre* (Stanford: Stanford University Press, 1950).

Another English immigrant, Frederick Weight, arrived in Springville within a month of the Harrisons. Weight became a prominent member of the Church and community and later wrote, "I passed through all the scenes of the reformation in Springville . . . having seen many things take place here – some good, some not so good. I always tried to mind my own business and find that it is the best policy."[61] William and Hannah probably shared Weight's sentiments.

Others in the polarized community of Springville were more vocal about the murders. Four years later, Brigham Young visited the town and felt compelled to discuss the subject. Young told the congregation not to whine about Parrish's death.[62] Addressing the infamous murders and other crimes, he said, "I cannot be implicated in any of them." John Turner wrote that while Young denied culpability, he condoned extralegal justice. "[T]here has been a great deal done," Young commented, "quite a number killed, and, I believe, many more ought to have been."[63]

Disagreement in Springville over the Reformation, the Parrish-Potter murders, and the bishop's role continued for many decades. Susan Bartholomew, Director of the Springville Pioneer Museum, recalls a spirited discussion among "old-timers," but believes that few of today's Springville residents know about the incident.[64] The location where William Parrish was killed for daring to renounce the LDS Church is well known to Springville historians. A small park sits between the north and south lanes of Main Street between 700 and 800 South. There is a memorial on the spot. but not to recognize the victims of religious fanaticism. Instead, a plaque at the bottom of a tall flagpole has a curiously uninspired inscription: "In appreciation of the citizens who contribute to the growth and progress of Springville. Dedicated September 18, 1979."

Garland Hurt, a federal Indian agent who was in nearby Spanish Fork at the time of the murders, is usually given the last word on Springville's most memorable historical event. He wrote, "The tragical murder of Potter and the two parishes, in the spring of 1857, must ever cleave like bird-lime to its [Springville's] history."[65]

61. Fredrick Weight, "A Short History of the Life Of Fredrick Weight By Himself," available online at http://weightfamily.net/FamHist/Pioneers/weight/weightf.htm.

62. Turner, *Brigham Young*, 260.

63. Ibid.

64. Personal communication, Susan Bartholomew, Springville, Utah, Aug. 2015.

65. Barney, *One Side by Himself*, 342n45.

8

George's Indian Family

Duing the winter of 1857, George Harrison was unaware of the tumultuous Mormon Reformation that his parents witnessed in Springville. The "white skeleton" was regaining his health in the company of a kind, mixed-race family that fed and protected him. Harrison did not assume a friendly reception when he intruded into an Oglala teepee. He later described his action to Howard Driggs as a "desperate chance with the savages."[1]

In Howard Driggs' "Handcart Boy," published in 1944, the Frenchman who headed the family is referred to only as the mountaineer and the French trader.[2] Eight years later in *George The Handcart Boy*, Driggs identified the Frenchman as Jeff Baker.[3] Baker is an unlikely name for a French trapper. Possibly, the author was thinking of the famous mountain man and trader, Jim Baker. By whatever name, the family's father was one of a cadre of former beaver trappers and traders who were integral to the Indians' exchange of buffalo hides and buckskin for pots, knives, rifles, ammunition, wool blankets, calico, glass beads, and whiskey. George Hyde wrote that the traders exerted great influence over the Oglalas in the 1850s and 1860s. Hyde continued, "Most of these men were Frenchmen from St. Louis; they married into the tribe and spoke the language, and it was through them and their retainers that the agent and other officials communicated with the Indians."[4]

The Oglala were one of seven tribes that composed the Teton Sioux, also known as Lakota Sioux.[5] By the 1850s Oglala numbered no more than 3000.[6] They lived in "lodge groups" or "bands," each consisting of about a hundred extended family members. A band stayed together throughout the year and was largely autonomous.[7] Bands cooperated mostly to make war against their perennial Indian enemies.

When George Harrison encountered the Oglala in 1856, the traditional hunter/warrior bands no longer lived along the North Platte. They moved away the previous year following General William Harney's massacre of nearly a hundred Sioux at

1. Driggs, "Handcart Boy," Sep 1944, 390.
2. Ibid. 390-91.
3. Driggs, *George The Handcart Boy*, 43.
4. George Hyde, *Red Cloud's Folk, A History of the Oglala Sioux Indians* (Norman, OK: Oklahoma University Press, 1987), 95.
5. Edward S. Curtis, *The North American Indian*, vol. 3, The University Press, Cambridge, Massachusetts, 1908, 12. Available online at curtis library.northwestern.edu.
6. Raymond J. DeMallie, "Sioux Until 1850," in R. J. DeMallie, ed., *Handbook of North American Indians: Plains*, vol. 13, part 2 (Washington D. C.: Government Printing Office, 2001), 734-35.
7. Ibid., 734.

Ash Hollow. The general's action was retaliation for an incident in 1854, in which thirty US Army troops, led by Lieutenant Grattan, were slaughtered. The foolish and ambitious young lieutenant manufactured the debacle when he unnecessarily provoked a large camp of Indians near Fort Laramie.[8] Harney's brazen retribution against Indians that probably included no one who had participated in the Grattan Massacre, taught the Sioux's warrior bands that the Platte River Valley was the white man's land.[9] Unwilling to live in submission to the US Army, warrior bands, including young braves such as Crazy Horse, moved away from the emigrant trail and prolonged their culture for two more decades.

Other Oglala bands were tired of the rigors of traditional Sioux life. "They hunted close to the emigrant road and then hurried back, to follow the wagon-trains and beg from the whites or to go to Fort Laramie and live off what they could get from the soldiers," wrote George Hyde.[10] These Indians were sneered at as "Waglukhe," translated as "loafers," by traditional warrior bands. According to Hyde, the loafers returned the scorn of the "wild" Sioux and treated them like country bumpkins with naïve ideas about fighting the obviously more powerful white men.[11]

The family and band that took in George Harrison differed from both the traditional Oglala and the loafers. A family of mixed-race children, headed by a French trader, certainly was not a part of a warrior band. Yet George Harrison's description of the family suggests they were not "loafers." The band was a hundred miles from Fort Laramie when George entered their camp. They were still nomadic, making long trips to hunting ranges in the summer and to sheltered valleys in the winter. The Frenchman who headed George's Indian family continued to be an active hunter and trapper. The squaws continued the difficult work of preparing hides and buckskin for trading.[12]

Not long after George's father departed the Oglala camp to return to the Martin Handcart Company in November 1856, the band moved its tepees to a warmer location for winter. The journey was difficult for George. Still emaciated and weak, he was walking through the same winter storms that the Martin company and its rescuers were experiencing to the west. Fortunately, an old squaw who was a part of the family gave George a pair of moccasins.[13] Harrison told Driggs that the rest of his clothing soon wore out. The Indian mother came to the rescue by making him a suit of buckskin that was fringed and beaded. She also made a new pair of moccasins that were shaped to George's feet and came up to his ankles. George reminisced, "With all these fine fixings, I felt myself a handsome young Indian."[14]

8. Two years later Aaron Harrison joined the still depleted Company G when he left the Martin Handcart Company at Fort Laramie.

9. Hyde, *Red Cloud's Folk*, 85.

10. Ibid., 86.

11. George Hyde, *Spotted Tail's Folk: A History of the Brule Sioux* (Norman, OK: University of Oklahoma Press, 1987), 116.

12. Driggs, "Handcart Boy," Nov 1944, 484.

13. Driggs, "Handwritten notes," 11.

14. Driggs, "Handcart Boy," Nov 1944, 484.

The Indians' new camp was probably in the Powder River Basin, a frequent wintering ground for Oglala. George Harrison remembers the spot as well sheltered from the winds, and supplied with plenty of wood and water. At the beginning, Harrison spent most of his time in the tent because he was "wretchedly ill." He described the tent as "cold and dirty at best."[15] Even as George regained his health there was little fun for a white boy around the Indian camp.[16] The French father, who was the only one in the family who spoke English, was often gone—hunting, trapping or trading. When he was around, the trader told tales of his adventures as a mountain man. George reciprocated with stories of his boyhood in England. Harrison later recalled that one of the things he missed most was "books to read and pictures to see."[17]

George Harrison's Indian experience was not entirely boring. He and Tabi, the young boy George first encountered, became good friends. They rigged up a crude sled and "took some jolly rides with it."[18] Papooses also joined in the fun of going over bumps and racing over the smooth slopes. Tabi taught George how to shoot with a bow and arrow, though his skills remained well short of the Indian boy's expertise. George tried to learn to ride a horse "injun style," without a saddle, but gave it up after some hard landings. Harrison told Driggs, "All the while I was learning the ways of the Indians and their language."[19]

The Oglala had a good supply of jerked buffalo meat cached in different locations and were skillful at bringing in fresh antelope and deer meat throughout the winter. The steady meat diet was supplanted with dried berries, but in five months with the Indians George saw no flour. He wished at times for a bit of English plum pudding or a helping of vegetables. All in all, he ate well, and before long, George began to feel "fat and fine."[20]

In late winter of 1857, about the time of the Parrish-Potter murders in Springville, the Indian band broke camp to travel to a trading post. George told Howard Driggs, "Our family used two travois, several pack ponies, and even some dogs with small travois to take our outfit with buckskins and furs we had to trade."[21] The Oglala band was stringing along the trail, and George began to think about his handcart journey. This time he was sturdy again, so he did not mind the walking. When the Indians were on the trail for a little over "twenty sleeps," Tabi went racing up a hill and waved for George to join him. George recalls that the sight from the top gave him a thrill that he never felt before. He told Howard Driggs that in the valley was old Fort Laramie, and above it, in the golden rays of the setting sun, waved the Stars and Stripes—"It was the prettiest sight of my life."[22]

---

15. Driggs, "Handcart Boy (First Draft)," 13.
16. Driggs, *George The Handcart Boy*, 57.
17. Ibid., 58.
18. Driggs, "Handcart Boy," Nov 1944, 484.
19. Driggs, "Handcart Boy (First Draft)," 13.
20. Driggs, "Handcart Boy," Nov 1944, 484.
21. Ibid., 485.
22. Ibid.

Edward S. Curtis captured this image of an Oglala woman in 1907. In 1856-57 George Harrison's "Indian mother" nursed him back to health when he was near death from starvation. *Credit: Northwestern University Library,* Edward S. Curtis's "The North American Indian," *2003*

George's Indian mother reacted angrily when she realized that he and Tabi were looking down at the fort.[23] She called George back rather sharply and started to chide him. His Indian mother told him that he came to her poor and starving and that she fed him until he was strong. She accused him of wanting to run away to his white people. George responded that he did not think of leaving the Indians, and that Tabi called him to climb the hill. Tabi confirmed George's story, and his Indian mother said no more. The deep disappointment, even betrayal, felt by the Indian mother shows that she developed strong affection for the boy she took in as a white skeleton. Perhaps she believed that George would stay and become a part of her racially mixed family.

After the Oglala band set up camp and enjoyed a dinner of broiled antelope, George, with permission of his "red guardians," visited Fort Laramie. He quickly found his brother Aaron, and "What a surprise I gave him!" recalled George. They enjoyed a good visit, and George learned that Aaron knew nothing of the fate of the Harrison family. Reports of the suffering of the Martin Handcart Company came to the fort through mountain men, but they did know how many or who perished.[24]

George told Aaron how he left the handcart company and lived with the Indians. He emphasized, "They certainly saved me from starvation."[25] The next day George

23. Driggs, "Handwritten notes," 15.
24. Driggs, "Handcart Boy," Dec 1944, 526.
25. Ibid.

returned with Tabi to Fort Laramie, and they watched the soldiers drill. For half an hour the friends sat on the steps of the barracks observing the maneuvers. Aaron joined them when the drills ended, and they all went to the Indian camp. George Harrison remembered, "My red mother in her quiet way, made him [Aaron] feel at home. I had to act as interpreter for what little talk went on."[26]

That evening Aaron's sergeant invited George to dinner at the barracks. George recalled how good the flapjacks, bacon and beans, with a bit of jam to top off the meal, tasted after months of Indian food.[27] During dinner the sergeant suggested that George meet Tom Blakely, who was wagon master at the fort. The soldier was going to the Missouri River for freight and needed a boy to do chores for his wife. Blakely married Mary Brown at Fort Laramie the previous June, and she was about three months pregnant with their first child.[28] George jumped at the opportunity and was hired to begin work the next morning. Further, he was to live at the Blakely home, a three-room cabin just outside the fort. As much as George was grateful to the Indian family who saved his life, he wished to return to his own culture as soon as possible. He told Driggs, "After four months away from home, parents and civilization, I was mightily happy to get back, I tell you."[29]

George returned to the tepee to tell his Indian mother, while trying not to show how happy he was. She took the news sadly, and the papooses cried when he left. Harrison was able to bring his red mother and the children to the Blakely cabin soon after he moved. Mrs. Blakely gave some cookies and trinkets to the papooses and a piece of bright calico to the mother. George gave a pocketknife to Tabi. A few days later, after trading some furs and buckskins for supplies at the sutler's store, the family joined its Oglala band travelling west to spend summer in the mountains.[30] George did not know if he would ever see them again.

George Harrison's stay with a nomadic family whose life was a mixture of the white man's culture and traditional Oglala culture was brief. However, the intimate experience gave him knowledge of, and empathy for, Indian life that few of George's contemporaries shared. Those traits served him well in future contacts with the Goshute, Paiute and Ute tribes.

---

26. Ibid.
27. Ibid., 527.
28. "The Thiede's and Allied Families of North Dakota: Information about Thomas M. Blakely," Genealogy.com. Available online at http://www.genealogy.com/ftm/t/h/i/Kenneth Thiede/WEBSITE-0001/UHP-0040.html.
29. Driggs, "Handwritten notes." 14.
30. Driggs, "Handcart Boy," Dec 1944, 527.

9

Fort Laramie and America's First Civil War

As his family was settling into Springville in the spring of 1857, George Harrison was five hundred miles away at Fort Laramie. He later recalled that wagons from the Salt Lake Valley were the first traffic through the fort that year. Howard Driggs wrote that these were ox trains going east to the Missouri River to bring back Mormon immigrants.[1] Actually, the "down and back" practice did not start until 1861.[2] Most of the travelers observed by George in early 1857 were Mormons and Gentiles fleeing Zion because of the scrutiny of the Reformation or the hardscrabble living conditions. In July, Brigham Young was pleased to write that the territory took an emetic and was spewing "Lawyers, Loafers, Special pleaders, Apostates, Officials and filth."[3] One of the officials who left was US surveyor David S. Burr. He wrote to his superior in Washington that the slaying of the Parrishes convinced him that his own life was in danger.[4] Some of the refugees were apparently from Springville, as George and his brother learned that their family survived the handcart journey to Utah.[5]

In addition to helping Mrs. Blakely, George found work at the sutler's store in Fort Laramie.[6] The establishment was a fabled oasis on the western frontier, and was visited by almost every traveler on the overland route. The essential character of the trading post changed little from the 1840s to the 1880s. The wife of an army colonel described the store's patrons as "Indians, dressed and half dressed and undressed; squaws, dressed to the same degree of completeness as their noble lords; papooses, absolutely nude, slightly not nude, or wrapped in calico, buckskin, or furs, mingled with soldiers of the garrison, teamsters, emigrants, speculators, half-breeds, and interpreters."[7]

Legendary trader and sutler Seth Ward acquired the store early in 1857.[8] Harrison possibly learned a few things observing Ward and other traders, though the fifteen-year-old did not imagine that trading would later be his vocation. George observed practices that took advantage of the natives, who "would get the worst of the bargain usually, for most of the white traders seemed to think it all right to

---

1. Driggs, "Handcart Boy," Dec 1944, 526.
2. William G. Hartley, "'Down and Back' Wagon Trains: Bringing the Saints to Utah in 1861," *The Ensign* (Sep 1985), available online at https://www.lds.org/ensign/1985/09/.
3. Turner, *Brigham Young*, 263.
4. Aird, *Mormon Convert*, 177.
5. Driggs, "Handcart Boy," Dec 1944, 527.
6. "Story of Utah's Biggest Indian War," *The Deseret Evening News*, August 26, 1899, 9.
7. Merrill J. Mattes, "The Sutler's Store at Fort Laramie," *Annals of Wyoming* 18, no. 2, 109.
8. Daniel Coleman, "Seth Ward, Frontier Trader, 1820-1903," Missouri Valley Special Collections, available online at http://www.kchistory.org/u?/Biographies, 156.

Oldest surviving photograph of Fort Laramie taken by Samuel C. Mills in late July to early August 1858. The original adobe walled fort (built as a fur trading post in 1834 by William Sublette) is seen on the left and "Old Bedlam" is prominent in the center. George Harrison left the fort in the early spring of 1858 attached to Colonel William Hoffman's relief train to resupply the Utah Expedition at Fort Bridger.

cheat the poor Indians."[9] The sutler's store included a bar where liquor flowed prodigiously. Fort Laramie historian Merrill Mattes wrote, "Here the whole of the fantastic social strata of the frontier assembled, and tossed coins at the bartender, blew clouds of foam, gurgled barrels of whisky, engaged in occasional knifings and shooting scrapes, plotted robberies and assassinations, boasted of Indian scalps and gold-nuggets; and dreamed of (or dreaded) a time when this vast wild land would be tamed and civilized."[10]

Unexpectedly, a handcart company from Utah passed through Fort Laramie in early summer. The travelers turned out to be seventy-one Mormon missionaries on their way to the eastern United States and Europe.[11] Howard Driggs quotes George as saying that the missionaries were using handcarts because they had little money.[12] The never-to-be-repeated use of handcarts to travel east was, in fact, a well-financed public relations campaign. Historian Karen Ann Griggs wrote

---

9. Driggs, "Handcart Boy (First Draft)," 17.

10. Merrill J. Mattes, "Fort Laramie, Guardian of the Oregon Trail," *Annals of Wyoming* 17, no. 1, 15.

11. Hafen and Hafen, *Handcarts to Zion*, 144.

12. Driggs, "Handcart Boy," Dec 1944, 527.

that following the handcart disasters of 1856, the Church "needed a dramatic demonstration of the efficiency of the handcart method of emigration to restore 'the humble vehicle to favor.'"[13]

Members of the company visited Fort Laramie's sutler store for provisions on May 20.[14] Harrison recalled them as young and vigorous fellows.[15] George and his brother Aaron went to the missionaries' camp after dinner, and "a glad welcome was given to us stranded handcart boys." The brothers stayed as long as they could that evening, visiting and singing songs from "bonny England."[16] The elite company was equipped with well-built handcarts and benefitted from frequent resupplies of food during their travel. The missionaries required only forty-eight days to reach the Missouri River from Salt Lake City. While exhausted, none of them suffered. The demonstration's official report concluded, "We had a time of general good health & happiness, and the most of us gained 10 lbs. in weight on the trip."[17]

Discussing his early days at Fort Laramie, Harrison told Howard Driggs that he and Aaron talked frequently.[18] The pleasant visits came to an end three months after George's arrival at the fort. On June 22, US Army Colonel Edwin Sumners reached Fort Laramie leading the Cheyenne Expedition. His mission was to punish the Indians for attacks along the emigrant trail during 1856.[19] Sumners added three companies of the 6th Infantry to his cavalry. One of the companies was Company G, which included George's brother, Aaron Harrison.[20] Sumners spent four days provisioning the regiment and training the newly attached soldiers, before the expedition departed southward to Colorado. George did not see Aaron again for three years.

After a month of searching for the Cheyenne, Sumners' scouts found the Indians near the Solomon River in northwest Kansas.[21] The cavalry took off in pursuit without waiting for the slower infantry and artillery. A large force of warriors prepared for battle in the early morning with prayer, songs, and body paint. Their medicine man gave them a special blessing, "that when they raised their hands against the weapons of the white man their bullets would drop."[22] Sumners' cavalry charged the Cheyenne with their sabers drawn—the only such attack in the history of western Indian campaigns.[23] The Indians, expecting a volley of harmless bullets, were confused by the tactic and broke their line. A running fight ensued in which

13. Karen Ann Griggs, "Handcarts Going East," *Journal of Mormon History* 35, no. 2, 192.

14. Ibid., 216.

15. Driggs, "Handcart Boy," Dec 1944, 527.

16. Ibid.

17. Griggs, "Handcarts Going East," 216.

18. Driggs, "Handcart Boy," Dec 1944, 527.

19. William Y. Chalfant, *Cheyennes and Horse Soldiers: The 1857 Expedition and the Battle of Solomon's Fork* (Norman, OK: University of Oklahoma Press, 1989), 61.

20. Clifford L. Swanson, *The Sixth United States Infantry, 1855 to Reconstruction* (Jefferson, NC: McFarland & Company, Inc., 2001), 9.

21. Chalfant, *Cheyennes and Horse Soldiers*, 177.

22. Ibid.

23. Douglas C. McChristian, *Fort Laramie, Military Bastion of the High Plains* (Norman, OK: The Arthur H. Clark Company, 2008), 109.

nine Cheyenne were killed and an unknown number wounded. Sumners' troops suffered two dead and nine wounded. One of the wounded was First Lieutenant J. E. B. Stuart, who was shot in the middle of his chest from point-blank range. The ball, from an antique pistol, glanced off Stuart's breastbone and lodged under a rib. Stuart survived to become a legendary cavalry commander and general in the Civil War.

Aaron Harrison and his fellow foot soldiers arrived after the battle at the Solomon River. Colonel Sumners later wrote that it was a matter of deep regret for the 6th Infantry as well as himself that he could not wait to bring them into the action.[24] Aaron, who did not join the US Army seeking glory, was unlikely to share the Colonel's regrets. The next day, Sumners' soldiers found the Cheyenne's large abandoned camp and destroyed all the lodges, as well as the Indians' winter supply of buffalo meat. The colonel embarked upon an unsuccessful three-month pursuit of the fleeing Cheyenne before returning to Fort Leavenworth.

By the end of Sumners' campaign, the infantry marched fifteen hundred miles across uninhabited plains in the middle of the summer, while suffering severe shortages of food and water.[25] The men were reduced to killing and eating any form of wildlife they could find, including coyotes, skunks and buzzards, according to historian Curtis R. Allen. He added, "Many soldiers deserted, perhaps justifiably, including two recruits from the Martin Company, Aaron Harrison and Samuel Blackham."[26] Army records show that they deserted on October 17, 1857, near the Missouri River.[27] The working conditions were not the only reason that Harrison and Blackham deserted. A month earlier, Colonel Sumners received orders to send the 6th Infantry companies to join the Utah Expedition. The expedition was en route to Utah to remove Brigham Young as governor.[28] Aaron and his friend, who were non-citizen mercenaries, were forced to contemplate the possibility of armed conflict against their families.

While Aaron Harrison marched in pursuit of the Cheyenne, George remained busy at Fort Laramie. Tom Blakely returned with army freight, probably in late July. Harrison was fortunate to line up a job as a cook for US Army Surgeon, Thomas M. Getty. "It was just the work I wanted," he later told Howard Driggs.[29] The army surgeon was attached to General William Harney's expedition against the Sioux in 1855, before assignment to Fort Laramie.[30] Dr. Getty occupied an apartment in "Old Bedlam," that also housed the fort's colonel and his family. Built in 1849,

24. Chalfant, *Cheyennes and Horse Soldiers*, 339.

25. Curtis R. Allen, "William Ashton: Handcart Pioneer and Five-Year Foot Soldier," p. 3. Available online at http://www.tellmystorytoo.com/pdf/handcartpioneerandfootsoldier2.pdf.

26. Ibid. 3-4.

27. The record of Aaron Harrison's enlistment and his desertion is found in Register of Enlistments, United States Army, NARA microfilm 233, roll 25, (1856 series), 91, line 311. Private communication from Curtis R. Allen, 2011.

28. Chalfant, *Cheyennes and Horse Soldiers*, 260.

29. Driggs, "Handcart Boy," Dec 1944, 527.

30. Guy V. Henry, *Military Record of Civilian Appointments in the United States Army*, vol. 1 (New York: D. Van Nostrand, 1873), 74. Available online at https://archive.org/details/cu31924092906134.

Fort Laramie's restored "Old Bedlam," where George Harrison learned to cook under the tutelage of an English mentor.

the structure still stands as the oldest in Wyoming. Originally, Old Bedlam housed single officers and reportedly was named after their raucous parties. The building was later converted to four apartments for the most senior officers. Two wings that housed four kitchens were built on the back of the apartments.[31]

Post Commander Colonel William Hoffman, employed an English "cockney" cook who took an interest in young George. Harrison recalled that his friend often slipped into his kitchen to show him how to prepare and serve meals. He added, "The work was not very hard."[32] Only a year removed from the glassworks in Manchester, George's perspective on work probably differed from that of most fifteen-year-olds. Though not physically taxing, Harrison told Driggs that the cooking job required strict attention to business. Sometimes Dr. Getty invited friends to dinner, and George did his best to please them. He probably served some meals that tried the doctor's patience, but Harrison was learning the profession that would make him famous. George observed that Dr. Getty was a bachelor, but "not one of the cranky kind." He liked the doctor very much, and for a pastime they would go fishing in the Laramie River.[33]

---

31. McChristian, *Fort Laramie*, 113.
32. Driggs, "Handcart Boy (First Draft)," 16.
33. Ibid.

Fort Laramie was not particularly busy with emigration in 1857, possibly due to Indian hostilities during the previous three years. About 5500 emigrants passed through on the way to California and Oregon. Mormons gathering to Utah numbered another 1300 emigrants.[34] At least seven LDS wagon trains and two westward bound handcart parties visited the fort.[35] Though Harrison could not fail to notice the passage of the Mormon handcart companies through the small community of Fort Laramie, he offered no comment to Driggs. Only three handcart companies subsequently crossed the plains. Brigham Young abandoned the experiment in 1860, conceding that it was a "hard task" for emigrants to pull their own provisions.[36]

The real story on the emigrant trail in 1857 was a juggernaut known as the "Utah Expedition." Soldiers were sent by the federal government to suppress a perceived Mormon rebellion and replace Brigham Young with a new governor. The army of over two thousand troops and three hundred large freight wagons dwarfed any other previously assembled in the American West.[37] Harrison and others at the fort learned of the approaching army no later than July 16, when Lieutenant and Quartermaster Peter Plympton hired Jim Bridger to serve as the expedition's guide.[38] George Harrison was probably puzzled by the trouble. He was new to the United States, isolated at Fort Laramie, and in no position to understand the Mormon theocracy's disagreements with the US government. Fifty years later, Howard Driggs wrote that George's characterization of the conflict was "more or less trumped up trouble."[39]

Historian Daniel Boorstin described the conflict between Brigham Young and the United States as the country's "first civil war."[40] Given Young's unyielding determination to create a sovereign government, a showdown was inevitable. After only three months in office, President James Buchanan clandestinely put the military in motion in late May 1857. Historian William MacKinnon wrote that Buchanan acted without consulting Congress and without a formal investigation of accusations of Mormon rebellion.[41] Though the Church continually denigrated the United States' elected leaders, harassed the territory's federally appointed officials, and was generally inhospitable to Gentiles, Buchanan probably was unable to prove rebellion. Even the Church's open practice of polygamy, though it appalled Americans, was legal.

---

34. John D. Unruh, Jr., *The Plains Across* (Urbana and Chicago: University of Illinois Press, 1993), 120.

35. Mormon Pioneer Overland Travel database, available online at http://www.lds.org/churchhistory/library/pioneercompanylist-chronological/.

36. Turner, *Brigham Young*, 254.

37. J. Cecil Alter, *Jim Bridger* (Norman, OK: University of Oklahoma Press, 1962), 266.

38. Ibid.

39. Driggs, "Handcart Boy," Dec 1944, 527.

40. Daniel H. Boorstin, *The Americans, The National Experience* (New York: History Book Club, 2002), 64.

41. William P. MacKinnon, *At Sword's Point, Part 1: A Documentary History of the Utah War to 1858* (Norman, OK: The Arthur H. Clark Company, 2008), 137.

Perhaps Buchanan's precipitous instigation of the "Utah War" was primarily motivated by political calculations. Despite his party's aggressive anti-Mormon rhetoric during the 1856 political campaign, Democrats were unable to counter Republican claims that they supported polygamy. Buchanan's victory was unexpectedly narrow, "signaling his need to deal in some way during 1857 with the 'Mormon problem,'" according to William MacKinnon.[42] The President probably believed that sending an army to remove Brigham Young from office would change the perception of his party.

A few weeks after Buchanan ordered military action, the country's top general, Winfield Scott, wrote that the army could not safely invade Utah before the following summer.[43] Apparently under pressure from the Secretary of War, John B. Floyd, the general abandoned his concerns and committed to enter Utah in 1857. Scott informed General William Harney to expect an appointment as the commander. With characteristic brashness, Harney said that he would capture Brigham Young and his apostles and execute them.[44] Harney reiterated General Scott's concerns about becoming trapped in the mountains by winter weather. Referencing the handcart companies of 1856, he wrote, "Between Fort Laramie & Salt Lake, snow generally falls from the middle of October to the 1st of November—Last year a number of Mormon women died, en route, in that part of the country, from cold & starvation."[45] President Buchanan and the War Department remained stubbornly committed to their original strategy. Wishful and irrational planning proved to be as dangerous as the Mormon prophecies of the previous year.

General Harney moved quickly to assemble troops and supplies for the expedition, though still assigned to quell hostilities between abolitionists and slaveholders in Kansas.[46] Colonel Edmund Alexander became the titular commander of the expedition. Alexander was an effective leader in the Mexican-American War from 1846-1848. However, during the Utah Expedition in 1857 he was seldom seen outside his horse-drawn ambulance. One of his officers, Captain Jesse Gove, described Alexander as "interested only in the health of his wife and entirely neglectful of his command."[47] The leaderless army dribbled piecemeal out of Fort Leavenworth and was soon spread over six hundred miles of the overland trail.

When Alexander's 10th Infantry reached Fort Laramie on September 2, Colonel Hoffman summoned the ladies and gentlemen in the garrison to join the expedition's officers at a banquet.[48] George Harrison certainly assisted his English mentor in preparing the meal for what was a festive and carefree affair. Army policy

---

42. Ibid., 58.

43. Ibid., 132.

44. Wilford Hill LeCheminant, "A Crisis Averted? General Harney and the Change in Command of the Utah Expedition," *Utah Historical Quarterly* 51, no. 1, 30.

45. MacKinnon, *At Sword's Point*, 158.

46. Ibid., 162.

47. Otis G. Hammond, ed., *The Utah Expedition, 1857-1858; Letters of Jesse A. Gove, 10th Inf., U.S.A.* (Concord, NH: New Hampshire Historical Society, 1928), 12.

48. Ibid., 50.

decreed that weather was no threat, and the officers did not believe the Mormons would fight. Captain Gove wrote, "It will be soon over. They [the Mormons] will offer no resistance." The same day, the US troops learned that highly respected Colonel Albert Sidney Johnston would replace Alexander as leader of the campaign. "Good!" wrote Gove, "the old woman [Alexander] feels it sensibly. He grows more worthless every day he lives."[49]

At the time of his new appointment, Colonel Johnston was commander of the Second United States Cavalry in Texas. His second-in-command, Robert E. Lee, wrote in a letter to Johnston, "I consider it highly complimentary to you to be selected for this service over others more convenient and accessible."[50] Unfortunately, Johnston was in Washington, D.C. when he received his orders and did not catch up to the floundering Utah Expedition for two months.

As George Harrison watched the military traffic pass through Fort Laramie in the fall of 1857, he had to be concerned about the welfare of his family. Unknown to him, the Utah War already intruded into their lives. Springville historian Mary Chase Finley described the small town's preparation for what was known locally as the "Echo Canyon War." Finley wrote, "Early in August warlike preparations began. The two grist mills ran night and day grinding all the wheat in the village."[51] The flour was saved in barrels for transport in case the Saints needed to flee the territory. Men under forty-five and boys over eighteen years of age were drilled daily. About the middle of October, wrote Finley, two companies marched from Springville to Echo Canyon to join the Nauvoo Legion.[52] George's forty-two-year-old father, William, probably participated in the military drills, though no record indicates that he served in Echo Canyon.

The Mormon militia tried to make the canyon impassable by building dams to flood trails, constructing breastworks, digging trenches, and piling boulders on the high cliffs to roll down on the enemy. As was the case with the companies sent to rescue the Willie and Martin handcarters the year before, communities throughout Utah were asked to provision the Nauvoo Legion with arms, ammunition, horses, bridles, clothing, bedding, food, and camp equipment. Finley wrote, "This meant much sacrificing for their stores were already depleted by the two previous years of near famine."[53]

A contemporary observer could plausibly argue that the Utah War was "all trumped up trouble" when President Buchanan ordered military action in May. That position became indefensible on September 15, 1857, when Brigham Young issued a proclamation of martial law.[54] Young portrayed the approaching US Army as a mercenary mob—no different than those that persecuted Mormons years before in Missouri and Illinois. He forbade entry into Utah by any armed force and ordered

49. Ibid.
50. Charles P. Roland, *Albert Sidney Johnston, Soldier of Three Republics* (Lexington, KY: University Press of Kentucky, 2001), 185.
51. Finley, *History of Springville*, 31.
52. Ibid.
53. Ibid.
54. MacKinnon, *At Sword's Point*, 286.

his militia to prepare to fight. Young also forbade travel into or through the territory without a permit, essentially severing the United States.[55] The document was a clear statement of rebellion against the US government. Young, who as territorial governor took an oath to uphold federal law, was committing treason.

Brigham Young's proclamation did not reach Colonel Alexander for two weeks. Even then, Alexander's staff remained skeptical that the Mormons would engage in a military confrontation. That assessment changed dramatically a few days later. On October 4, Lot Smith and twenty-three Mormon cavalry worked behind Alexander's advance position on Ham's Fork and surprised teamsters camped near the Green River. Though greatly outnumbered, Smith's militia convinced the freighters to surrender.[56] The Nauvoo Legion torched fifty-two large US Army supply wagons. The next day Smith encountered a train of twenty-six wagons camped at noon along the Big Sandy River about ten miles southwest of present-day Farson, Wyoming. Again, Smith's cavalry disarmed the teamsters and burned the wagons.[57] In both encounters, the teamsters were given food and sent westward on foot to join Alexander's force. Lot Smith's two raids destroyed 450,000 pounds of freight—food needed for a large army in the wilderness.

With hostilities a reality, Alexander belatedly took command of the Utah Expedition and called a war council. The inept colonel made a decision that later astonished Johnston.[58] In order to avoid the entrenched Mormons in Echo Canyon, Alexander chose to take the army over a seldom-traveled trail to enter Utah from the north.[59] The narrow route up Ham's Fork toward present-day Kemmerer, Wyoming, became increasingly impassable as the seven-mile-long column progressed. A foot of snow on October 17 brought the struggling army to a complete halt.[60] The blizzard arrived two days earlier on the calendar than the brutal winter storm that struck the Martin and Willie handcarters the year before.

Brigham Young, who received daily reports on Alexander's activity, ordered the Nauvoo Legion to fall back, "as the enemy continue to keep baffling about on Ham's Fork, like a flock of geese without a leader."[61] Alexander decided that the expedition would backtrack. The soldiers and four thousand animals struggled back down Ham's Fork to the main emigrant trail to wait for Johnston's arrival. Thousands of animals perished from cold and starvation, and the soldiers were demoralized by the three-week misadventure.[62]

Colonel Johnston caught up to the Utah Expedition on November 3 near today's Granger, Wyoming. He realized that the mission was no longer to enter

55. Ibid., 288.

56. "Narrative of Lot Smith," in Leroy R. Hafen and Ann W. Hafen, eds., *Mormon Resistance* (Lincoln, NE: Bison Books, 2005), 222.

57. Ibid., 226.

58. Norman F. Furniss, *The Mormon Conflict, 1850-1859* (New Haven, CT: Yale University Press, 1966), 113.

59. Roland, *Albert Sidney Johnston*, 193-4.

60. Furniss, *Mormon Conflict*, 114.

61. Donald R. Moorman with Gene Sessions, *Camp Floyd and the Mormons: The Utah War* (Salt Lake City: The University of Utah Press, 1992), 27.

62. Ibid., 28-29.

the Salt Lake Valley but to survive the winter.[63] The best option was to establish a camp near Fort Bridger where adequate water, forage, and wood was available. The thirty-five-mile trip to the fort was across a flat, open sagebrush desert that offered no protection from storms. As Johnston's column started the march, a ferocious blizzard struck. In blinding snow and intense cold, the troops moved only a few miles a day. Historian Charles Roland wrote, "Grease froze on the axles of moving wagons and caissons, and horses, mules and oxen died by hundreds."[64] Colonel Johnston, fifty-four years old and partially lame from an old bullet wound, led his army on foot through the blizzard. His willingness to share hardship endeared him to the troops.[65] The regiment took thirteen days to travel thirty-five miles. The chastened Utah Expedition erected its tents near Fort Bridger and prepared for a winter in the high country without a sufficient food supply.[66]

The arrival of winter was also difficult for twelve hundred Mormon soldiers camped in Echo Canyon awaiting Johnston's advance. Mary Chase Finley described the experience of the Springville contingent—"Owing to the severity of weather, the men suffered greatly from the cold . . . A piece of rag carpet, when not in use as a saddle blanket, was used for an overcoat over a heavy jeans shirt. Many of the boys had their feet badly frozen."[67] Young released most of the Nauvoo Legion once he was convinced that Johnston's force was pinned down for the winter. Finley wrote that there was great rejoicing in Springville when they arrived home in time for the Christmas holidays.[68]

There was little activity at Fort Laramie after six companies of US cavalry under the command of Captain Philip St. George Cooke passed through on October 23.[69] Cooke was also escorting the newly appointed Governor of Utah, Alfred Cumming. The trailing cavalry, which normally would be at the front of the Utah Expedition to protect supply trains, was a fitting comment on the campaign's dysfunction. George Harrison continued to cook for Dr. Getty and soon learned, along with the rest of the fort, that the US Army was unable to advance into the Salt Lake Valley. George certainly viewed that as good news for his family in Springville. He probably heard talk about a relief party in early spring that would take food to the stranded soldiers at Fort Bridger. Perhaps he would be able to join and get closer to Utah. Harrison could only wonder about his brother Aaron's circumstances. Reports about the Cheyenne Expedition's moderate success and return to Fort Leavenworth was received at Fort Laramie, though information on specific soldiers was probably unavailable.

Back in Washington, D.C., President Buchanan was under relentless political attack for his military debacle. He provided a *post hoc* rationale for the war to the

63. Roland, *Albert Sidney Johnston*, 193-94.
64. Ibid., 194-95.
65. Ibid., 196.
66. Fred R. Gowans and Eugene E. Campbell, *Fort Bridger: Island in the Wilderness* (Provo: Brigham Young University Press, 1975), 108.
67. Finley, *History of Springville*, 31.
68. Ibid., 31.
69. Hafen and Hafen, eds., *Mormon Resistance*, 295-96.

US Congress in December 1857. The president said, "This is the first rebellion which has existed in our Territories; and humanity itself requires that we should put it down in such a manner that it shall be the last."[70] Buchanan's political troubles did not prevent him from gaining congressional approval of nearly four thousand additional troops to join Johnston's force. With the added troops the Utah Expedition comprised a third of the US Army.[71]

In Salt Lake Valley, Brigham Young was thinking about how events might unfold the following spring. The Kingdom was a cash poor, agrarian society that lacked manufacturing capability. The Nauvoo Legion possessed little artillery and was critically short of rifles, gunpowder and bullets. Young and his counselors were debating whether to arm the Mormon militia with traditional Indian longbows or try to manufacture crossbows.[72] Church leaders knew that they would be facing a well-armed force led by a competent and respected officer. Apparently, Brigham Young prophesized divine intervention when he told his followers, "Our enemies will not be able to come within a hundred miles of us. I know that ten men, such as I could name and select, could stop them."[73] The Harrisons and 40,000 other Saints could only wonder what sacrifices would be required in the spring.

---

70. MacKinnon, *At Sword's Point*, 484.

71. David L. Bigler and Will Bagley, *The Mormon Rebellion: America's First Civil War, 1857–1858* (Norman, OK: University of Oklahoma, 2011), 266.

72. Ibid., 270.

73. Brigham Young, "Present and Former Persecutions of the Saints," October 8, 1857, in *Journal of Discourses*, vol. 5 (London: Asa Calkin, 1858), 339. Available online at http://scriptures.byu.edu/jod/jodhtml.php?vol=05&disc=57.

10

Invasion of the Kingdom
and Camp Floyd

T
he brutal two-week march to Fort Bridger led by Colonel Johnston was the first step in salvaging the Utah Expedition. The next was underway in the spring of 1858 when Lt. Colonel William Hoffman left Fort Leavenworth with wagons carrying food and supplies for Johnston's troops.[1] When Hoffman reached Fort Laramie in late April, he picked up additional soldiers, including Dr. Getty. The doctor asked George Harrison to accompany the relief column to Fort Bridger and, ultimately, Utah. George recalled the cold, raw weather, the same kind that he encountered the year before when returning to Fort Laramie with his Indian family.[2] Snowstorms made the trail impassable, and the column halted for two full weeks at La Bonte Creek. George remembered that on one bitterly cold night he was called out of his small tent to get more blankets for Dr. Getty.[3] Once the army was moving again, Harrison was on foot, trudging through snow and ice, as he retraced the trail he travelled with the Martin Handcart Company.

At Horseshoe Bend, east of where the white skeleton stumbled into a teepee eighteen months earlier, George saw a familiar looking camp. He did not take long to find his Indian mother and her family. The French father was out hunting, and George learned that the family was out of food.[4] Harrison went to Dr. Getty and said that the Indians who saved his life were across the creek and needed food. The army surgeon reminded George that even the relief party was on half rations to help Johnston's troops. George offered to pay for food, but Dr. Getty told him that money was not the issue. The kind doctor went to the quartermaster's tent and somehow came back with a sack full of supplies—bacon, flour, beans, and some sugar. George later told Howard Driggs that you never saw happier, more grateful people than his red friends. He considered the provisions small pay for all the Indians did for him. Harrison visited with them until it was time for taps. His Indian mother showed her appreciation by giving him a fine pair of beaded moccasins. "That was the last I ever saw of these dear Indian friends," recalled George, "but I have kept them close to my heart through all the years."[5]

---

1. Robert B. Coakley, *The Role of Federal Military Forces in Domestic Disorders, 1789-1878* (Washington, D.C.: Center of Military History, U.S. Army, 1988), 210.

2. Driggs, "Handcart Boy," Dec 1944, 527.

3. Ibid.

4. Ibid., 528.

5. Ibid.

The relief column reached Deer Creek, and George felt sad as he viewed the ashes of the Martin company bonfire. He knew that he was following the route travelled by his family, but did not know the full story of their disastrous journey. George passed many points of serious trouble for the handcarters such as the North Platte Crossing, without sensing the significance.[6] Harrison recalled several broken handcarts scattered about at Devil's Gate. Along the Big Sandy River, where the Nauvoo Legion burned a US Army supply train, he saw the irons of the wagons lying with the ashes. Some of the soldiers were angered because the destruction of supplies put the men at Fort Bridger and Fort Laramie on short rations. When one of the soldiers asked George if he was afraid that the army would kill his father and mother, he responded that they would not kill anything. The soldiers joked with him a good deal about being a Mormon boy. Nonetheless, George remembered them as "pretty kind."[7]

As Hoffman's relief train progressed to Fort Bridger, preparations for war took a new turn in the Salt Lake Valley. Brigham Young decided not to engage in a futile battle with the US Army. If necessary, he would lead the Saints out of the territory after destroying all the buildings and crops. Young said, "Before I will suffer what I have in times gone by, there shall not be one building, nor one foot of lumber, nor a stick, nor a tree, nor a particle of grass and hay, that will burn, left in reach of our enemies."[8]

Young's first step was to relocate the Mormons south to Utah Valley where they would have no contact with Johnston's troops before the US Army's intentions were clear.[9] An exodus of 30,000 people, three quarters of Utah's population, began on April 1, 1858. When a snowstorm struck two days later, the road "was lined with people and teams to Provo for 50 miles. Many suffered and some came near perishing."[10] The weather was cold enough that horses died by the road. Historian Richard Poll wrote that the move was costly to participants, whose abandoned homes and fields deteriorated and whose energies were used up in the sheer effort of relocating and surviving.[11]

Because William Harrison's family was living in Springville, they were spared the difficult evacuation. Instead, they were on the receiving end of the stream of refugees. Springville took in enough evacuees that the population of a thousand temporarily doubled.[12] The citizens opened their homes to the dislocated Saints. The bastions at the four gates of the town's adobe wall were roofed in to create shelter. "Houses were built all along the banks of the creek, on the public square, and on vacant lots . . . Wagon boxes also served for habitations," wrote Springville

6. Ibid., 10. Jan 1945.
7. Ibid.
8. Richard D. Poll, "The Move South," *BYU Studies* 29, no. 4, 66.
9. Furniss, *Mormon Conflict*, 182–83.
10. Bigler and Bagley, *Mormon Rebellion*, 295, citing Wilford Woodruff.
11. Poll, "Move South," 84.
12. Johnson, *History of Springville*, 50.

historian Mary Chase Finley.[13] Don Carlos Johnson remembered many of the new houses as small circular structures built of cane and thatched roofs.[14]

On June 7, more than two months after "the move south" from Salt Lake Valley began, Colonel Hoffman's relief train reached Fort Bridger. Rationing and improvising stretched the army's meager supplies through the winter. Charles Roland wrote, "To spare the few weakened horses that remained alive, Johnston ordered soldiers to draw wagons to procure wood for the camp . . . He reduced the flour ration by one half, and even slaughtered draft oxen for meat."[15] George Harrison remembered finding a hungry band of men whom he described as "poor devils."[16]

While at Fort Bridger, Colonel Johnston received a promotion to brigadier general in recognition of his leadership upon assuming command of the failing Utah Expedition. As the general organized his troops to advance upon Salt Lake City, Dr. Getty was ordered to stay with several companies remaining at Fort Bridger. George wanted to move closer to his family in Utah and pressed to go ahead with Johnston's troops.[17] Initially, the doctor urged Harrison to stay. However, Getty understood the young man's wishes and found two officers who wanted a cook. George remembered them as Captain Lee and Lieutenant Kelly.[18] Historian Roger Nielson shows them as officers in Company A of the 10th Infantry.[19] Before George departed, Dr. Getty gave him $85 in gold for his ten months of service.

George Harrison faced a new problem once he took possession of the gold. In a letter to Howard Driggs many years later, he said that soldiers were continually trying to borrow the money for gambling. "I knew my parents in Springville were very poor, and I wished to aid them with what I had managed to save," he wrote.[20] George asked an officer he recalled as Lieutenant "Plumstead" to hold his money. The officer was one he often met at Dr. Getty's quarters at Fort Laramie. The soldier, who was actually Lieutenant Peter Plympton, agreed to hold George's money.[21]

Johnston's force, bulked up to about 2500 soldiers, including cavalry and artillery units, started toward Salt Lake City on June 13, 1858. George Harrison was traveling with an angry army that looked forward to fighting its way into the valley. Peace negotiators, Benjamin McCulloch and Lazarus Powell, were in Salt Lake City to deliver an ultimatum from President Buchanan. Church authorities were offered pardons for any previous violations of law if they agreed

13. Finley, *History of Springville*, 32.

14. Johnson, *History of Springville*, 50.

15. Roland, *Albert Sidney Johnston*, 198.

16. Driggs, "Handcart Boy (First Draft)," 20.

17. Driggs, "Handcart Boy," Jan 1945, 10.

18. Driggs, "Handcart Boy (First Draft)," 20.

19. Roger Nielson, *Roll Call at Old Camp Floyd* (Springville: by the author, 2006), 62-63.

20. George Harrison, "The Story of the Vented Brand," Howard R. Driggs collection, box 17, fld 9, Gerald R. Sherratt Library, Southern Utah University.

21. Harrison, "Story of the Vented Brand." Roger Nielson reviewed the officers who were present at Fort Laramie and subsequently at Old Camp Floyd and concluded that the soldier who accepted George Harrison's money at Fort Bridger was Lieutenant Peter Plympton. Personal communication from Roger Nielson, Springville, Utah, 2013.

to submit to federal authority. This included offering no resistance to the entry of the US Army and the establishment of a military post in Utah. In his offer, President Buchanan tersely dismissed Young's dream of a sovereign Kingdom— "The land you live upon was purchased by the United States and paid for out of their treasury . . . It is absurd to believe that they [the people of the other states and territories] will or can permit you to erect in their very midst a government of your own."[22] Fortunately, a shooting war was averted when Young, aware that Johnston's troops had departed Fort Bridger, accepted Buchanan's ultimatum.

While camped on the Bear River south of present-day Evanston, Wyoming, General Johnston learned that Brigham Young accepted President Buchanan's terms. Before the army reached Salt Lake City, Johnston issued orders that no one would leave the ranks of the march or damage any private property.[23] George Harrison was probably at the dusty end of the ten-mile-long column when it entered the city on June 26, 1858. He witnessed an eerie sight. Harrison described the capital to Driggs as a city of the dead—"I saw only two persons as we marched through the quiet town. An old lady who had preferred to stay at home, peeped from behind a curtain, but drew back quickly as she caught me looking at her. A man on a sorrel mule also rode slowly along the street as the soldier boys tramped by."[24] The horseman was probably one of the Mormon operatives assigned to torch the city if the US Army did not act as promised. George Harrison was likely not the only Mormon attached to Johnston's Army as it marched into the valley. William MacKinnon wrote that contemporary accounts of Brigham Young's intelligence capabilities suggest that several unidentified Mormon spies were among the civilian workers in the column.[25]

One Mormon who was not present in the invading army was George's brother. Aaron Harrison was not mentioned as a part of Johnston's force in Howard Driggs' first draft of "Handcart Boy."[26] By the story's 1944 publication, Driggs placed Aaron in Johnston's army marching into Salt Lake City and subsequently staying at Camp Floyd.[27] No record exists to suggest that Aaron ever served in the US Army after his desertion in October 1857, near Fort Leavenworth. Furthermore, as documented by Curtis Allen, Aaron's company, Company G of the 6th Infantry, never entered the Salt Lake Valley.[28] None of Aaron's Mormon contemporaries would ever fault him for deserting an army that intended to invade Utah. For reasons that are not clear today, either George Harrison or his descendants promoted the idea of Aaron's participation in the Utah Expedition.

During the US Army's march through the capital, General Johnston, who considered the Mormons to be traitors, was heard to say he "would give his

22. Hafen and Hafen, eds., *Mormon Resistance*, 335.
23. Roland, *Albert Sidney Johnston*, 213.
24. Driggs, "Handcart Boy," Jan 1945, 10.
25. MacKinnon, *At Sword's Point*, 137.
26. Driggs, "Handcart Boy (First Draft), 20.
27. Driggs, "Handcart Boy," Jan 1945, 10-11.
28. Allen, "William Ashton," 4.

plantation for a chance to bombard the city for fifteen minutes."[29] His well-disciplined troops felt the same animosity, but they passed through Salt Lake City without incident. After camping on the west bank of the Jordan River for three days, the occupying army meandered for several weeks before establishing "Old Camp Floyd" in the Cedar Valley.[30] During their march, the US Army shared roads crowded with Mormon refugees returning north to their homes. Charles A. Scott, an enlisted artillery man wrote, "They are the most destitute looking set I ever saw, pigs, poultry, whiteheaded children. Mothers and Wives all heaped promiscuously together in the wagon, with barely sufficient clothing to cover their nakedness."[31]

Another officer in Johnston's regiment was less sympathetic when he observed the dislocated and impoverished Saints. While newspapers and cartoonists characterized Mormons as physically deformed and debauched for decades, a US Army surgeon lent a patina of scientific legitimacy to the silliness. Dr. A. Roberts Bartholow, riding with the 10th Infantry, wrote in an official report that Mormon men were a "new race" of human being that was the "production of polygamy."[32] The new breed, according to Bartholow, could be distinguished at a glance. The lank, angular persons were characterized by a "yellow, sunken, cadaverous visage; the greenish-colored eyes; the thick protuberant lips; the low forehead; the light, and yellowish hair." The doctor's most interesting claim was that these "physical peculiarities," once acquired through the practice of polygamy, were passed on to offspring.[33] Bartholow's bizarre observations and nonscientific conclusions were discussed in numerous medical journals and professional meetings for decades.[34]

The army initially located at "Old" Camp Floyd, while the permanent post was built about ten miles south near Fairfield.[35] Johnston was determined to get his troops out of tents after the difficult winter they spent at Fort Bridger.[36] In September enlisted men started moving to Camp Floyd's permanent location. The soldiers, assisted by Mormon contractors, built their new quarters with adobe brick.[37] Other buildings such as workshops, barns, stables, warehouses and a social hall were built of wood. Before long, the camp held almost four hundred buildings. Constructing the camp and feeding the soldiers was a windfall for the Saints. Don Carlos Johnson wrote, "A vast amount of supplies of every kind was needed ... Nearly every man in Springville went over to the camp to work or to sell farm produce to

---

29. Moorman with Sessions, *Camp Floyd*, 49.

30. Nielson, *Roll Call*, vi.

31. Robert Stowers and John M. Ellis, eds., "Charles A. Scott's Diary of the Utah Expedition, 1857-1861," *Utah History Quarterly* 28, no. 2, 174-5.

32. *Statistical Report on Sickness and Mortality in the Army of the United States, January 1855 to January 1869*, (Washington, D. C.: George W. Bowman, 1860), 302.

33. Ibid.

34. W. Paul Reeve, *Religion of a Different Color: Race and the Mormon Struggle for Whiteness* (New York: Oxford University Press, 2015), 16-19.

35. Nielson, *Roll Call*, viii.

36. Roland, *Albert Sidney Johnston*, 218.

37. Thomas G. Alexander and Leonard J. Arrington, "Camp in the Sagebrush: Camp Floyd Utah, 1858-1861," *Utah Historical Quarterly* 34, no. 1, 7.

the soldiers."[38] According to Donald Moorman the windfall came none too soon for the Saints, "already reduced to proud poverty by a decade of agricultural and commercial disasters.[39] George Harrison observed that the Army's arrival proved not to be a calamity as first feared, "but was in many ways a blessing."[40]

Not long after settling at Camp Floyd, Harrison received an unexpected visitor. His father, having walked forty miles from Springville, arrived at George's tent.[41] This was their first reunion since William left his son in the care of Indians and trudged back to the handcart company. George took his father to meet Lieutenant "Plumstead" [Plympton].[42] He asked the lieutenant for the eighty-five dollars he was holding for the young man. George gave eighty dollars to his father who stood and looked at him with tears rolling down his cheeks. The lieutenant told William that he should be proud of his son—"It is not many boys who could live in an army and keep himself straight and save his wages as he has done."[43] George's father used sixty-five dollars to purchase a yoke of oxen from the US Army. The Englishman named them Prince and Albert.

A few years later, William's oxen became the subjects of a morality tale that provides insight into George's respect for his father. George related the story in a letter to Howard Driggs.[44] Before the US Army sold oxen, the agents vented (destroyed) the brand. The "US" brands on the oxen that William purchased were not vented well and reappeared when the hair grew back. On advice of neighbors, William tried to destroy the brands with a flat iron. Sometime later a friend told George's father that Prince and Albert were in a corral in Provo. US agents were collecting oxen that wandered or were rustled from government herds. William Harrison walked to Provo and started to take down the corral bars. An agent said, "Old man what are going to do?" William told him that he bought the oxen with "money which my Georgie gave me, which he earned cooking for the officers. I gave $65.00 in gold for them, and I am going to have them." The agent asked who had burned off the brand. William said he did because the original venting was not deep enough. The agent looked at William and said, "old man you are the most honest man I ever saw, you can have your oxen." George's father called, and the oxen came trotting up to him.[45]

George likely enjoyed a reunion with Dr. Getty at Camp Floyd. A registry of 1858-1859 accounts at the sutler's store lists Dr. Getty.[46] In January 1860, the doctor was still at the camp, serving as Asst. Surgeon for the 7th Infantry.[47] In April,

38. Johnson, *History of Springville*, 50.

39. Moorman with Sessions, *Camp Floyd*, 261.

40. Driggs, "Handcart Boy (First Draft)," 25.

41. Driggs, "Handcart Boy," Jan 1945, 11.

42. Harrison, "Story of the Vented Brand."

43. Driggs, "Handcart Boy (First Draft)," 23.

44. Harrison, "Story of the Vented Brand."

45. Ibid.

46. "Book A, Camp Floyd Mining District," Hickman Family Museum site, index available at http://hickmansfamily.homestead.com/campfloyd.html. The same index lists an account for Lt. Kelly, for whom George Harrison was cooking.

47. "The Army at Camp Floyd – Mormon News – Losses of Cattle – Statement of the

Dr. Getty accompanied troops that were transferred to Fort Clark, Texas, along the Mexican border. George Harrison remained at Camp Floyd for the nearly three years of its existence. Though only forty miles from Springville, he was seldom able to visit his family. George recalled that his employers were demanding regarding their meals.[48] The Mormon workforce of day laborers and skilled craftsmen at Camp Floyd typically earned fifty dollars a month, according to historian Donald Moorman.[49] Harrison was probably earning at least three times the eight dollars a month that Dr. Getty paid him when he was first learning to cook. Whatever George's income, much of it went to his parents.

In contrast to George Harrison's willingness to save money, almost all of the wages paid to Camp Floyd's soldiers were quickly spent in "Frogtown." The boomtown, separated from the camp by a small river, was typical of those that sprung up across the American West to entertain soldiers, miners, and railroad workers. Moorman wrote, "The dusty, smoky streets of Fairfield [Frogtown] became, in the eyes of many spokesmen, a refuge for all of society's outcasts and criminals . . . Front Street was lined with a dense network of connected gambling dens, dance halls, brothels, and other second-rate establishments."[50] A *New York Times* correspondent observed, "It is, perhaps, safe to say that scarcely twenty men in the village earn an honest livelihood."[51] Moorman described Frogtown's hygiene as consistent with the transient population—"the habitants moved ankle-deep in the mud after heavy rains or suffocated in talcum dust seldom escaping the pungent odors of uncollected human and animal waste."[52] Camp Floyd and Frogtown quickly grew to a combined population of more than seven thousand, the second largest city in Utah.[53]

One establishment in Frogtown was an unlikely island of civility. John Carson and four brothers were among the original settlers of Fairfield in 1854. When the US Army arrived and built Camp Floyd nearby, most of the Mormon settlers left. Carson stayed to convert his home into the Stagecoach Inn, a small hotel and restaurant.[54] The inn was located just one block west of an Overland Stage and Pony Express Station, where stage drivers, passengers and pony express riders were fed. A small number of the passengers were privileged to dine and stay at the nearby Stagecoach Inn.

Thomas Alexander wrote that by refusing to serve alcohol or cater to a rowdy clientele, Carson was able to fill his hotel with prominent visitors, actors and actresses on their way to California.[55] Donald Moorman described Carson's hotel

---

Military Force in Utah" (correspondent dated article Jan. 17, 1860), *New York Times*, 15 Feb 1860.

48. Driggs, "Handcart Boy (First Draft)," 24.

49. Moorman with Sessions, *Camp Floyd*, 264.

50. Ibid., 63.

51. "Army at Camp Floyd."

52. Moorman with Sessions, *Camp Floyd*, 63.

53. Alexander and Arrington, "Camp in the Sagebrush," 9.

54. The original structure is restored and is part of the Camp Floyd/Stagecoach Inn State Park and Museum.

55. Alexander and Arrington, "Camp in the Sagebrush," 10.

—"the innkeeper presided at meals and led the conversations, the sitting room was the center of the inn's social life. The bread was freshly baked, the food always abundant, well cooked, and consumed rapidly and silently . . . For five hundred miles west of Fairfield no accommodations matched the Stagecoach Inn, which seemed opulent in comparison to the verminous way stations that dotted the Great Basin."[56] George Harrison probably visited both the stage station and Carson's hotel periodically if only to talk to his fellow cooks. Perhaps, he filed away a few observations of the Stagecoach Inn that he later used at his own hotel and restaurant.

Despite fears of hostilities between the occupying army and the Saints, no serious incidents occurred initially.[57] Johnston kept his troops close to Camp Floyd and maintained strict discipline. The calm period was also promoted by Governor Cumming's conciliatory relationship with Brigham Young. Cumming was aligned with President Buchanan, who did not want any further confrontation between the US Army and the Mormons.[58] Seemingly unaware of Buchanan's agenda, federal judge John Cradlebaugh arrived in Utah at the end of 1858 and embarked upon a very different course. By the following March, the judge convened a court in Provo and stated his bewilderment that authorities did not prosecute recent murders in Utah.[59] His list included the Parrish-Potter assassinations in Springville. Cradlebaugh asked General Johnston to provide troops to guard the individuals he would hold for trial. Johnston dispatched a company of infantry to camp near the makeshift courthouse in Provo. The presence of US Army troops caused anxiety and distrust among the citizens. Mormons poured into Provo to protect their leaders, and the city's marshal warned that he was adding two hundred policemen to his force. Johnston sent eight hundred additional troops to dissuade hostilities. Governor Cumming, under pressure from Brigham Young, asked Johnston to remove all troops in and around Provo. Johnston bluntly refused. The two sides were closer to a shooting war than any time since Mormon guerillas under Lot Smith attacked and destroyed army trains in 1857.[60]

The dangerous standoff was defused when Cradlebaugh shut down the court, allowing troops to be withdrawn. The frustrated judge harshly rebuked the grand jury for their failure to issue indictments based upon testimony regarding the Parrish-Potter murders.[61] Cradlebaugh relocated to Camp Floyd where he took a different tack. The judge issued bench warrants for the arrest of a dozen men in Springville and Provo suspected of involvement in the murders. Without informing Governor Cumming, General Johnston approved troops to aid federal marshals in apprehending the suspects.

The first target was Bishop Aaron Johnson. On the night of March 25, 1859, two hundred soldiers breached Springville's city wall and surrounded the bishop's

56. Moorman with Sessions, *Camp Floyd*, 63.
57. Furniss, *Mormon Conflict*, 211.
58. Coakley, *Role of Federal Military Forces*, 211.
59. Bigler and Bagley, *Mormon Rebellion*, 334.
60. Furniss, *Mormon Conflict*, 217.
61. Bigler and Bagley, *Mormon Rebellion*, 339-340.

home.[62] Don Carlos Johnson, who was eleven-years old and present in the house, later wrote a first hand account.[63] At daybreak a loud knock was heard on the front door. The young boy looked out the window to see hundreds of soldiers in blue with glittering guns and sabers. Mary Ann Johnson answered the door and was presented with a warrant for her husband's arrest. Marshal's deputies searched the thirty-five-room house plus cellars and attics without success. Johnson and scores of church officials from several towns were already hiding in the canyons of the Wasatch Mountains. A number of these roosts, including the one up Hobble Creek Canyon, were named "Kolob," a heavenly body that is closest to the throne of God in Mormon scripture.[64] The uproar caused by the US Army's forcible intrusion into Springville certainly awakened many citizens. George Harrison's parents and sisters lived only two blocks north of the bishop's home and probably spent a restless night.[65]

The confrontations precipitated by Judge Cradlebaugh and supported by General Johnston made officials in the Buchanan administration nervous. The War Department ordered Johnston not to use federal troops to enforce federal law unless requested by Utah's governor. Robert Coakley wrote that this order ended the law enforcement mission of the Army in Utah as Governor Cumming never requested military assistance.[66] Judge Cradlebaugh and other federal judges were put out of the business of prosecuting alleged Mormon crimes. After a summer hiding in the mountains, the "Kolob Boys" were able to return to their communities. None of those involved in the Parrish-Potter murders were held accountable. However, the impetuous judge created an important record of contemporary testimonies and affidavits that document an instance of church-sponsored murder for the sin of apostasy.

During 1860, a more frightening civil war than the Mormon Rebellion was imminent. George recalled that the feeling at Camp Floyd was tense as Southern sympathizers in the US Army were ordered to leave.[67] General Johnston, who as George pointed out, was well liked by the soldiers, was one of the first to depart.[68] He travelled to California and then to Texas via the isthmus of Panama. As much as Johnston claimed to despise Brigham Young as a traitor, the US Army general also took up arms against his country. Johnston died from a bullet wound on April 6, 1862, as he led a charge on Union lines at the Battle of Shiloh. The Confederate slaveholder was the highest-ranking general from either side to die fighting in the Civil War.

---

62. Ibid., 340.

63. Johnson, *History of Springville*, 56.

64. Ibid., 57.

65. The 1860 US Census shows the family renting near 400 North and Main Street. 1860 US Federal Census, Utah, Utah County, Springville (post office), page 303. Available online at https://www.ancestry.com/interactive/7667/4297342_00490?pid=34795458 (subscription required).

66. Coakley, *Role of Federal Military Forces*, 224.

67. Driggs, "Handcart Boy (First Draft)," 26.

68. Ibid.

George Harrison and Howard R. Driggs at Camp Floyd in 1918 (date per Camp Floyd historian, Chuck Mood). Behind them is the camp's Commissary building, the only structure to survive. The building has been restored and now serves as the Camp Floyd State Park Museum. *Courtesy of Gerald R. Sherratt Library, Southern Utah University.*

By August of 1860, the number of troops at Camp Floyd dropped to 320 from a high of nearly 2,800 two years before.[69] George Harrison remained at the camp as long as possible because the income was the best way to help his struggling parents.[70] After rebels bombarded Fort Sumter in April 1861, the remaining federal soldiers were called eastward. Colonel Philip St. George Cooke, the camp's last commander, disposed of $3,000,000 to $4,000,000 of assets. George Harrison remembered, "Wagons, harnesses, and other equipment were sold to the settlers for next to nothing."[71] Frogtown quickly disappeared.

The Utah War, frequently referred to as "Buchanan's Blunder," actually accomplished its intended mission. A federal appointee assumed the governorship, and the US Army took up residence. At Buchanan's insistence, the troops proved to be more of a reminder of federal authority than an active instrument of law enforcement against the Mormons.[72] Young's acquiescence to the US Army made it clear that there would never be an autonomous Mormon kingdom. A forty-year process of separating church from state, labeled by historians as the "Americanization" of Utah, was set in motion.

The war was also the last of a series of expensive and difficult events that exacted a heavy toll on the Mormon people. The food and income lost to the droughts and cricket plagues of 1855 and 1856; the costs of rescuing the handcart parties;

---

69. Alexander and Arrington, "Camp in the Sagebrush," 19.
70. Driggs, "Handcart Boy," Jan 1945, 11.
71. Driggs, "Handcart Boy (First Draft)," 27.
72. Coakley, *Role of Federal Military Forces*, 218.

the costs of supporting the Nauvoo Legion in the Utah War; and the costs of the "Move South" combined to impoverish the Mormons, according to Leonard Arrington. He wrote, "it was clear that a decade and more of achievement and social independence in the face of hostile nature and hostile humanity had ended in poverty and disappointment."[73]

When the US Army departed from Utah, George Harrison lost dependable, cash-paying customers whom he served for nearly four years. As the nineteen-year-old walked or hitched a wagon ride to Springville, he probably had no knowledge of his next job. George saw little of his family after separating from them and the Martin company at Deer Creek. He later told Howard Driggs that the break was a good opportunity to visit with his parents and siblings.[74]

73. Arrington, *Great Basin Kingdom*, 194.
74. Driggs, "Handcart Boy," Jan 1945, 27.

11

Fish Springs Overland Stage Station
and Patrick Connor

One of the siblings George caught up with after leaving Camp Floyd was his brother Aaron. The 1860 Census shows the Harrison family living in a rented house near 400 North Main Street.[1] Strangely, the same census listed a "George Harrison," age nineteen, as a resident in the William Harrison home. However, George worked at Camp Floyd until July 1861 and was seldom able to visit Springville. The man who was identified as George Harrison on the census was, in all likelihood, Aaron Harrison.

When Aaron deserted the US Army near Fort Leavenworth in 1857, he was faced with the considerable problem of another thousand-mile trek to Utah. Money was undoubtedly an issue. He also worried about being identified and apprehended by the US Army, which was unpredictable in its treatment of deserters. Aaron's best option was to assume an alias and join an LDS Church company departing Florence, Nebraska. Records show that the only Aaron Harrison to ever travel overland in an LDS Church company was a member of the 1856 Martin Handcart Company.[2] Records also document that an 1860 company led by LDS Patriarch John Smith, included a lone traveler, a twenty two-year-old named "George Harrison."[3] No George Harrison who was of a similar age in 1860 is found on any of the Mormon ship rosters, nor in the 1860, 1870 or 1880 Utah censuses. The Smith Company arrived in Salt Lake City on September 1, 1860.[4] Aaron had ample time to travel to Springville before the census taker visited the Harrison residence on September 8.

Soon after his arrival in Springville, George's brother found a kindred rebel spirit in Tryphena Ursula Goddard Carson. In 1854, Tryphena, also referred to as Ursula, Sula or Zula, was seventeen and working for the William Huff Carson family in Salt Lake City.[5] William's wife became ill and, shortly before dying, asked Tryphena to take care of her five children. Tryphena stayed with the family,

---

1. Their approximate location can be determined because the census shows the family living near Martin P. Crandall, whose lot was at the southeast corner of 400 North and Main.

2. Mormon Pioneer Overland Travel database. Search results available online at https://history.lds.org/overlandtravel/search?first-name=aaron&last-name=harrison&birth-year=&death-year=.

3. John Smith Company (1860), Mormon Pioneer Overland Travel database, available online at https://history.lds.org/overlandtravel/companies/272.

4. Ibid.

5. Shirley Carson Hogenson, comp., *Tryphena Ursula Goddard—Second Wife of William Duff Carson, Her Ancestors and Progenitors* (Salt Lake City: The George Carson and Anna Hough Family Organization, 1981). 2-5. Obtained at the Daughters of Utah Pioneers Library in Salt Lake City.

and about a year later she married William Huff Carson. The same year, William was one of five Carson brothers who participated in the establishment of Fairfield, Utah, the first settlement in Cedar Valley.[6]

At the beginning of the Tintic War in February 1856, Utes killed two Carson brothers, George and Washington. Their deaths left two widows and children who needed support. William Carson announced that he would marry his brother Washington Carson's widow, though Tryphena threatened to "walk out the back door the day a second wife walked in the front door."[7] Tryphena did not leave immediately, but within two years made good on her threat. Despite "some little trouble with who was to take the children," she departed with the three children conceived with William Carson.[8] Family tradition holds that Tryphena also took the "big Carson Family Bible with all the information written on the fly leafs of the families, births, marriages deaths etc."[9] Tryphena settled in Springville in a house next to the William Harrison residence.[10] She and Aaron were married in about 1863.

Though George enjoyed his visit with Aaron and family, he knew that he did not want to work in the cashless agrarian economy. Springville residents subsisted mainly on farm products and vegetables from their own gardens. Historian Mary Chase Finley wrote, "Laborers, such as adobe makers and lumbermen, were in good demand, but were usually paid in kind as there was little money in circulation."[11] George found another opportunity in the Gentile economy. He took a job as a cook with the Overland Stage Company.[12]

Working at a stage and pony express station was among the most dangerous jobs in North America in the early 1860s.[13] George was aware of the risk. While he was at Camp Floyd, Indians carried out a campaign of death and destruction along the emigrant and mail route in western Utah. Seven stations were burned to the ground and sixteen station employees were killed.[14] Troops dispatched by General Johnston from Camp Floyd responded with brutal reprisals in what became known as the "Paiute War." By the end of the year, the US Army achieved a temporary truce with Indians along the mail and emigrations routes through Utah.

Not surprisingly, the dangerous duty at isolated stage stations paid well. A station keeper made $100 per month plus room and board, and other personnel

6. Ibid.

7. Ibid.

8. Lynn R. Carson, *The Tintic War and the Deaths of George and Washington Carson* (Salt Lake City: George Carson-Ann Hough Family Organization, 1979), 29. Available online at https://familysearch.org/photos/artifacts/1921181.

9. Hogenson, *Tryphena Ursula Goddard*. 8.

10. Ibid., 7.

11. Finley, *History of Springville*, 44.

12. Driggs, "Handcart Boy," Jan 1945, 27.

13. "The Story of the Pony Express and the Paiute War/High Danger in the Desert," WesternHistory. No longer available online.

14. Raymond W. Settle and Mary Lund, *Saddles and Spurs: The Pony Express Saga* (Lincoln, NE: University of Nebraska Press, 1955), 160.

The Fish Springs Overland Stage and Pony Express Station was about a year old when
George Harrison arrived as a cook in 1861. The structure was still inhabited when this photo
was taken in 1914.
Used by permission, Utah State Historical Society

earned about half that wage.[15] Even at the low end of the range, Harrison probably
doubled his income at Camp Floyd. The stage outposts employed rough, sometimes
desperate characters, described by LeRoy R. Hafen as "the dregs of society, many of
whom were fugitives from justice."[16]

George was assigned to the Fish Springs Station, located 100 miles west of
Camp Floyd on the "Central Route." The previously infrequently traveled route
became the country's primary choice for mail delivery to and from California
when President Lincoln shifted stage lines away from Confederate troops in the
Southwest.[17] Fish Springs Station was located in the Great Salt Lake Desert, one of
the least inhabitable areas of the North American continent. After passing through
the barren landscape in 1860, Horace Greeley wrote, "If Uncle Sam should ever sell
that tract for one cent per acre, he will swindle the purchaser outrageously."[18] To
those crossing the bleak inferno, the prospect of "Fish Springs" probably sounded

---

15. Joseph J. Di Certo, *The Saga of the Pony Express* (Missoula, MT: Mountain Press Publishing
Company, 2002), 44.

16. Leroy R. Hafen, *The Overland Mail, 1849-1869* (Norman, OK: University of Oklahoma
Press), 304.

17. Mary Jane Woodger, "Abraham Lincoln and the Mormons," in Kenneth L. Alford, ed.,
Civil War Saints (Provo and Salt Lake City: RSC/Deseret Book, 2012), 15.

18. Philip L. Fradkin, *Stagecoach: Wells Fargo and the American West* (New York: Free Press,
2002), 49.

promising. In fact, the springs were a collection of warm, sulfurous potholes. Adventurer Richard F. Burton stayed a night at Fish Springs in 1860 and was struck by the "rotten water." Burton and his fellow travelers were served a breakfast, "which the water rendered truly detestable."[19]

Fish Springs was a "home" station where drivers for daily east and west bound mail coaches were rotated and lodged. The Pony Express was still operating when George Harrison began cooking at Fish Springs, and the riders changed horses and bunked at the station. Typically a station keeper, a cook, and from two to four stock tenders manned these larger outposts.[20] George told Howard Driggs that the station was a busy place.[21] Two months after George's arrival the transcontinental telegraph line was completed. The Pony Express went out of business, and a telegraph operator was added to the station.[22]

Harrison provided Howard Driggs with a good estimate of when he started cooking on the Overland Stage Route. The yet unknown Samuel Clemens passed through Fish Springs Station on August 9, 1861.[23] Years later, after Harrison apparently read Mark Twain's description of the journey in *Roughing It*, he recalled beginning employment at the station at about the same time.[24] Twain described Fish Springs as an outpost in the middle of an alkali desert whose "concentrated hideousness shames the diffused and diluted horrors of Sahara."[25]

The United States was immersed in the Civil War throughout Harrison's tenure at Fish Springs. Though Brigham Young believed that slavery was a divinely ordained institution, he did not align with either side.[26] Young viewed the war only in his religious terms and promised the Saints that the conflict would destroy the United States government. The Mormons, he said, would survive to establish the Kingdom of God and rule over all mankind.[27] Young made one short-lived contribution to the Union's cause. In May 1862 he offered a company of cavalry led by Lot Smith to protect the overland mail route in Wyoming from Indian attacks.[28]

Not long after Young's conciliatory gesture, Abraham Lincoln signed the Morrill Act, the nation's first anti-polygamy statute.[29] Lincoln was too preoccupied with the Civil War to enforce the legislation. He informed Young that he would

19. Sir Richard F. Burton, *The City of Saints; Among the Mormons and Across; the Rocky Mountains to California* (Torrington, WY: The Narrative Press, 2003), 338.

20. Settle and Lund, *Saddles and Spurs*, 115.

21. Driggs, "Handcart Boy," Jan 1945, 27.

22. Driggs, "Handcart Boy," Jan 1945, 27.

23. Mark Twain, *Roughing It* (Oakland: University of California Press, 1995), 776.

24. Driggs, "Handcart Boy," Jan 1945, 27.

25. Twain, *Roughing It*, 122.

26. Turner, *Brigham Young*, 317.

27. Will Bagley, "A Terror to Evil-Doers: Camp Douglas, Abraham Lincoln, and Utah's Civil War," *Utah Historical Quarterly* 80, no. 4, 318.

28. William P. MacKinnon, "Utah's Civil War(s): Linkages and Connections," *Utah Historical Quarterly* 80, no. 4, 300.

29. Ibid., 304.

leave the Mormons alone if they caused him no difficulties.[30] However, the President hedged his bet by ordering the relocation of the "California Volunteers" to Utah after receiving reports of disloyal rhetoric by Young and other Church officials. The army was tasked to protect the Union's mail route, but also to keep an eye on the Mormons.

Another impending intrusion of federal troops into Utah combined with legislation criminalizing polygamy put the Church president in a foul mood. When asked in August 1862 to renew the enlistment of Mormon cavalry to protect the country's mail route to Utah and California, Young declined. Utah's brief role in the Civil War ended. William MacKinnon wrote, "Compared to the participation, if not carnage, experienced by virtually every other state and territory, Utah's absence from the fray was unparalleled."[31] Many Americans viewed Utah's unwillingness to participate in the war as additional evidence of disloyalty and rebellion.

Colonel Patrick Connor, who led the California Volunteers out of Stockton, California, in July 1862, was among those with a poor opinion of Brigham Young. Connor looked forward to the opportunity to fight Indians and, hopefully, Mormons. By late August, his regiment was camped near the Ruby Valley Overland Stage Station. Connor left his troops and, in civilian dress, traveled two hundred miles by stagecoach to Salt Lake City. After a short visit, the belligerent soldier wrote to his superior in California that the Mormon capital was a "community of traitors, murderers, fanatics and whores," and that Church leaders were preaching treason.[32] Connor originally planned to reoccupy Camp Floyd. After visiting the location, he believed the camp was too remote from Salt Lake City. Connor successfully lobbied for approval to construct a new camp on a plateau three miles east of the capital. The Colonel promised that once entrenched he would "say to the Saints of Utah, enough of your treason."[33]

George Harrison was probably not aware of Connor when the soldier, without uniform, paused at Fish Springs going to and from Salt Lake City. But, there was no mistaking the colonel a month later when he arrived at Fish Springs leading seven hundred infantry and three companies of cavalry. The California Volunteers marched twenty-two miles on October 11, and the army's chaplain looked forward to the springs as a chance for relief from the heat. Unfortunately, he found the sulfurous brine to be "like a seat in the California Legislature . . . excruciatingly nauseous."[34]

By chance, George Harrison was on leave from Fish Springs Station when the California Volunteers camped nearby. George and his brother Aaron were part of an improbable cricket match played two days before in Salt Lake City. The Harrison brothers probably learned the game in Manchester. They scored a third of the Springville Union Cricket Club's runs. The Springville men prevailed in a close

30. George U. Hubbard, "Abraham Lincoln As Seen By The Mormons," *Utah Historical Quarterly* 31, no. 2, 103.

31. MacKinnon, "Utah's Civil War(s)," 301.

32. James F. Varley, *Brigham and the Brigadier* (Tucson: Westernlore Press, 1989), 49.

33. Ibid., 59.

34. Ibid., 62.

six-hour match, and Salt Lake City's Deseret Union Club treated the winners to dinner. A reporter wrote that the meal at the "Valley House" reflected great credit on the host "as a caterer for the inner man."[35]

Colonel Connor continued eastward from Fish Springs without revealing his plans. His troops assumed that the abandoned Camp Floyd was their destination. When the weary California Volunteers arrived at the camp on October 17, Connor announced that they would spend the winter closer to the Mormon capital.[36] A twenty-mile march on the following day brought the army to the west bank of the Jordan River. Rumors that the Mormons would use force to oppose the army's crossing of the river ran unchecked among the soldiers. While no evidence emerged that the stories were true, Connor sent a message to Young saying that he would "cross the river Jordan if hell yawned before him."[37] On October 20, 1862, having met no opposition, the California Volunteers marched up Main Street and turned east onto 100 South. The large crowds were silent as the soldiers passed to a plateau at the mouth of Red Butte Canyon. Connor named the new military post Camp Douglas and trained his cannons on the city below.[38] Historians Alford and MacKinnon noted that the camp is the only military installation in the United States sited for the purpose of keeping an eye on American citizens.[39] Camp Douglas became Fort Douglas in 1878 and was not closed until 1991 when the property became part of the adjoining University of Utah campus.

As Connor's regiment marched to Salt Lake City in 1862, Indian attacks upon the emigrant trail reached a new intensity. Travel west of Fort Hall, near present-day Pocatello, Idaho, was "a particular type of hell."[40] While camped at Ruby Valley, Connor received a report that Indians murdered twenty-three emigrants. Chaplain Anderson wrote that the Colonel made arrangements "for putting several grains of very hot corn in the ears of the Indians."[41] Connor sent a cavalry expedition to proceed to Salt Lake City with instructions to make a lasting impression on all tribes. When the unscathed cavalry rejoined Connor at Camp Douglas on October 29, the soldiers reported that they killed "a veritable potpourri of redmen."[42]

Three months later Colonel Connor was presented with another opportunity for glory. He received new reports of immigrants murdered by Shoshone Indians north of Salt Lake City. Federal Judge John Kinney received the same reports and issued a warrant for the arrest of several Shoshone chiefs thought to be in Cache Valley. Kinney gave the warrant to a federal marshal who promptly went to Colonel

35. "Cricket Match." *Deseret News*, 15 Oct 1862, 3.
36. Varley, *Brigham and the Brigadier*, 63.
37. Ibid.
38. Bigler, *Forgotten Kingdom*, 227.
39. Kenneth L. Alford and William MacKinnon, "What's In a Name? The Establishment of Camp Douglas," in Kenneth L. Alford, ed., *Civil War Saints* (Provo and Salt Lake City: RSC and Deseret Book, 2012), 161.
40. Varley, *Brigham and the Brigadier*, 53.
41. Ibid., 59.
42. Ibid., 75.

Connor for help. The colonel told the marshal that he was welcome to join the US Army's expedition, but that he should not expect any Indian survivors.[43]

The expedition's target was the winter camp of an estimated 400 Shoshone near the Bear River in what is today Idaho. After a very cold march of 110 miles, the California Volunteers, led by Connor, were ready to attack the village at dawn on January 29, 1863.[44] The Shoshone were never going to win the battle, but they held their own until they ran out of ammunition after two hours of fighting. A massacre ensued, including numerous atrocities committed against women and children.[45] Connor wrote in his official report that his troops found 224 Indian fatalities. A group of local citizens walked the battlefield the next morning and counted 368 dead Indians.[46] Twenty-three California Volunteers were fatally wounded and seventy-five suffered severe frostbite. The slaughter marked the end of the Northern Shoshone as an independent tribe. Connor received a promotion to brigadier general and national fame as an Indian fighter. In Denver, the *Rocky Mountain News* recommended employing a few more men such as Colonel Connor to "wipe the treacherous vagabonds from the face of the earth."[47]

Within two months of the Bear River Massacre, angry Indian reprisals began along the Central Overland Route west of Salt Lake City. On March 22, a band of Goshutes took possession of Eight Mile Stage Station, fifty miles west of Fish Springs.[48] The Indians killed the two station keepers and then hid to wait for a stagecoach. When the stage arrived, the Goshutes killed the driver and severely wounded a passenger sitting next to him. One of three other passengers managed to get to the reins and drive the coach to safety at Deep Creek Station. The following morning a party rode back to the site of the attack to determine the fate of the station keepers. The cook was stripped and scalped. He suffered multiple knife wounds, and his tongue was cut out. The naked body of the other station keeper was found nearby.[49]

The attacks moved closer to George Harrison at Fish Springs. Harrison told Howard Driggs that Goshutes continually hung around his station begging for something to eat. George found it difficult to turn them away as he remembered who saved him from starvation.[50] In order to control the requests, he asked the Indians to do chores for him in exchange for food. One old Goshute who frequently worked for George slipped up to the kitchen the day after the Eight Mile Station murders and excitedly told him to get out as Indians were coming.[51] George alerted station personnel, including the telegraph operator who sent the message along the

43. Ibid., 97.

44. Brigham D. Madsen, *Glory Hunter: A Biography of Patrick Edward Connor* (Salt Lake City: University of Utah Press, 1990), 80.

45. Ibid., 84.

46. Brigham D. Madsen, *The Northern Shoshoni* (Caldwell, ID: The Caxton Printers, Ltd., 1980), 36.

47. Hafen, *Overland Mail*, 249.

18. Varley, *Brigham and the Brigadier*, 126.

49. Ibid.

50. Driggs, "Handcart Boy," Jan 1945, 27.

51. Ibid.

wires. The Indians did not bother Fish Springs Station, but thirty miles west they burned down Canyon Station and killed the keeper.[52] George later told Howard Driggs, "things looked dismal for cooks at the stage stations."[53] The twenty-one-year-old wisely resigned his job and returned to Springville.

The hostilities in March 1863 that caused George Harrison to leave employment with the Overland Stage are considered the beginning of the "Goshute War"—an arbitrary name as Paiutes, Shoshone and Utes also participated.[54] During a seven-month period, the stage company lost nearly twenty stations, and sixteen employees were killed.[55] Patrick Connor ordered cavalry units to kill any warriors found in the general vicinity of the stage and mail route. The natives recognized the futility of fighting, and by October, Connor signed separate treaties with each tribe involved.[56] The treaties marked the end of any significant Indian resistance to emigration and the overland stage in Utah.

Patrick Connor was left with no Indians to subdue, and President Lincoln prohibited him from picking a fight with the Mormons. He looked for other ways to make life difficult for Brigham Young. Connor believed that discoveries of gold and other valuable minerals would bring a flood of Gentile miners to Utah.[57] The strategy enjoyed the added attraction of potential riches for Connor and his soldiers.[58] With encouragement from their general, the California Volunteers started prospecting in the summer of 1863. The industry did not develop overnight, but mining gradually became a significant part of Utah's economy while attracting many Gentiles to the state. General Connor is remembered as the "Father of Utah Mining" and an early force in the Americanization of Utah.[59] Connor's efforts to stimulate mining later presented George Harrison with a life-changing opportunity as a trader.

52. Sam Post Davis, ed., *The History of Nevada*, Volume I (Reno/Los Angeles: The Elms Publishing Co., 1913), 158. Available online at https://archive.org/stream/historyofnevada01davirich.

53. Driggs, "Handcart Boy," Jan 1945, 27.

54. Dennis R. Defa, "The Goshute Indians of Utah," in *A History of Utah's Native Americans*, Utah History to Go. Available online at http://historytogo.utah.gov/people/ethnic_cultures/the_history_of_utahs_american_indians/chapter3.html.

55. Ibid.

56. Varley, *Brigham and the Brigadier*, 155.

57. Leonard J. Arrington, "Abundance From the Earth: The Beginnings of Commercial Mining in Utah," *Utah Historical Quarterly* 31, no. 3, 200.

58. Varley, *Brigham and the Brigadier*, 155.

59. Madsen, *Glory Hunter*, 276.

12

Freighting, Marriage and the Black Hawk War

G eorge Harrison's eighteen-month stay at the Fish Springs Overland Stage Station was lucrative. Much of his income probably went to help his parents become established as farmers, a vocation that never interested George. Fortunately, Springville offered a burgeoning freight industry, developed largely because farming was limited by insufficient water.[1] One history of Utah County noted, "The colonists had early to look to some other occupation beside tilling the soil to eke out a livelihood . . . Before the railroad came, Springville had attained success as a freighting center."[2]

George learned his new job on the difficult "Southern Route" to California. Before the completion of the transcontinental railroad, much of Utah's imported goods were shipped around the tip of South America to San Pedro, today's port of Los Angeles. The goods were then hauled by wagons to Utah. From 1855 to 1869, the trail was one of the busiest freight routes in the West.[3] The US Army at Camp Floyd and later at Camp Douglas received a significant portion of these shipments. In an article published many years later in the *Deseret News*, Harrison recalled going to southern California in 1862 [actually 1863]—following freighting as a vocation.[4]

While travel on the overland trail between the Missouri River and Utah relied upon oxen, mules were the unanimous favorites on the Southern Route. Mules were able to subsist on desert feed and the inconsistent and often saline water.[5] The first four hundred miles of the southern end of the trail crossed a series of uninhabited deserts, the most challenging of which was named "Death Valley." Dreary landscapes passed by at two miles an hour—assuming the mules were healthy and cooperating. The eight hundred-mile freighting trip from San Pedro to Salt Lake City lasted two months. A historian wrote, "Freighting was a hard and grinding life. There was work, hard work, loading and unloading at each end of the trip, and there was the never ending exposure to sun, wind, snow, rain, mud, cold, and the hard bed on the ground, wet or dry, at the end of each strenuous day."[6]

1. Glenn L. Alleman, *The Legacy of the Springville Contractors* (Springville: Springville Historical Society, 2014), 2.

2. Emma N. Huff, comp. *Memories That Live, Utah County Centennial History* (np: Daughters of Utah Pioneers of Utah County, 1947), 354-56.

3. Edward Leo Lyman, *The Overland Journey From Utah to California* (Reno: University of Nevada Press, 2004, 152.

4. "Story of Utah's Biggest Indian War."

5. Lyman, *Overland Journey*, 165.

6. "Fox, a Champion Puller," William R. Palmer Collection, Gerald R. Sherratt Library,

When a freighting outfit hired George he had limited experience with draught animals and wagons. To become a "real" freighter he needed to learn the skills of a muleskinner. The entry-level job for working for a freighting company was a "swamper," who did odd jobs such as feeding the mules, setting up camp and cooking. George's skill as a cook was probably helpful in obtaining his new opportunity. Over time, and with experience, swampers learned how to repair harnesses and wagons, hitch up a team, and use a whip and reins to guide the animals.

Decades later George, entertaining diners at his restaurant, recalled "hair-raising stories" of experiences with the Southern Paiutes. A guest wrote, "His favorite story is how he cooked sap, or flour mush, for very hungry Indians in return for certain work bargained for, and the chief held as hostage until both sides complied with the bargain to the letter."[7] George described his diet in those early days as "Sorghum and sowbelly and Sowbelly and sorghum."[8] Sorghum was a widely consumed cereal grain valued for its drought resistance, while sowbelly was salt pork made from the least desirable parts of a hog carcass. Harrison also recalled how he handled the alkali water that was common in the deserts. He put a handful of flour in a bucket of water; the alkali adhered to the flour and made the water so it would not hurt the mules' stomachs.[9]

Muleskinning was anything but a reputable profession. Harold Schindler wrote that teamsters in general were the also-rans in frontier communities—"teamsters had a lock on the lowest rung of the social ladder . . . this included bullwhackers and muleskinners, men who could curse their animals in a vile stream of profanity for ten minutes straight without repeating themselves."[10] George worked alongside grown men since age eight and probably commanded the necessary vocabulary. Muleskinners were also notorious for their "various abhorrent odors," occasioned in part by close proximity to mules, but also by an aversion to washing or bathing.[11]

As was the case with cooking at Fish Springs, George Harrison chose the rough and difficult job because it paid well. Newly hired swampers earned at least thirty dollars a month, and as George gained experience he may have approached the fifty dollars a month he probably earned at Fish Springs. Edward L. Lyman wrote, "Drivers handling the largest wagon outfits often commanded pay of $75-$100, plus expenses, and sometimes netted $175 monthly."[12] Harrison probably did not make sufficient trips on the Southern Route to ascend to driver of one of the big rigs, but he earned a living and acquired valuable skills that he used for decades.

Southern Utah University.

7.   Roger V. Roper, "Hotels Revisited, Retracing a 1919 Utah Road Trip," *Utah Preservation*, 2. Available online at https://collections.lib.utah.edu/details?id=418888&q=*&page=1&rows=200&fd=title_t%2Csetname_s%2Ctype_t&sort=&gallery=&facet_setname_s=dha_hpp.

8.   Ibid.

9.   Ibid.

10.   Hal Schindler, "Bullwhacking Was No Snap; Occupied Lowest Rung on the Social Ladder," *The Salt Lake Tribune*, 29 Oct. 1995. Available online at https://heritage.utah.gov/history/uhg-slt-bullwhacking-snap.

11.   Lyman, *Overland Journey*, 165.

12.   Ibid., 166.

Photo of Rosella Damon White taken in a studio in Keene, New Hampshire, a small town
near her family's home in Marlborough. The photo was found in suitcase in the attic of her
home in Springville, Utah.
Copy given to author by Barbara Lee.

In between his trips to California, George Harrison found time to start
building a life in Springville. He joined a vocal quartet that performed around Utah
County. At one concert, George met Rosella Damon White who lived in Provo.
Rosella was born on September 16, 1838, in the small village of Marlborough,
New Hampshire. She was the sixth of seven children. Her father, Noah White,
was a farmer and carpenter who became an invalid during her childhood. Rosella
later told her daughter, Anna May, that he was paralyzed and was so helpless that
he needed to be led around. She added that her girlhood was not very pleasant.[13]
Rosella married Jonathan Milan Russell on April 25, 1854—six months before
her sixteenth birthday. Her mother, Arvilla Lewis White, died in November of the
same year, at the relatively young age of fifty-one.[14]

Rosella did not move far from home when she married. The 1860 US Census
shows that she and Jonathan Russell were living in Dublin, New Hampshire, nine
miles east of Marlborough. Jonathan is listed as a potter and Rosella as a dressmaker.
In November 1861 she received a letter from her brother Everett, who was head

<hr>

13. May Harrison Smith, "History of Rosella Damon White Harrison," Camp Aaron
Johnson, Daughters of Utah Pioneers of Utah County, Springville, Utah. Copy in possession of
author (gift of Shirley Smith, Springville, Utah).

14. Arvilla White death certificate, New Hampshire, Death and Disinterment Records,
1754-1947, Ancestry.com. Available online at http://ancstry.me/2n9yUHK (subscription required).

bugler for the Ohio Volunteers camped at Romney, Virginia. Everett addressed Rosella as "My ever dear but absent sister," and noted that he had "many a bullet whistle by me." He was pleased to hear from Rosella "because you have ever been a good sister to me."[15]

Within a few months after this letter, Rosella took a step that caused a dramatic change in her brother's affections. Years later, Rosella wrote, "I left all my friends and relatives for the sake of the Gospel."[16] The gospel that caused Rosella to leave family and friends was the Mormon religion. Prior to her conversion, she probably worshiped in the Congregational Church as did her paternal grandfather, William White.[17] Once Rosella and Jonathan decided to follow Mormonism, they did not take long to gather to Zion. The couple travelled 1400 miles by rail and steamship to Florence, Nebraska. Church elder James McKnight baptized the couple in the Missouri River on July 20, 1862.[18] McKnight's most notable contribution to Utah history came four years earlier, when he and apostle George A. Smith authored the first official report of the Mountain Meadows Massacre.[19]

Ten days after baptism, Rosella and Jonathan Russell departed for Utah as members of the Isaac Canfield Company.[20] To help pay their way across the plains, Rosella cooked for the wagon train.[21] The company of eighteen wagons and 120 Saints elected three captains, including Rosella's husband.[22] Coincidentally, Samuel Blackham, his wife and a one-year-old child were also travelling in the same party.[23] Six years before, Samuel and Aaron Harrison left the Martin Handcart Company to enlist in the US Army at Fort Laramie. The Canfield Company enjoyed an "exceedingly prosperous journey" across the plains with little sickness, no deaths and very few losses of cattle.[24] Though the trip went as well as possible, Rosella and her husband experienced an exhausting 1000-mile walk across the plains and mountains to Salt Lake City. Four days after their arrival on October 16, 1862, the

---

15. Everett White (Romney, VA) to Rosella Damon White Russell, 16 Nov 1861. Copy of letter provided by Rosella's great-granddaughter, Barbara Lee, Springville, Utah, 2015.

16. Myrl Storrs Stewart, "Biography of Rosella Damon White Harrison," Daughters of the Utah Pioneers Camp 49, Weber County. The letter is reproduced as an attachment. The original was placed in a Relief Society Box, which was sealed for fifty years in 1892. The box was opened on March 17, 1942. Biography obtained from George Harrison's great-grandson, Jan Storrs, 2012

17. Thomas White and Samuel White, *Ancestral Chronological Record of the William White Family from 1607 to 1895* (Concord, NH: Republican Press Association, 1895), 57. Available online at https://archive.org/details/ancestralchrono00whitgoog.

18. Smith, "History of Rosella Damon White Harrison."

19. Juanita Brooks, *The Mountain Meadows Massacre* (Norman, OK: University of Oklahoma Press, 1970), 165. The report, given to Brigham Young and placed in the Journal History of the Church, attributed the massacre to Indians.

20. Isaac A. Canfield Company, 1862, Mormon Pioneer Overland Travel database, available online at https://history.lds.org/overlandtravels/companyPioneers?lang=eng&companyId=83.

21. Smith, "History of Rosella Damon White Harrison."

22. Isaac A. Canfield Emigrating Company, Journal, 1862 July-Oct., Isaac A. Canfield Company, 1862, Mormon Pioneer Overland Travel database. Available online at https://history.lds.org/overlandtravel/sources/4937.

23. Isaac A. Canfield Company.

24. "Arrival of Trains," *Deseret News*, 22 Oct 1862, 132.

couple was able to watch Colonel Patrick Connor and the California Volunteers march through the capital to set up camp below Red Butte.

Rosella initially did housework in Salt Lake City. As related by her daughter, Jonathan Russell would not work and did not support his wife. Rosella stood it as long as she could, then went to see Brigham Young to gain approval for a divorce. The Church president was not in his office when she arrived, so she waited. As time went by, Rosella began to think that she was not meant to get a divorce. President Young did come, and Rosella explained her troubles to him. He said, "don't you live with that man another minute," and the divorce was granted.[25] Historian Eugene Campbell wrote, "In the case of women, he [Young] seemed especially generous in freeing them from an unhappy marriage."[26]

Rosella moved to Provo where she did domestic work and struggled to make ends meet. She lived on potatoes and a little salt for seven weeks.[27] Rosella had a melodeon that she brought across the plains and subsequently to Provo. The small organ and musical talents that she developed as a young girl led to a chance meeting with "a splendid singer from Springville."[28] That singer was George Harrison, who was part of a group that included Aaron Harrison and David Wheeler.[29] Rosella became organist for the quartet as well as singing alto.

In early 1865, Rosella received a letter from her brother Everett that responded to one in which she probably described her life in Provo. She may have mentioned her friend, George Harrison. The location and date on Everett's letter, Sisters Ferry, Savannah River Georgia, January 30, 1865, placed him as part of the left wing of William Tecumseh Sherman's army. The army was resting after its scorched-earth march from Atlanta to Savannah, Georgia, and preparing to move north to Charleston, South Carolina.[30] Everett's reply captured the country's animosity toward Mormons and possibly the strain of war. He wrote, "Dear sister I have just received a letter from you . . . I am in sorrow over you because you have so acted within the last 2 years . . . As for my part, I had rather have heard of your death than to have heard of your going off with that damnable sect the Mormons . . . The situation that you are in now is no better than the most common whore . . . should you return to your duty as a sister then write and not until then."[31]

---

25. Smith, "History of Rosella Damon White Harrison."

26. Eugene E. Campbell and Bruce L. Campbell, "Divorce among Mormon Polygamists: Extent and Explanations," *Utah Historical Quarterly* 46, no. 1, 12.

27. Smith, "History of Rosella Damon White Harrison."

28. Ibid.

29. Mary L. Wheeler, "Biography of David Wheeler," Aaron Johnson Camp of Springville Daughters of the Utah Pioneers. The author states that the quartet included George, Aaron and "Rosena"[Rosella] Harrison. The history dated Feb. 3, 1930 found in David Wheeler file at Springville Pioneer Museum.

30. "Sister's Ferry," Wikipedia.

31. Everett White (Sister's Ferry) to Rosella Damon White Russell, 30 Jan 1865. The original letter is in the possession of Barbara Lee, great-granddaughter of Rosella, and resident of Springville, Utah. The letter was found in a suitcase that came from the attic of George and Rosella Harrison's home.

George and Rosella Harrison—possibly taken at their wedding in 1866.
Copy given to author by Barbara Lee.

Rosella ignored her brother's opinion and married George Harrison on May 4, 1865, with Bishop Aaron Johnson performing the ceremony.[32] On December 7, 1868, their marriage was solemnized in the Endowment House in Salt Lake City.[33] The purpose of this Mormon ordinance is to seal familial relationships throughout eternity.[34] Upon marrying, George and Rosella settled in Springville. The first of Rosella's nine children was born within a year of her marriage to George. George Harrison probably continued to freight to California. However, about a year after his marriage, that career was put on hold by another war between the Mormons and the Utes.

Despite the purported special relationship between the LDS Church and Indians, historian Warren Metcalf pointed out that Mormon settlers were relentless

32. "... and Mrs. George Harrison Celebrate Golden Wedding," newspaper clipping with a partial title and missing page number. Article is "Special Correspondence" from Springville and is dated May 6. Article describes anniversary party on May 4. Clipping given to author by Jan Storrs in 2012.

33. Stewart, "Biography of Rosella Damon White Harrison."

34. "Mormon Temple Endowment," Temples of the Church of Jesus Christ of Latter-day Saints, available online at http://www.ldschurchtemples.com/mormon/endowment/.

in their expropriation of land for farms and new colonies.[35] The Utes were expected to relocate without a fuss. Some of the natives tried to give up a nomadic lifestyle and settle on Indian farms that Brigham Young established following the Walker War. As early as 1856, Indian Agent Garland Hurt observed that the scale of subsidies to Utes at the farms was too great a burden on the Mormon rank and file.[36] Eventually the local Saints tired of feeding the Indians, and the farms were abandoned.[37] The Utes had no choice but to steal cattle to avoid starvation. Before long, Mormons were embroiled in their longest, bloodiest and final Indian war.

Historians mark April 9, 1865, as the beginning of the Black Hawk War.[38] On the same day that Robert E. Lee surrendered at Appomattox, a group of Utes rode into Manti, Utah, to meet with US officials and make reparations for Mormon cattle that they stole and butchered. One aggrieved settler showed up drunk and initiated a shouting match. He pulled a young chieftain off his horse. The angered Indian delegation, including a young leader named Black Hawk, rode away hurling insults over their shoulders.[39] Within a few days, Black Hawk and other Utes killed five Mormons. From 1865 to 1867 the Indians made over a hundred raids, while killing seventy settlers and stealing thousands of cattle. The Saints were forced to abandon dozens of small settlements in southern Utah and "fort up" elsewhere.[40] Both the Mormon militia and the Utes killed women and children when the opportunities presented. David Bigler described the war much like the previous Walker War—a "deadly series of atrocities and reprisals."[41]

Springville was not attacked during the Black Hawk War, though many alarms resulted from sightings of Indians in the mountains east of town. Don Carlos Johnson wrote that a high level of anxiety existed among the citizens. Sentries were stationed at the mouths of the canyons.[42] An armed squad accompanied the town's cattle when the herd was led out to graze. Militia patrolled the foothills of the Wasatch Mountains looking for the enemy.[43] The town's adobe wall, built during the Walker War, was still in place and afforded some protection to the anxious settlers.

During the summer of 1866, Daniel H. Wells, Commander of the Nauvoo Legion and Brigham Young's second counselor, requisitioned a contingent from Springville to travel to Sanpete County to defend settlers.[44] Major General Aaron Johnson mustered an infantry company of twenty-two men into service on June

---

35. Warren Metcalf, "A Precarious Balance: The Northern Utes and the Black Hawk War," *Utah Historical Quarterly* 57, no. 1, 25.

36. Ronald W. Walker, "Toward a Reconstruction of Mormon and Indian Relations, 1847-1877," *BYU Studies* 29, no. 4, 35.

37. Metcalf, "Precarious Balance," 26.

38. John Alton Peterson, *Utah's Black Hawk War* (Salt Lake City: University of Utah Press, 1998), 16.

39. Ibid., 13.

40. Ibid., 2.

41. Bigler, *Forgotten Kingdom*, 238.

42. Johnson, *History of Springville*, 65-66.

43. Ibid.

44. Ibid.

14, 1866. Franklin Whitmore captained the company. George Harrison was one of two sergeants.[45] Harrison's rank was unusual for a twenty-four-year-old with no military experience. The title probably reflected his service as an army cook, a role he almost certainly played for Whitmore's company. Harrison's relationship with Indians was complex, and he certainly did not relish fighting the natives. Nonetheless, George was realistic about the threat presented by the combative Utes. He was also politic enough to understand the value of participating in an effort that was important to the community in which he chose to settle.

The first in the Harrison family to enlist in the militia during the Black Hawk War was George's fifty-one-year-old father. William Harrison served in Captain A. Lambson's company from May 10 to October 20, 1866.[46] The company was probably a "home guard" for Springville. There is no record that George's brother, Aaron, who lived in Springville from 1860 to 1869, served in the Nauvoo Legion. After his 1500-mile march under Colonel Sumners in 1857, he apparently was uninterested in more military service.

Whitmore's infantry, including Sergeant George Harrison, spent a month marching in Sanpete and Sevier Counties without making contact with Indians. Contemporaneously, a Ute raiding party stole thirty-eight cattle and fifteen horses near Spanish Fork.[47] Major Creer and fifteen militiamen from Springville tracked the Indians up an almost insurmountable trail over Maple Mountain. The Mormons surprised the Utes near Diamond Fork River. A gun battle in trees and dense shrubs turned into a standoff. An unknown mounted chief, possibly Black Hawk, was struck by a bullet and retreated.[48] The other Utes followed, taking their dead and wounded. The Mormon soldiers recovered all of the stolen livestock. They later learned that five or six Indians were killed. Two settlers, including Albert Dimmick from Springville, lay dead. This successful battle and a similar result the week before in Thistle Valley turned the course of the war. John Peterson wrote, "it is clear the Mormon victories seriously weakened the raiders' solidarity; from that point on, Black Hawk's band began to disintegrate."[49]

In 1901 George Harrison applied for a pension for his participation in the Black Hawk War. His affidavit documented 110 days of service in 1866, which included "home service."[50] However, the time Harrison spent officially enlisted in the Nauvoo Legion was the least of his participation in the Black Hawk War. General Wells and his staff took up residence south of Manti in Sanpete County

---

45. Roger B. Nielson, *Utah's Black Hawk War Veterans* (Springville: by the author, 2009), 263.

46. William Harrison, "Utah, Veterans with Federal Service Buried in Utah, Territorial to 1966." FamilySearch database. Available online at https://familysearch.org/ark:/61903/3:1:S3HT-69D7-RS?mode=g&cc=1542862.

47. Peterson, *Utah's Black Hawk War*, 305-309.

48. Huff, *Memories That Live*, 315.

49. Peterson, *Utah's Black Hawk War*, 309.

50. George Harrison, "Commissioner of Indian War Records, Indian War Service Affidavits, 1909-1919," Series 2217, box 2, folder 2, Utah State Archives. Available online at http://images.archives.utah.gov/cdm/compoundobject/collection/2217/id/3583/rec/1.

Image of George Harrison with young child (probably George William, but possibly Rosella Arvilla). Tintype ca. 1867-1868. George was either still freighting on the Southern Route to California or was cooking for Nauvoo Legion militia engaged in the Black Hawk Indian War.

Tintype courtesy of Deanna Williams

late in 1866.[51] Wells employed George as a cook until the close of the war in 1868. George's duties foretold his future celebrity as "he showed a natural aptitude at both cooking and the leading of singing."[52] Nauvoo Legion members served without compensation, though perhaps the General paid something for George's extended services.

Black Hawk, suffering the effects of injury, made peace with the Mormons in 1867. Additional Ute chiefs followed in 1868.[53] Scattered hostilities continued into 1872. According to John Peterson, the final years of the Saints' last Indian war were notable for revealing the Church's diminishing military power. The war gave Brigham Young reason to train the Nauvoo Legion to the highest degree of efficiency in its history, which caused anxiety for some Mormon watchers. In 1870, under direction from President Ulysses S. Grant, Utah's federal governor outlawed gatherings of the Legion except upon his orders.[54]

---

51. Driggs, "Handcart Boy (First Draft)," 32.
52. "Chorister of Indian War Veterans Buried," *Deseret News*, 5 Feb 1921, clipping found in George Harrison file at Springville Pioneer Museum and is missing page number.
53. Peterson, *Utah's Black Hawk War*, 351-352.
54. Ibid., 360.

Two years later, more than 2000 Indians rode into Sanpete County for a "Ghost Dance."[55] Former Legion Commander Wells requested help from the US Army. Five companies from Camp Douglas, aided by two companies of the essentially defunct Nauvoo Legion, escorted the Indians back to the Uintah Reservation east and south of the Wasatch Mountains.[56] The event marked the official end of Utah's last Indian war.

After the war, George Harrison faced a familiar problem of finding profitable employment, but with the added responsibility of a wife and three young children. Possibly, he was able to renew freighting from southern California, but that was short-lived. The transcontinental railroad was completed in 1869 and quickly captured the business of transporting manufactured goods to Utah. A testament to the lack of work in Springville was that both George and his brother Aaron moved out of town in the late 1860s.

George Harrison did not migrate to California, as did Aaron and many other Utahns. The 1870 US Census placed George, Rosella and three children in Wahsatch, Utah. After completion of the transcontinental railroad in 1869, Union Pacific built shops at the top of Echo Canyon for maintenance of locomotives.[57] The railroad also built a roundhouse, warehouses, a boarding house, and a restaurant. The community of less than three hundred was better described as a camp than a town. The Census shows that George Harrison was cooking for railroad crews. His son, George William Harrison, recalled that the family lived in a tent. George William added that Wahsatch was such a rough place that Rosella and the children did not stay long before returning to Springville.[58] George stayed a little longer before he rejoined his family. By May 1871, the Wahsatch site was abandoned because the wooden structures did not hold up to strong winter winds. The shops were rebuilt from stone in a more sheltered location ten miles away in newly founded Evanston, Wyoming.[59]

When the Harrisons returned to Springville they probably did not anticipate that George's next job would be life changing. The mining industry in Utah was burgeoning—largely the result of Patrick Connor's early promotion. Opportunities were created, not only to freight food to the mining camps, but also to become a trader.

---

55. The Ghost Dance was a religious ceremony adopted by numerous Indian tribes in the latter part of the 19th century. The dance was thought to bring the spirits of the dead to fight on behalf of the Indians, make the white settlers leave, and bring prosperity to native peoples.

56. Peterson, *Utah's Black Hawk War*, 367.

57. "Eastbound To Wahsatch; Union Pacific's Route Through Weber and Echo Canyons," UtahRails.net. Available online at http://utahrails.net/articles/weber-echo.php.

58. George William Harrison, Autobiography, 1951, p. 1. Deanna Williams, great-granddaughter of George Beefsteak Harrison gave original document to author in June 2017

59. Ibid.

13

Trading, ZCMI and the United Order

O ne of Patrick Connor's earliest mining investments was in a location
initially known as "Mountain Valley." In 1864 small amounts of silver
were recovered, but little progress was made until a San Francisco
financier, Francois Pioche, bought the property in 1869. He invested in
better equipment and a redesigned process to separate silver from ore.[1] By 1871,
the mines were second only to the Comstock Lode in productivity. Six thousand
itinerant men moved to the location, renamed Pioche, about a hundred miles west
of Cedar City, Utah. The miners were unable to produce food and they presented
a financial windfall to Utah's farmers and freighters.[2] George Harrison employed
the freighting skills he learned on his California trips and started hauling produce
from Springville to Pioche—a round trip of six hundred miles.[3]

Pioche, in today's Nevada, was in a class by itself in terms of lawlessness.
Historian William Palmer wrote, "Outlaws, gamblers, saloon men, claim jumpers,
and bad men and wild women of every kind swarmed in, and Pioche soon became
the wildest, bloodiest, most lawless camp in the whole west . . . Pioche still boasts
that it had seventy-two killings before there was one natural death."[4] Mormon
peddlers from Utah were regarded as legitimate prey for the thieves. The freighters
could take their loads into Nevada safely, but coming back with cash was hazardous.
"Somewhere along the lonely road in the thick cedars, or in some rocky winding
canyon, many of them were held up at gunpoint and robbed," wrote Palmer.[5] He
added the need for money in Utah was so pressing that freighters were always
ready to take the chance.

While freighting to Pioche confronted George Harrison with the unavoidable
danger of robbery, he voluntarily accepted an additional risk. Pioche gave George
the opportunity to "trade" as well as freight. Previously, he was paid a set wage
to haul goods owned by somebody else. In his additional role as a trader, George
owned the food he transported and sold it at whatever price he could negotiate. The
game of arbitrage could be very profitable on the frontier, where shortages of food

---

1. W. Paul Reeve, *Making Space on the Western Frontier; Mormons, Miners and Southern Paiutes* (Urbana: University of Illinois Press, 2006), 27.

2. William R. Palmer, "Early Day Trading with the Nevada Mining Camps," *Utah Historical Quarterly* 26, no. 4, 354.

3. Mae [Anna May] Harrison Smith, and Ada Bissell Harrison, "History of George Harrison," Camp Aaron Johnson of Daughters of Utah Pioneers, Springville, Utah, published in Utah Pioneer Histories, Vol. 3, compiled by Margaret J. Miner, in the camp's Centennial Edition in 1950, p. 137- . A copy of the history was given to the author by George Harrison's great grandson, Jan Storrs, Spanish Fork Utah, 2012.

4. Palmer, "Early Day Trading," 355.

5. Ibid., 354.

and other goods were common. A contemporary of Harrison who accompanied freighters to the mining town of Virginia City, Montana, observed, "my Mormon friends sold the supplies they had hauled down from Salt Lake, and I wondered that day whether freighting supplies was not a gold mine without a rival . . . They bought flour at six dollars a hundred pounds and sold it at forty dollars, sugar at sixty cents a pound and sold it at fourteen dollars."[6]

George Harrison's granddaughter Myrl Storrs Stewart emphasized that his trading activities involved the whole family—"Grandmother [Rosella] and the children picked cucumbers and packed them in brine in 40-gallon kegs. They dressed chickens by the dozens. They bought butter and had to work it all over which was a very hard task. They picked beans and all kinds of fruits and vegetables and prepared them for grandfather to take in his wagon."[7]

In 1875 the silver mines in Pioche began a precipitous decline caused by flooding.[8] George was fortunate that mines at Ophir and Bingham Canyon in the Oquirrh Mountains, originally prospected by Connor's California Volunteers, became productive. He turned to the Utah mining camps to sell vegetables, eggs, butter and fruit.[9] George's oldest son, George William, recalled accompanying his father to the Utah mines in 1876—"We used to stop at the Jordan River and fill our 10-gallon keg with water which would last until we reached home."[10]

With the opportunity to profit from trading, George and his family enjoyed a significant improvement in their standard of living. Oldest son George William wrote, "While my father was peddling, he was buying farming ground which he rented out."[11] The best evidence for the Harrison's good fortune was a house that George purchased in 1873. Twenty years before, Lyman S. Wood built the two-room house at the southwest corner of 300 West and 300 South. A nomination form for the National Register of Historic Places states that the twenty-four foot by fourteen foot, one-story rectangular cabin was typical of residences in Springville during the initial years of settlement.[12] By 1877, George and Rosella had six children and were prosperous enough to add a two-story, four-room adobe brick house to the eastern end of the existing structure. According to the 1982 nomination form, "Harrison's new house, a hall-and-parlor I-house type, was a ubiquitous symbol of economic achievement in Utah during the second half of the nineteenth century."[13] The house built by George in 1877 still stands in the same location, is occupied, and is listed on the historic register. During the 1980s the original brick and adobe lining was covered with stucco, and the house now has a metal roof.

6. Betty M. Madsen and Brigham D. Madsen, *North to Montana: Jehus, Bullwhackers, and Mule Skinners on the Montana Trail* (Logan: Utah State University Press, 1998), 73.

7. Stewart, "Biography of Rosella Damon White Harrison."

8. Reeve, *Making Space*, 117.

9. Smith and Harrison, "History of George Harrison."

10. "Herald Salutes Springville's Older Residents with Picture and Story," *The Springville Herald*, 25 Oct 1951, 4.

11. George William Harrison, "Autobiography," 2.

12. Johnson and Knight, "Historic Resources."

13. Ibid.

Harrison's ability to buy a home and subsequently build an addition was facilitated by a radical change in land ownership in Utah. Until 1869, the Church effectively retained control of all land in Utah.[14] Only Mormons were allowed to occupy and cultivate assigned acreages, a privilege that was contingent upon what the Church deemed to be good behavior.[15] No property could be divided or sold without Church approval. Anticipating a surge of Gentile immigration upon completion of the transcontinental railroad, Brigham Young knew he would be unable to defend the status quo. In 1869 the Church and the US government cooperated in passing legislation to address the historical reality of "stewardship" rather than ownership in Utah. Soon after, the territory's first land office was established in Salt Lake City.[16] Don Carlos Johnson wrote that in 1872 and 1873 Springville citizens busily filed claims to gain legal title to property that they occupied for many years.[17] Also for the first time, non-Mormon residents of Utah were able to acquire land legally.

An early consequence of private property ownership in Springville was the demolition of the city's obsolete wall. Springville officials made a generous offer to those whose property abutted the wall. Upon tearing down the adobe structure, the landowners were given two rods (about thirty feet) of property on the other side. The last standing block of the iconic wall on 400 West was torn down in 1878.[18]

George Harrison was part of a small minority of Mormons, mostly traders, merchants and miners, who were fortunate to earn their living outside of the Church's controlled economy. However, a successful Mormon trader or merchant was always at risk of being labeled as unfaithful. Brigham Young never stopped preaching against those who exhibited "self-seeking individualism and personal aggrandizement."[19] Brigham's nephew, Joseph W. Young, targeted Mormons such as George Harrison, saying they "had no right to go to Pioche and trade off our lumber, chickens, eggs and grain."[20] Apostle Erastus Snow observed that traders were at the bottom of the list as far as tithing one-tenth of their profits to the Church.

Brigham Young never deviated from his intent, stated four days after first arriving in Utah, to have no trade or commerce with the Gentile world.[21] He had some success in promoting economic isolation and self-sufficiency, but private merchants—Mormon as well as Gentile—were adept at importing goods that Saints lined up to buy. In 1868, the imminent completion of the transcontinental railroad promised a flood of Eastern merchants and peddlers into Utah. In response, Young

14. "Original Land Titles in Utah Territory," Utah Department of Administrative Services, Division of Archives and Records Service. Available online at http://archives.utah.gov/research/guides/land-original-title.htm.

15. Bigler, *Forgotten Kingdom*, 53.

16. Ibid., 46.

17. Johnson, *History of Springville*, 82.

18. Finley, *History of Springville*, 19.

19. Arrington, *Great Basin Kingdom*, 93.

20. Reeve, *Making Space*, 93.

21. Arrington, *Great Basin Kingdom*, 47.

founded Zion's Cooperative Mercantile Institute (ZCMI) to import eastern goods, sell the merchandise through local Church cooperatives, and keep the profits in the territory. A critical part of the plan was to force the Saints to boycott independent stores.[22]

The story of ZCMI in Springville was representative of what happened in most of the approximately one hundred Mormon communities that established a cooperative. In 1868 Brigham Young decided that the store would be organized under the control of Bishop Aaron Johnson. Existing merchants were coerced into giving their merchandise to the cooperative in exchange for most of the shares. A few retailers, such as the Packards and the Haymond & Houtz partnership, refused to participate in the Church's takeover of merchandizing.[23]

Bishop Johnson located the store in his house and selected his fourth wife, Mary Ann, to operate the cooperative. Mary Ann was Johnson's fourteen-year-old niece when he married her in 1846.[24] She was always above the other wives in terms of organizational capabilities, and served as the bishop's "right hand" in many of his executive duties. Unfortunately, Mary Ann never operated a business.[25] Within two years, cooperative shareholders accused her of sloppy bookkeeping and embezzlement of funds. The store's directors cleared the bishop's wife of the worst charges, but found that "her accounts were somewhat loose and slack."[26] The directors recommended that she resign from the store, and Mary Ann complied.

The store's critics then went after Aaron Johnson. Johnson's opponents forced the bishop to give up his role in the cooperative and to move the store out of his house. That was not enough for Johnson's detractors. They presented a case for his mismanagement to a Church court outside of Springville. The bishop's close friend, Brigham Young, and five apostles presided. Johnson was cleared of the charges, and his accusers were found guilty of "unchristian like conduct" for accusing him. Conveniently, Johnson resigned as Springville's bishop within a month.[27]

Despite poor management, the Springville Cooperative was initially successful with more than four hundred Springville residents who became stockholders. Springville historian Mary Chase Finley wrote that the cooperative "was indeed the people's store."[28] As was the case with other Church stores, the sales were perhaps stimulated more by threats from the pulpit than the quality of the merchandise. Competition demonstrated the futility of the cooperative system. Milan Packard opened a new store in Springville in 1873, and the establishment quickly became

22. Turner, *Brigham Young*, 354.
23. Johnson, *Aaron Johnson*, 50-51.
24. Ibid., 301.
25. Ibid., 302.
26. Ibid., 594-5.
27. Ibid., 597.
28. Finley, *History of Springville*, 59.

profitable.[29] Other merchandisers followed, including Reynolds Brothers & Company and Deal Brothers & Mendenhall Company.[30]

Brigham Young grew frustrated with Saints who continued to make purchases outside the Church cooperatives. In 1874 he took a desperate step to reorganize Mormon society to emphasize communalism, equality, and obedience to the Church. As with the Consecration initiative of 1854, the Saints were asked to pledge all of their property, as well as "time, labor, energy and ability" to what he called the "United Order."[31] In turn, the Order, which was synonymous with the Church hierarchy, would give each family what was needed for a frugal and moral life. An expectation that the Saints would not engage in any commerce with Gentiles was reinforced. Wallace Stegner described the movement as "Christian Communism."[32]

In his history of Springville, Don Carlos Johnson wrote that the United Order was strongly opposed. The residents went to obligatory Church meetings, and, under duress, some committed to place their property into communal holding but only "when the time came."[33] George Harrison was just beginning to achieve economic success, and almost certainly did not support Young's social engineering. Most Mormon towns went through the motions of establishing communal societies but, with few exceptions, the idea did not take hold. The fact that Brigham Young publicly consecrated his property to the Order in June 1874 and reneged two months later undermined the nobility, and the feasibility, of the plan.[34] Similar to the quick demise of 1854's consecration movement, Young's United Order was abandoned by 1876. The attempt marked the last effort by the LDS Church to exert complete control over Utah's communal economy.

After the collapse of the United Order the Church mounted a campaign to collect Perpetual Emigration Fund debts. PEF officers prepared a list of over 18,000 debtors, which included William Harrison and his family.[35] William, despite relative success as a farmer and fruit grower, was probably never in a position to repay the debt he incurred to emigrate from England. In 1856 William committed to pay back £75 (equal to $375) to the PEF. The Church applied annual interest of up to ten percent. The amount that William owed was probably three to four times what he borrowed initially and was certainly more than his net worth. When he died in 1881, his will listed assets as his home, the furniture and his twelve-acre farm, which were valued at $500, $50 and $150 respectively.[36]

29. "History of Milan Packard, Utah," Online Utah.com. Available online at http://www.onlineutah.com/packard_milan_history.shtml.

30. Johnson and Knight, "Historic Resources of Springville City," section E, 5.

31. Arrington, *Great Basin Kingdom*, 328.

32. Stegner, *Mormon Country*, 110.

33. Johnson, *History of Springville*, 82.

34. Turner, *Brigham Young*, 400.

35. Richard L Jensen, "Names of Persons and Sureties indebted to the Perpetual Emigrating Fund Company 1850 to 1877," *Mormon Historical Studies* 1, no. 2, 141.

36. William Harrison, "Utah Wills and Probate Records, 1800-1945," Probate Estate Files, Case No. 249-267, 187. Ancestry database. Available online at http://ancstry.me/2mCEOV4.

Historian Richard L. Jensen observed that PEF recipients, such as William, faced many economic challenges including scarcity of cash in Utah. He wrote, "In fact, many never escaped what, even in those relatively austere times, was considered poverty."[37] William and Hannah may have been among them if not for George's steady support. Springville's bishop certainly spoke to William about repaying the PEF loan. A year later, when the *Deseret News* published a "List of Honor" naming those who recently repaid PEF debts, the Harrisons were not included.[38] Even if William was able to pay the loan, he possibly declined given the organizers' failure to fulfill critical promises made to the Martin company.

Brigham Young died in 1877, and in a series of 1878-79 newspaper articles, John Jaques published an early history of the disastrous handcart company. He wrote, in part, to promote the idea that the PEF should "cancel the indebtedness for passage, if any remains, of every member of this unfortunate and sorely tried emigrant [Martin] company."[39] Not long after, Church President John Taylor forgave the debts of a number of individuals "considered worthy of help and too poor to pay."[40] In effect, Taylor's message was the end of any serious effort to collect PEF debts.

John Taylor was less devoted to communalism and more open to capitalism and business than Brigham Young.[41] Other signs of the slowly developing Americanization of Utah during the 1870s included the demise of the Church's private militia and the adoption of federal law governing the private ownership of land. The emergence of a largely Gentile-controlled mining industry also weakened Church control of the economy and made way for free enterprise. Above all, the transcontinental railroad enabled a flood of Gentile immigrants. By 1880, Utah's 140,000 residents were no longer isolated from the other fifty million Americans.

George Harrison's transition from wage earner to trader and entrepreneur is captured by several documents from the period. In an 1868 gazetteer, he was still hauling goods for others and listed himself as a "freighter."[42] Eleven years later, George was supplying miners in Ophir and Bingham Canyon and gave his vocation as a "trader."[43] A year later on the 1880 Census he provided a more colorful description of his occupation as "huckster."[44] Within a few years, Harrison was never again referred to as anything but a hotelkeeper and restaurateur.

---

37. Jensen, "Names of Persons," 142.

38. "A List of Honor," editorial, *Deseret News*, 17 April 1878, 6.

39. John Jaques, "Some Reminiscences," *Salt Lake Daily Herald*, 19 Jan 1879.

40. Jensen, "Names of Persons," 142-43.

41. Reeve, *Making Space*, 99.

42. H. L. A. Culmer, ed., *Utah Directory and Gazetteer for 1868* (Salt Lake City: J. C. Graham & Co.). The author found this gazetteer on the shelves of the library at the Utah Historical Society in Salt Lake City and failed to write down the page number.

43. Henry L. A. Culmer, *Utah Directory and Gazetteer for 1879-80* (Salt Lake City: J. C. Graham & Co., 1879), 256. Available online at https://archive.org/stream/utahdirectorygaz00culmr ich#page/n5/mode/2up.

44. 1880 US Federal Census, Springville City and Precinct, Utah County, ED 82, 30. Available online at https://familysearch.org/ark:/61903/3:1:33S7-9YBR-K6?mode=g&i=29&cc=1417683.

14

A Pink Hotel, Drummers and
the Manifesto

George Harrison's freighting and trading career started to wane in the late 1870s as the spread of railroads displaced less efficient muleskinners. However, railroads created other opportunities including in Springville. The *Deseret News* reported on November 19, 1879 that a narrow gauge railroad was completed from Springville to the mining camp of Scofield in Carbon County. A year later an extension to Provo and the main rail line north to Salt Lake City ended Springville's relative isolation from the rest of the country. The article continued that the Scofield coal delivered to Springville and Provo was quite popular as it generated more heat than "the celebrated Rock Springs variety."[1] Construction of the sixty-mile-long Utah and Pleasant Valley Railroad (U&PVR) began in 1876 under the direction of prime contractor Milan Packard, who was also a significant investor. Another of Packard's businesses was his general store in Springville, which prospered competing against ZCMI. He was often short on cash to pay those building the railroad. Packard paid, in part, with merchandise from his store including calico, the standard cotton material used for clothing. Milan Packard's railroad became known as the "Calico Railroad."[2]

Martin Pardon Crandall procured a contract for grade work on the Calico Railroad.[3] He was one of a number of successful Springville freighters who learned "grading" while working on the Union Pacific route through Echo and Weber Canyons in 1868 and 1869.[4] The Springville contractors were among others in Utah who gained a reputation for the quality of their work. Glenn L. Alleman wrote, "Railroad men soon acknowledged that nowhere on the Union Pacific line could the grading compare in completeness and timeliness with the work done by the people of Utah."[5]

In 1883 ownership of the U&PVR passed to the Denver and Rio Grande Railroad (D&RG), which built a depot in the middle of Springville's Main Street

1. See Utah and Pleasant Valley Railroad section of "Utah Railroads" from *Our Pioneer Heritage*, vol. 10 (Salt Lake City: Daughters of the Utah Pioneers, 1967), 137–192. Available online at UtahRails.net, http://utahrails.net/utahrails/utah-railroads-dup.php.
2. Ibid.
3. Ibid. Though the author of this book largely resisted the temptation to research ancestors besides George Harrison, I did learn that Martin Pardon Crandall is also a great-great grandfather. He was an industrious businessman and his four plural wives enhanced his stature in religious and civil society in early Springville. See https://www.ancestry.com/genealogy/records/martin-pardon-crandall_18888197.
4. Alleman, *Legacy of the Springville Contractors*, 9–10.
5. Ibid.

between 2nd and 3rd South Streets. A steady stream of crews disembarked from the coal trains that stopped in Springville. George Harrison recognized an opportunity. Money that he earned as a trader enabled the forty-two-year-old to pursue a long held dream. George paid $300 for a half-acre of ground at 245 South Main Street.[6] Records in the Utah County Recorder's Office show that this transaction occurred on December 6, 1883. Daughter-in-law Mary (Myrtle) Harrison recalled that George Harrison paid $75 for a wood frame building that served as a saloon at First North. He paid twenty-five bushels of wheat to have it moved.[7] In early 1884 Harrison opened the doors to a restaurant directly across from the D&RG train depot. With Rosella's help, George started serving beefsteak meals to railroad crews.[8] Oldest son, George William, later wrote, "Father and I would remain there [in the restaurant] every night until 10 o'clock to feed a railroad crew of five men for which he charged 35 cents."[9]

Harrison soon identified a new hotel as another opportunity. Historian Robert Carter wrote, "Local and family histories found in the Springville Daughters of Utah Pioneers Museum reveal that for years Springville was without a hotel, and overnight visitors stayed in the homes of townspeople."[10] Many visiting dignitaries stayed in Bishop Aaron Johnson's large home. The first dedicated hotel came in the early 1870s when Philip and Sarah Ann Boyer built a two-story fifteen-room establishment that also served as their home.[11] The Boyer Hotel did well, indicating demand for more accommodations in Springville. In February 1886 the *Deseret News* reported, "Another notable improvement lately made in Springville is the erection of a large and well appointed hotel by Brother George Harrison."[12]

George built the hotel to abut the south side of his wood frame restaurant. The hotel's kitchen, which housed a huge coal stove, remained in the rear of the wooden building. The dining room was moved into the hotel. The emptied space became a sample room for travelling salesmen.[13] Long tables were placed along the walls and down the center of the room enabling the salesmen to display their merchandise to local merchants.

The Harrison Hotel was unusual, even eccentric, in its construction. A massive stone foundation supported adobe-lined deep pink brick walls. George Harrison's sons, George William and Lewis hauled the rock, brick, and adobe to the building site.[14] George's daughter-in-law Myrtle Harrison recalled that George Harrison

6. Bertrand F. Harrison, *The History of The Harrison Hotel*, np, 1984, p. 4. Copy held in Special Collections at the Harold B. Lee Library, Brigham Young University, Provo, Utah.

7. Myrtle Harrison, "Harrison Hotel," in Kate B. Carter, comp., *Heart Throbs of the West*, vol. 5 (Salt Lake City: Daughters of Utah Pioneers, 1944), 345.

8. Bertrand Harrison, *History of The Harrison Hotel*, 4.

9. George William Harrison, "Autobiography," 3.

10. D. Robert Carter, "Mysterious Fires Plagued Springville Hotel," *Springville Daily Herald*, 1 Apr 2006.

11. Ibid.

12. "Local News," *Deseret News*, 3 Feb 1886, 41.

13. Harrison, *History of The Harrison Hotel*, 7-8.

14. George William Harrison, Autobiography, p. 3

Photographer George Anderson is standing on top of the Reynolds Building in 1900. Across Main Street is the white wooden building that was George Harrison's original restaurant in 1884. Behind is the three-story brick hotel that George built in 1886.
Courtesy Harold B. Lee Library, Brigham Young University

and Jim Clark did the carpentry.[15] Walter Wheeler did the masonry work, and his brother David did the plastering. The walls were sixteen inches thick, making the building cool in the summer and warm in the winter.[16] Eight guest rooms were on the second floor. The fifteen-foot-high ceilings required constant attention to coal stoves that heated rooms during cold weather. Smoke from the coal made it necessary to climb a twelve-foot ladder to wash the ceilings at least twice each year.[17] A steep stairway led to two rooms on the third floor, where George and Rosella lived.

By the time George Harrison opened the hotel in 1886, Rosella's health was significantly compromised. Anna May Harrison Smith recalled that her mother was a very small woman who experienced pneumonia three times.[18] The illnesses sapped her strength. Oldest daughter Rosella Arvilla (always known as Arvilla

---

15. Myrtle Harrison, "Harrison Hotel," 345.

16. Ibid.

17. Martha Fereday Harrison, "Autobiography" (ca. 1980), p. 38. Copy given to author by Kent Bernard Harrison, Provo, Utah.

18. Smith, "History of Rosella Damon White Harrison."

or "Villa") was frequently unable to attend school because of the need to care for the younger children.[19] In 1879 and 1883 Rosella lost infant sons after difficult pregnancies. In both instances she suffered from "gathered breasts" (infection and abscesses).[20] Arvilla went around Springville picking up "buffalo chips," to make poultices to put on her mother's breasts. Rosella was unable to nurse either Ralph Damon or Charles Bertrand. Her daughter wrote that there was not any other way to feed babies in those days, and the infants died within four or five weeks of birth.[21]

The year before the hotel opened, Rosella, at age forty-six, was challenged with the birth of her last child, Winfred. She may have taken Winfred with her when she joined George in moving three blocks away into the new hotel. Rosella helped with the cooking and taught George Harrison how to make many things—especially pastries.[22] At the beginning, Rosella bottled all the fruit used in the restaurant. She cut and hemmed bolts of linen purchased from travelling salesmen to make all the sheets, pillowcases, tablecloths and napkins, as well as making quilts from samples left by salesmen. Particularly strenuous was the daily chore of changing bedding and cleaning the guest rooms on the second floor. After a few years, Rosella was forced to give up the hotel work.[23] She moved back to the Harrisons' house, probably in 1888 or 1889. At home, Rosella continued to make the hotel linens and quilts for many years.[24] Her granddaughter wrote that Rosella was also an expert dressmaker, and sewed hundreds of tiny buttonholes down the front of basques.[25]

While feeding steaks to railroad crews jump-started the restaurant, George Harrison's grandson, Bertrand Harrison, wrote that "drummers," were the mainstay of the hotel.[26] These salesmen worked for large wholesalers and carried samples to solicit orders from local retailers.[27] From 1870 to 1920 drummers were the foot soldiers for eastern manufacturers who wanted to convince rural families to buy mass-produced substitutes for products they previously made or did without. The drummers travelled constantly, worked hard, and many had no domestic life.[28] They were also the most experienced and discerning of hotel guests. According to an article in *The New York Times*, "Railroads and hotels have for the most part taken peculiar pains to propitiate the drummer, who alone of mortal men dares return the stare of the proud hotel clerk with a haughtiness equal to his own."[29]

19. Stewart, "Biography of Rosella."
20. Ibid.
21. Ibid.
22. Smith, "History of Rosella."
23. Ibid.
24. Martha Harrison, "Autobiography," 19.
25. Stewart, "Biography of Rosella Damon White Harrison."
26. Bertrand Harrison, *History of The Harrison Hotel*, 7.
27. Bill Long, "Drummers, Canvassers, Knockers, et. al.." Archived at http://archive.is/KdZBx (original article no longer available).
28. "On the Road, 1885-1897," The American Menu. Available online at http://www.theamericanmenu.com/2011/03/on-road.html.
29. Ibid. The article quotes from the *New York Times*, 26 June 1887.

A depiction of a group of drummers gathered at a hotel on Thanksgiving. The drawing was originally published in *Frank Leslie's Illustrated Weekly*, November 28, 1885.

Though the drummers' purpose was to sell merchandise, they unconsciously brought urban attitudes about capitalism, consumerism and modernity to rural communities. Timothy Spears quotes from a 1929 article, "To those of us who lived in the little inland towns in the Gay Nineties, the Drummer was not primarily interesting in his capacity as salesman. Rather, he commanded attention because he was 'a brilliant bird of passage,' 'a connecting link with the great outside world,' 'a sentimentalist,' a 'purveyor of stories,' and a 'political prophet.'"[30] The cosmopolitan salesmen embodied much that was antithetical to the communitarian and non-materialistic society that Brigham Young envisioned. Drummers were equally undesirable to officials in other parts of the country—"From the perspective of the South ... the salesmen were perceived as purveyors not so much of goods but of a cultural lifestyle (as Northerners) that they despised."[31] Authorities in many cities and states implemented significant fees upon drummers until the US Supreme Court prohibited the practice in the late nineteenth century.[32]

Dorothy Buchanan wrote that the travelling salesmen congregated at establishments where they could expect to enjoy the company of other drummers.[33]

30. Timothy B. Spears, *100 Years on the Road: The Traveling Salesman in American Culture* (New Haven, CT: Yale University Press, 1995), 12.

31. Ibid.

32. Stanley Hollander, "Nineteenth Century Anti-Drummer Legislation in the United States," *The Business History Review* 38, no. 4, 479-500.

33. Dorothy J. Buchanan, "Life on the Road; Reminiscences of a Drummer," *Utah Historical*

George's guesthouse and restaurant quickly became one of their favorite stops in Utah. Howard Driggs described the Harrison Hotel as clean, though "just a plain pioneer home."[34] The real attraction of the hotel for the drummers was the restaurant. Beefsteaks were the foundation of that success. George Harrison said in a newspaper article in 1905 that he never failed to have a porterhouse steak for anyone who came to his restaurant, and "in the olden times we had to hustle for them."[35]

Part of the popularity of Harrison's beefsteaks was that he dry-aged the meat. Family stories tell that George hung meat until it "nearly spoiled." Another report is more specific—"His secret for tenderness was to hang the meat in a cool place until it grew 'whiskers.'"[36] The whiskers were mold that grows on the outside of meat when hung for three to four weeks at cold temperatures, ideally 34 to 38 degrees.[37] As much as fifty percent of the weight of the meat evaporates, creating a concentrated beef flavor. Natural enzymes make the meat tender by breaking down connective tissue. The fungus, which grows on the meat's surface and is scraped off before cooking, produces additional enzymes that contribute to tenderness and flavor.[38]

Harrison carefully selected the cattle he bought and he oversaw the butchering of the meat. He had an ideal facility for hanging beef—an icehouse that was part of a barn on the back of his lot. The northeast section of the structure was built with double walls separated by ten inches of sawdust.[39] Ice was cut during the winter, hauled to Harrison's ice house and packed in sawdust. George's son, George William, recalled helping to haul the blocks of ice from Utah Lake. One of the uses was to make ice cream that was sold from the restaurant on Sundays.[40] Springville historian Helen Beardall remembered learning that when Harrison ran out of ice, he sometimes moved his aging beef to the cold room at Walter Wheeler's mortuary.[41]

When George Harrison was ready to cook a steak, he went to the barn to cut an aged porterhouse that weighed fourteen to sixteen ounces.[42] Kent Harrison, George's great-grandson, wrote that the steaks were seared initially on very hot cast iron and then further cooked at a lower temperature. Salt and pepper were used,

Quarterly 34, no. 1, 25.

34. Driggs, "Theirs Was the Handcart Way", 202.

35. "Little Romance of a Utah Pioneer," *Salt Lake Telegram*, 19 Oct 1905, 4.

36. "Springville Heritage Quilt Found," *Daily Herald*, 13 Aug 2009. Available online at http://www.heraldextra.com/news/local/south/springville/springville-heritage-quilt-found/article_0c7f62e2-75a0-594f-9e8e-b596dcfa26a5.html.

37. "Beef aging," *Wikipedia*, last modified 27 Feb 2017, https://en.wikipedia.org/wiki/Beef_aging. Derrick Riches, "Aging Beef – Dry Aging: The nearly lost art of the great steak," The Spruce, last modified 22 Feb 2017, https://www.thespruce.com/dry-aging-beef-331496.

38. Ibid.

39. Harrison, *History of The Harrison Hotel*, 8.

40. "Herald Salutes Springville's Older Residents."

41. Personal communication from Helen Beardall, Springville, Utah, March 2016.

42. Bertrand Kent Harrison, "Remembrances of the Harrison Hotel of Springville, Utah," August, 2004, 3. Copy given to author by Kent Harrison in 2012.

"Black Bass" Harrison circa late 1880s.
Family photo given to author by Barbara Lee.

and butter was added when the steaks were served.[43] George left no doubt that his English mentor at Fort Laramie taught him how to cook beefsteaks—"He helped me learn the art of broiling steak to 'a queen's taste.'"[44]

Porterhouse steaks were not the only notable entrée on the hotel's menu. George also served black bass that came from Utah Lake. He occasionally did his own fishing, but usually bought from one fisherman who supplied him with high quality fish.[45] A newspaper article in 1896 said, " . . . late arrivals at his hostelry are considering the advisability of re-dubbing him 'Black Bass' Harrison."[46] In 1909, a newsman reporting George's stay at a Salt Lake City hotel, wrote that he was known as "Black Bass" Harrison during the fishing season and as "Beefsteak" Harrison at other times.[47]

Another signature of the restaurant was a glass jar of sugar cookies on each table where guests could help themselves.[48] George also kept a jar in the drummers' sample room. For a time, Kitty Woods, the daughter of long-tenured mayor Lyman

---

43. Ibid.
44. Howard R. Driggs, "Beefsteak was a Handcart Boy," *Millennial Star* 120, no. 7, 209.
45. "A Little Journey to the Home of Beefsteak Harrison," *Salt Lake Tribune*, 17 Jul 1915, 5.
46. "Campfire Brevities," *The Salt Lake Tribune*, 21 Aug 1896, 5.
47. "In Hotel Corridors," *Salt Lake Tribune*, 2 Feb 1909, 4.
48. Harrison, *History of The Harrison Hotel*, 9-10.

Woods, entered the room, sat down, and ate cookies till they were gone.[49] Though not pleased, George probably accepted Kitty's fondness for his cookies as a cost of doing business. Harrison went to great lengths to not disclose the cookie recipe, which he probably learned from Rosella. In an interview, great-granddaughter Barbara Lee said, "He made these secret sugar cookies, and he would not let anyone know how to do it. The story goes that my grandma spied on him one day when he was making the cookies, just trying to figure out what the ingredients were, and he threw flour on her."[50]

A staple of the restaurant was soup, and a large kettle was always cooking on the back of the stove. Cooking stock for the soup began early each morning when bones from the previous day's steaks were simmered for several hours.[51] No hungry person was turned away from the hotel without food—especially if he or she were an Indian.[52] Harrison always recalled the kindness that the Oglala Sioux showed him when he was in a bad way in Wyoming. While George was generous toward the unfortunate, he was practical enough to insist that they not mingle with paying customers in the restaurant. Beefsteak's granddaughter, Arlena, worked in the hotel and recounted that the soup line formed at the back door to the kitchen.[53] Also, whenever George learned of someone who was ill in Springville, he sent a small bucket of hotel soup to the ailing individual. One Springville resident said that George Harrison gave away enough soup to "float him right to Heaven."[54]

George's gifts as an entertainer were probably as important to his reputation as his culinary skills. The *Deseret News* noted at Harrison's death, "Rarely was there a party in his famous little hotel that Mr. Harrison did not, at sometime during the meal, come from the kitchen, still wearing his white apron, and start what is now known as 'community singing.'"[55] Howard Driggs wrote that Harrison loved a "choice story," and he was always ready to join guests and friends in swapping yarns.[56] Utah born Henry C. Jacobs, who worked as a drummer in the 1890s, recalled the restaurant fondly—"'Beefsteak' had a way with people and was a real cook."[57] Beefsteak's daughter-in-law, Mary Myrtle Harrison, wrote that he was "full of fun," and he told his customers, "This is no hospital, if you can't eat, there's the door."[58]

Harrison's celebrity as a cook, singer and storyteller came quickly. Ten years after opening his hotel, an article observed that he "is known by every drummer

49. Personal communication from Barbara Lee, Springville, Utah, 2012.

50. Ann Whiting Allen, "Mother Keeps Traditions Alive by Passing Along Her Piemaking Skills to the Next Generation," *Deseret News*, 5 May 1991, http://www.deseretnews.com/article/161029/.

51. Personal communication from Suzanne Fulmer (great-granddaughter of Beefsteak Harrison), Sandy, Utah, February, 2016.

52. Harrison, *History of The Harrison Hotel*, 10.

53. Personal communication from Colleen Thatcher (daughter of Arlena), Mapleton, Utah, 2012.

54. Smith and Harrison, "History of George Harrison."

55. "Chorister of Indian War Veterans Buried."

56. Driggs, "Handcart Boy (First Draft)," 1-2.

57. Buchanan, "Life on the Road," 27.

58. Harrison, "History of the Harrison Hotel."

who carries a grip between Chicago and the Golden Gate as 'Beefsteak' Harrison."[59] The travelling salesmen were the source of his nickname. Harrison told a reporter, "Those pesky fellows the drummers ages ago called me 'Beefsteak Harrison' and I'll go down to my grave that way. The rascals!"[60] Drummers were not the only clientele of the hotel and restaurant. An article in *The Instructor* recalled that Church officials often enjoyed George's hotel rooms, cooking and story telling when travelling to and from southern Utah during the first quarter of the twentieth century.[61] As time passed, the restaurant also attracted locals. Notable among them was Springville artist John Hafen. One of his paintings, "Sunset, Great Salt Lake," a pastel painted in 1890, hung in the hotel lobby. The painting was payment for restaurant debt.[62] Bertrand F. Harrison and his wife Lorna, donated the painting to the Springville Museum of Art in 1999.[63]

An advertisement in a 1903-04 Utah gazetteer shows that the Harrison Hotel was operating on the "American Plan." George charged $2.50 a day for a room and three meals. The Boyer Hotel, which always had a good reputation and offered livery service and a drummer's room as did Harrison, charged $1.50 daily.[64] Only Beefsteak's cooking and entertainment skills can account for his ability to charge a sixty-seven percent premium over the competition.

Because of his unsolicited celebrity, Beefsteak was often the subject of news coverage. In 1905 a reporter learned he was staying at the Kenyon Hotel in Salt Lake City and managed a short interview. Two distinguishing traits of Beefsteak, according to the article, were that he maintained his inky black hair and that he wrote poetry. The reporter added that Beefsteak denied authoring the following verse

"A good wig hides a head that's bare,
And black ink darkens up gray hair."

The article closed by saying that another axiom of "Doc" Harrison is, "You better weigh your own faults before you measure those of others."[65]

As George established his restaurant and hotel in the 1880s, the Americanization of Utah quickened. The primary battleground was the LDS Church's refusal to abandon the practice of polygamy. Despite anti-polygamy legislation signed by Abraham Lincoln in 1862, the Church continued to promote celestial marriage. Following the Civil War, the Mormons no longer argued that polygamy was a

59. "Mimic Field of War," *The Salt Lake Tribune*, 21 Aug 1896, 5.

60. "Little Romance."

61. Review of "George, the Handcart Boy," *The Instructor* 87, no. 11, 338-39. Available online at https://archive.org/stream/instructor8711dese.

62. "Remembrances of the Harrison Hotel," 3.

63. The Springville Museum of Art also holds a painting of the Harrison Hotel done in 1938 by Inez Chader. She evokes an earlier period by painting a muddy street in front of the hotel. Chader also gave the hotel a sand colored stucco exterior. Family historians say the hotel's deep pink brick exterior never changed.

64. *Utah State Gazetteer and Business Directory, 1903-1904*, vol. 2 (Salt Lake City: R. L. Polk and Co., 1903). Available online at https://babel.hathitrust.org/cgi/pt?id=njp.32101074870112;view =1up;seq=33.

65. "'Doc' Harrison of Springville is Here," *Salt Lake Telegram*, 8 Apr 1905, 12.

"domestic issue" relegated to the discretion of the states. Instead, the leadership maintained that the practice was protected under the first amendment as the "free exercise of religion." By 1875, both Mormons and Gentiles wished to test the constitutionality of that idea.[66] George Reynolds, secretary to Brigham Young, was an acknowledged polygamist who volunteered to be the defendant in a trial. A Utah jury found Reynolds guilty and he was sentenced to two years in prison and fined. In 1879 the US Supreme Court upheld the territorial court's decision. The Court stated that, while the Constitution protects freedom of beliefs and opinions, actions (including the practice of polygamy) are subject to governmental laws and sanctions. To think otherwise would in effect "permit every citizen to become a law unto himself."[67]

The judicial ruling set the stage for severe anti-polygamy legislation and enforcement. In 1882, the Edmunds Act increased the penalty for polygamy to five years imprisonment and a $500 fine. Those believed to be polygamists were disenfranchised and prohibited from holding any public office. As importantly, the legislation defined polygamy as simple cohabitation, which required a very low burden of proof.[68] Don Carlos Johnson wrote that by 1884-85 in Springville many persons "were compelled to take to the Underground or go to prison and quite a number chose the latter."[69]

The Edmunds-Tucker Act was adopted by the US government in 1887 to destroy the LDS Church financially. The Church was disincorporated, and the federal government claimed all property in excess of fifty thousand dollars. Federal law also dissolved the Perpetual Emigration Fund, viewed by its critics as a tool to recruit ignorant aliens who would never learn American values.[70] Dismantling the PEF was largely symbolic, as the Church already ceased encouraging immigration. By the early 1880s, wrote Leonard Arrington, "in every valley there were signs that the continued flow of immigration and the natural increase in population had filled up the land."[71] The "Gathering," which was a "first principle" of the Mormon faith when the Harrisons emigrated in 1856, was discarded.

In September 1890, with 600 Mormon polygamists in jail, many others in hiding, and the government seizing Church property, Wilford Woodruff issued the "Manifesto." The Church's fourth president proclaimed an end to the performance of celestial marriage, without addressing already existing polygamous marriages. Perhaps the concession seemed a small step, but as David Bigler wrote, "it accepted for the first time the supremacy of laws enacted by the representatives of the people over laws revealed from God."[72] Another capitulation came soon after when Utah

66. Gustive O. Larson, *The Americanization of Utah for Statehood* (San Marino, CA: The Huntington Library, 1971), 77-78.

67. Ibid.

68. Larson, *Americanization of Utah*, 95.

69. Johnson, *History of Springville*, 88.

70. Dean L. May, *Utah: A People's History* (Salt Lake City: University of Utah Press, 1987), 127.

71. Arrington, *Great Basin Kingdom*, 354.

72. Bigler, *Forgotten Kingdom*, 355-56.

became the last state or territory to establish tax-supported, free elementary schools. Public schools were opposed for forty years because, as stated by Brigham Young, "schools supported by general taxes cannot be conducted on a religious basis."[73]

Seven months after the Manifesto, United States President Benjamin Harrison, riding in a five-car train, arrived in Salt Lake City. The long-time outspoken foe of Mormons was returning to Washington, D.C. from California—part of a nineteen-day, 9,000-mile tour of the country.[74] The President was greeted enthusiastically at every stop in Utah, signifying a change in attitude toward the federal government. The most dramatic reception came as President Harrison's party travelled up 100 South Street to Liberty Park. The procession encountered a gentle hillside where six or seven thousand school children were waving small American flags and cheering the President.[75] The children sang "America" and the "Star Spangled Banner" while keeping time with their flags. In a tremulous voice, Harrison thanked the children. When the President said they were preparing themselves for "usefulness, citizenship and patriotism," three cheers interrupted him.

At Liberty Park, Harrison addressed statehood—the issue of prime importance to Utahns. The President told the audience, which included the Church's leaders, that it was his pleasant duty the year before to welcome the Dakotas, Washington, Montana, Idaho, and Wyoming into the great sisterhood of the States. Despite being softened up by the school children, Harrison reminded the audience of why Utah's forty-year quest for statehood was unsuccessful. "I have no discord as a public officer with men of any creed or politics if they will obey the law," said the President, "My oath of office, my public duty, requires me to be against those who violate it."[76]

The train left Salt Lake City going south and stopped four times in Utah Valley. Springville, still not quite three thousand in population, was honored to be included. The presidential party stopped at the depot in the middle of Main Street. President Harrison stepped onto the back of his observation car to an enthusiastic crowd. He noted only three substantive buildings in the vicinity—the train depot, the Deal Brothers & Mendenhall Mercantile Store, and the pink Harrison Hotel.[77] The President offered a brief speech, commenting on the productivity of the Utah Valley and the kindness with which the citizens received him.[78] George Harrison

---

73. Larson, *Americanization of Utah*, 55.

74. "All Aboard: Making Tracks with the Presidential Train," Benjamin Harrison Presidential Site. Available online at http://www.presidentbenjaminharrison.org/index.php/learn/exhibits/past-exhibits/19-learn/exhibits/past-exhibits/62-all-aboard-making-tracks-with-the-presidential-train.

75. Orson Ferguson Whitney, *Popular History of Utah* (Salt Lake City: George Q. Cannon & Sons, 1904), 492. Available online at https://archive.org/details/popularhistoryof00byuwhit.

76. Charles Hedges, comp., *Speeches of Benjamin Harrison, twenty-third president of the United States; a complete collection of his public addresses from February, 1888, to February, 1892* (New York: United States Book Company, 1892), 430-34. Available online at https://archive.org/details/speechesofbenjam00harrrich.

77. Sanborn Fire Insurance Map of Springville, Utah, 1890.. Digitized by the J. Willard Marriott Library, University of Utah. Available online at https://collections.lib.utah.edu/details?id=320874.

78. Hedges, *Speeches of Benjamin Harrison*, 436.

(no relation to the president) was certainly among those in the cheering crowd. As the train departed by the route of the Calico Railroad up Spanish Fork Canyon, George and others probably sensed that Utah's relationship with the rest of the United States was changing rapidly.

15

Music, Indian War Veterans and Family

George and Rosella Harrison met through their love of music and they continued to perform in public for much of their lives. Rosella was most active during her first three decades in Springville, when she was also raising children and preparing food for George's trading activities. She was especially noted for excellence in playing the organ in church. Her daughter wrote that Rosella played for the Springville Church Choir for twenty-five years.[1] Rosella did not obtain the appointment without the approval of Fredrick Weight, an unusually talented musician from England who was chosen church chorister by Springville's bishop in 1856.[2] When her children were very young, Rosella took them to choir practice as well as the church services. She usually had a baby on her lap and three or four grouped around while she played the organ.[3]

Rosella's daughter Anna May wrote that in the early days her mother and father travelled throughout the state giving concerts.[4] One performance in the White Meeting House in Springville included all of the children. Rosella played the organ while George led the singing of "I am happy as a birdie in its nest." The older children sang softly in the chorus, while Gertrude, only three years old, sang as loudly as she could above the rest. The audience was very pleased, and an elderly man rose up and said, "That's the best thing I ever heard."

Some of the older children learned to read music at the Evan Stephens' singing class, which was held weekly in Springville. Stephens was a prominent Latter-day Saint composer and hymn writer who travelled from Salt Lake City. The weekly trip was impractical before Springville was accessible by rail in 1880. Stephens was a good friend of George and Rosella and always stayed at the family's house.[5] Anna May recalled that her father and the musician talked while Rosella fixed dinner. In 1890 Stephens began a twenty-six-year tenure as director of the Mormon Tabernacle Choir.

Though Rosella gave up the position of Springville's church organist after twenty-five years, her musical influence outlasted her performances. Her granddaughter wrote that Rosella taught George Harrison "all the music he knew."[6] George was naturally gifted at "carrying a tune." As a young man he developed his talent

---

1. May Harrison Smith, "History of Rosella."
2. Johnson, *Aaron Johnson*, 359.
3. Smith "History of Rosella Damon White Harrison."
4. Ibid.
5. Ibid.
6. Stewart "Biography of Rosella."

The "Glee Club Quartet" ca. 1915. George Harrison, Walter Wheeler, David Wheeler and Joseph Tuckett (L to R) made up Springville's first all male quartet.
Courtesy Harold B. Lee Library, Brigham Young University

in church and at home, where the Harrison family often sang together.[7] People often attested to Harrison's skill as a singer, and throughout his life he was able to perform on request. In Los Angeles, at a 1905 dinner celebration of early freighters on the Southern Trail, the sixty-four-year-old pioneer was called on for a song. A reporter wrote that George Harrison "rose, and took the pitch, and in a strong clear voice, sang a ballad of early days."[8]

However, unlike Rosella, George never received formal musical training. Tellingly, no mention is ever made that he played an instrument. Rosella taught her husband enough about reading musical scores to enable him to succeed Fredrick Weight as Church chorister around 1882.[9] George Harrison held that position in Springville's lone ward for the succeeding decade. When four wards were created in 1892, he continued as chorister of the Second Ward for many years.

Harrison was also a member of the long-lived "Glee Club Quartet," Springville's first all-male group. The quartet formed in about 1870.[10] George joined David

7. Driggs, *George The Handcart Boy,* 11.

8. "Give Pioneers Farewell Dinner," *Los Angeles Herald.* October 17, 1905, p. 2.

9. Johnson, *Aaron Johnson,* 359.

10. "Walter Wheeler, the Undertaker and Embalmer," *Springville Independent,* 1906, precise date and page number missing from clipping. Copy given to author by Jack Parker of Springville, 2016.

Wheeler, Walter Wheeler and Joseph Tuckett as fixtures in civic performances for decades. The men were born within six years of each other in England, where they learned their musical skills. The four singers were instrumental in convincing Evan Stephens to teach vocal classes in Springville, and they were among his pupils.[11]

Harrison's experience as a singer and chorister led to a prominent role in the Utah Indian War Veterans organization. On July 4, 1893, a number of Springville men, including George, were reminiscing about war experiences in the 1860s. They decided to arrange a statewide reunion for veterans of the hostilities.[12] The first reunion of the Black Hawk War Veterans was held at Reynolds Hall in Springville on January 15, 1894. One hundred and eleven veterans from Utah County accepted invitations to attend.[13] Visiting delegations were greeted by sleighs, under the direction of George Harrison, and taken to Springville homes.[14] The supper that evening, accompanied by singing, speeches and dancing, was a great success.

The Black Hawk War Veterans reunion grew into an annual statewide event, which expanded to include veterans of all Utah Indian conflicts. In 1896, the location was the Geneva Resort on the northeast shore of Utah Lake. A newspaper reported attendance of 5000 veterans and families and noted, "George Harrison, the Springville hotel-keeper, is a prominent figure of the reunion. He has been dubbed 'professor' because of his leadership of the choir from his town."[15] The Springville "professor" served as the chorister for the statewide organization for more than two decades. The number of newspaper articles and photographs documenting George's participation in local and statewide reunions is voluminous. His involvement with War Veterans activities became another component of his celebrity in Utah. An article about the 1907 reunion described him as "the noted Indian fighter and singer of Indian songs," which probably overstates Harrison's military role in the conflict.[16] While the reunions served primarily to preserve memories and friendships, the members successfully lobbied for pensions that were granted in 1918.[17]

Rosella left the hotel and returned to her home in about 1889. She had more time with her children and members of the extended family. Part of that extended family was Hannah Harrison. After William's death in 1881, Hannah continued to live at home and take care of the garden. Hannah was a regular at Sunday services where she was one of "seven lovable old ladies" who took possession of the bench in front of the stove. They upholstered their pew with soft pillows. Even if the sisters were not present, no one presumed to occupy the vacant seats.[18] On Thursdays,

---

11. Huff, comp., *Memories That Live*, 324-25.

12. Johnson, *History of Springville*, 92-93.

13. Finley, *History of Springville*, 78.

14. Johnson, *History of Springville*, 92-93.

15. "Mimic Field of War."

16. "Indian War Veterans of Utah Will Sing Old Battle Songs," *Salt Lake Telegram*, June 7, 1907, p. 6

17. Roger B. Nielson, *Utah's Black Hawk War Veterans*, Self-published, Springville, Utah, 2009, vii.

18. Finley, *History of Springville*, 28.

Hannah attended a meeting where she interpreted the testimonies of those who spoke in tongues.[19] When the Relief Society was organized in Springville in 1868, Hannah was chosen as a counselor to the first president, Cynthia Clyde.[20]

In 1887 Hannah sold her home and moved a block away to live with Rosella.[21] Records at the Utah County Recorder's office show that Hannah's son George was the buyer.[22] When Hannah moved into Rosella's home, a granddaughter, Drucilla Kast, may have come with her. In 1866, Drucilla's mother, Alice Harrison, married Eric Kast. Kast returned from a mission to Sweden in 1873 with a second wife. Alice divorced him and left five-year-old Drucilla with her parents.[23] In rejecting polygamous marriage, Alice was among the majority of Mormons who disliked the practice. During the nineteenth century in Utah, about twenty percent of Mormon families were polygamous.[24] Many accepted the practice grudgingly. Historian Davis Bitton wrote that men who aspired to significant religious or civil positions [known as Utah society's "big bugs"] almost inevitably succumbed to the pressure to take plural wives.[25]

Drucilla's stay with William and Hannah Harrison was not always happy. She later told her granddaughter, Dorothy Miner, that she was treated like a slave.[26] William expected Drucilla to clean neighbors' houses, and he kept the money that she earned. He was very strict and sometimes punished his granddaughter with a switch.[27] Corporal punishment was prevalent at the time, though less often used for girls than boys. Drucilla also recalled that her mother, Alice, had tried to take her back, but William and Hannah refused.[28]

Rosella's two oldest children probably moved out before Rosella returned to the home. Arvilla married Joseph Henry Storrs in October 1888. The couple lived in Springville for ten years before moving permanently to nearby American Fork.[29] Arvilla raised a large family, while Joseph was a successful businessman and a long-serving LDS bishop.

George William Harrison married Ada Bissell in 1889. About that time, possession of the house and property that belonged to William and Hannah

19. Myrl Storrs Stewart, "Biography of Hannah Ellis Harrison."

20. Huff, *Memories That Live*, 322. The Relief Society is an all-female auxiliary of the LDS Church. The purpose is charity and education.

21. Ada Bissell Harrison, "Biography of Hannah Ellis Harrison," Camp Aaron Johnson, DUP, Springville Utah.

22. The "Block Abstract for Springville City," Utah County Recorder's Office, Provo, Utah, 2015.

23. "Biography of Alice Harrison (Kast) Catlin," on file at the Daughters of Utah Pioneers Museum, Salt Lake City.

24. William Volf, "Mormon Polygamy in the Nineteenth Century: The Practice of the Principle in Reality," *Nebraska Anthropologist* 15, 41. Available online at http://digitalcommons.unl.edu/nebanthro/126.

25. Davis Bitton, "Mormon Polygamy: A Review Article," *Journal of Mormon History* 4, 112.

26. Personal communication from Dorothy Miner; Springville, Utah, October 2014.

27. Ibid.

28. Ibid.

29. Stewart, "Biography of Rosella Arvilla Harrison Storrs."

passed from George Harrison to his oldest son.[30] In about 1897, George William completed a rock, brick and adobe home that remains occupied at 341 South 200 West in Springville.[31] He also took over William's farm, and was a successful life-long farmer and cattleman. George William and Ada were active Church members. When they celebrated seventy-two years of marriage in 1961, a newspaper noted them as Utah's longest married couple.[32]

Rosella's other children were slower to leave home than the two oldest and several returned years after they initially departed. Most of the children remained in or near Springville and actively practiced the Mormon religion. Third child, Lewis, was an exception. He separated from the Church in dramatic fashion, as described by grandson, Douglas Bird.[33] When Lewis was about fifteen, he announced to his family that he was finished with religion. Failing to convince his son otherwise, George Harrison took Lewis to the front yard to discipline him. Whatever struggle ensued, family legend holds that Lewis got the better of his father and never again attended church. In 1895 he married Mary (May) Madsen, and two children were born in Springville. The family moved to southern Utah but, by 1904, Lewis moved back to Springville without his first wife or the children. In 1908 he married Clara Stewart. The 1910 US Census shows Lewis, Clara and their first child, Idona, living with Rosella. The rift between Lewis and his father was not permanent. Lewis inherited the family home when George died.[34]

Rosella's fourth child Anna May left home to marry Andrew Bjorkland in 1893. Two years later she moved back. Anna May filed for divorce, citing extreme cruelty and habitual drunkenness on Andrew's part.[35] The separation was more sensational than most because Anna May's husband filed a lawsuit against George and Rosella. Andrew alleged that they coerced their daughter into divorcing him. As reported in a Provo newspaper, Burkley [he changed his last name] also charged the Harrisons with "attempting to commit an abortion upon Mrs. Burkley." Burkley retracted this claim along with the rest of the suit two weeks later. He stated that he received erroneous information. With the help of medical men whom he trusted, Andrew stated that his accusation was entirely wrong. He added that Mr. and Mrs. Harrison are well known to the public as respectable, moral and law-abiding citizens, and that he craved the public's pardon.[36]

---

30. "Block Abstract for Springville City."

31. Newspaper article in George William Harrison file at Daughters of Utah Pioneers Museum, Salt Lake City.

32. "Springville Couple Note 72 Years in Marriage." Newspaper article emanates from Springville and someone wrote Aug. 24, 1961 at the top of the clipping. No other information. Clipping found in George William Harrison file at Daughters of the Utah Pioneers Museum, Salt Lake City.

33. Personal communication from Douglas Bird (great-grandson of George Harrison), Springville, Utah, October 2014.

34. Personal communication from Barbara Lee (great-granddaughter of George and Rosella), Springville, Utah, 2012.

35. "District Court," *The Evening Dispatch*, 13 Mar 1895, 4. Available online at https://newspapers.lib.utah.edu/details?id=3141663.

36. "A Card," *The Evening Dispatch*, 30 Mar 1895, 1. Available online at https://newspapers.

The Harrison family ca. 1892. From left to right: Rosella Arvilla, Anna May, George "Beef-steak," George William, Winfred, Lewis, Rosella, Gertrude, William "Willie."
Courtesy Harold B. Lee Library, Brigham Young University

Anna May reconciled with Andrew and delivered her second child six months later. The couple had a third child in February 1897, but subsequently separated. In 1903 Anna May married George Preston Smith. They raised the children from Anna May's first marriage as well as two children they conceived. George Smith drove the Harrison Hotel's hack for years. By the 1920 census, he was working as a foreman for the railroad.

Willie White Harrison was the fifth of Rosella's children. He was living at home in 1900 and probably stayed there until he married Mary Myrtle Hall in 1902. The 1910 census shows them with a home in Springville and three young children. Willie noted that he was employed as a chemist at Springville's sugar factory. He was very active in the Church, including a mission to the Eastern States.[37] Willie received a diploma in bookkeeping from the Brigham Young Academy in Provo and served as ward clerk in Springville for twenty-three years. He was also active in civic affairs, serving three terms as city recorder.

---

lib.utah.edu/details?id=3139817.

37. Willie White Harrison, Early Mormon Missionaries database. Available online at https://history.lds.org/missionary/individual/willie-white-harrison-1874?lang=eng.

Rosella's two youngest children married in 1904, but neither moved away from home initially.[38] Winfred and his wife, Martha Fereday Harrison, added their first child, Vivian, to Rosella's household in June 1905. Martha wrote that Rosella expected her to clean the house.[39] Martha was also asked to do the laundry using either a washboard or a hand-powered washing tub. Previous to Martha's arrival in the home, Rosella sent laundry out to be washed. Martha remembered that the heavy woolen underwear that George Harrison wore over a lighter set of undergarments was particularly difficult to wash.[40] Winfred and Martha moved out and back to Rosella's home several times. In 1919 they lived in the house of Winfred's aunt Martha Noakes. Martha, known affectionately as Aunt Mattie, was Hannah Harrison's last child, born in Springville in 1858. At age eighteen, she married William Huntington. A year after he died in 1896, Martha married George Noakes who was sixteen years her junior. Again, Mattie outlived her husband—the second time by twenty-five years.

Gertrude Harrison married William M. Packard in 1904. Unlike Martha, Gertrude was never asked to do housework in Rosella's home. In fact, Gertrude thought it was strange that Martha knew how to make bread and sew.[41] William and Gertrude left Rosella's home a few years after their marriage, but by 1910 returned. Eventually, they moved permanently to Salt Lake City.

Rosella became active in the Young Ladies Mutual Improvement Association and served as president for several years.[42] Her daughter wrote that she also became very involved in temple work. She also did research to document the genealogies of her ancestors. Rosella was concerned that none of her family had accepted the Mormon gospel.[43] The LDS Church teaches that only those who are baptized as Mormons will enter heaven. Proxy baptism of deceased persons who were not Church members is allowed, but requires documentation of genealogy.

Rosella's younger sister Elvira White Burgess and brother Everett Edward White moved to Springville in 1902.[44] Both were widowed and neither of them became members of the Mormon Church. Perhaps financial difficulties were the reason for relocating close to Rosella. Everett died in Springville in 1907.[45] Elvira was living with Rosella at the time of the 1910 census. She stayed in Springville until her death in 1928.

Despite the nasty letter that Everett White wrote to Rosella in 1865, he came to terms with her conversion to the Mormon faith well before his move to Utah. Everett was closely involved with the authors of a book that traced the White family back to William and Susanna White who emigrated on the *Mayflower*. The book contains the names and birthdates of Rosella's nine children, which required

38. Martha Harrison, "Autobiography," 16.
39. Ibid., 18.
40. Ibid., 19.
41. Ibid.
42. Stewart, "Biography of Rosella Damon White Harrison."
43. Ibid.
44. Personal communication from Barbara Lee, Springville, Utah, May, 2015.
45. Ibid.

"The Four Georges." George "Beefsteak" Harrison (b. 1841) is seated. His firstborn was George William (G. W., b. 1866). G. W. is standing to the viewer's left of his father. Also standing is G. W.'s firstborn, George Bissell Harrison (b. 1890). In front of Beefsteak is George Myron Harrison, firstborn of George Bissell (b. 1915). Photo ca. 1918-1920 in Springville, Utah.
Family photo in possession of author.

contact between Everett and Rosella prior to the 1895 publication.[46] When Rosella and George Harrison first met Howard Driggs on a train in 1909, Rosella emphasized that she was "a real daughter of the *Mayflower*."[47] Her obituary and biographies state that she was a seventh generation descendant of Peregrine White, who was born on the ship ten days after arrival at Cape Cod in November 1620.[48] Peregrine is celebrated as the first European child born in New England.[49]

On May 4, 1915, Rosella and George Harrison commemorated their golden wedding anniversary. The event can be viewed as a capstone to a rewarding and

46. White, *Ancestral Chronological Record*, 65-66.

47. Driggs, "Theirs Was the Handcart Way to Zion," 202. The author wrote that this first encounter with George Harrison occurred soon after Driggs returned from a trip along the Mormon Trail. A photo album dated May 13, 1909, which is held at the Church History Library in Salt Lake City, documents the Driggs' journey.

48. The "Ancestral Chronological Record" referred to in footnote 43 is difficult to follow. The author contacted the Mayflower Society, which led to Barbara Williams, historian for The Pilgrim William White Society. She took little time to determine that Rosella was a descendant of William and Susanna White's son Peregrine. The genealogy can be traced back from Rosella in the online "Geni" database.

49. "Peregrine White," Pilgrim Hall Museum, Plymouth, Massachusetts. Available online at http://www.pilgrimhallmuseum.org/peregrine_white.htm.

sometimes challenging family life. As published in the *Deseret News*, fifty-five guests assembled at their home for a celebration.[50] The report notes the presence of all seven of their children, twenty-one of thirty-one their grandchildren, and one of their two great-grandchildren. The great-grandchild in attendance was probably George Myron Harrison, who was born to George Bissell Harrison and Alta Viola Crandall in Springville a month before. Rosella and George were certainly pleased that the newspaper article described them as "sturdy pioneer stock and known to be among the most respected citizens of Springville."

---

50. "... and Mrs. George Harrison Celebrate Golden."

16

Statehood, Motor Cars and Patriotism

Several weeks after US President Benjamin Harrison departed Utah in May 1891, Mormon leaders took their first concrete step to separate church and state. The Church dissolved its political arm, the People's Party, and surrendered absolute control of secular government in Utah.[1] The Saints were instructed to join either of the two national parties. Most Utahns identified with the Democrats because Republicans sponsored the legal persecution of Mormons during the 1880s.[2] However, Utah leaders recognized that support of national Republican leaders was necessary to gain admission to the Union.[3] While no longer in strict control of politics, Church leaders used their influence to encourage a somewhat equitable division of party membership. Historian Glenn Bird recalls learning from "old-timers" that Springville bishops walked through the community instructing citizens on one side of a street to join the Democrats and those on the other side to register as Republicans.[4]

In early 1893, mindful of the changes occurring in Utah, President Harrison pardoned Mormons who were previously in polygamous marriages.[5] The amnestied polygamists were again able to vote and hold office. Later the same year, the Saints were given an opportunity to present the best side of Mormonism to the nation. On August 29, 250 members of the Mormon Tabernacle Choir boarded a train to perform outside of Utah for the first time.[6] The occasion was a choral competition at the World's Fair, the Colombian Exposition in Chicago.[7] The Mormon choir finished second and earned great acclaim. However, according to Reid L. Neilson, the celebrated musical talent of the choir was not what primarily captured the public's imagination. The national press had denigrated Mormons as sub-human for fifty years. Neilson wrote, "Most Chicago residents and cosmopolitan fairgoers simply wanted to see what an 'exotic' Latter-day Saint looked like up close and in person."[8] A local newspaper reported, "there will be not a little disappointment when they discover that these musical Mormons are just the same as other people."[9]

1. Larson, *Americanization of Utah*, 287.
2. Holzapfel, *History of Utah County*, 110.
3. Larson, *Americanization of Utah*, 286.
4. Personal communication from Glenn Bird, Springville, Utah, 2016.
5. Bigler, *Forgotten Kingdom*, 358.
6. Reid L. Neilson, *Exhibiting Mormonism: The Latter-day Saints and the 1893 Chicago World's Fair* (New York: Oxford University Press, 2011), 107.
7. The exhibition's name commemorated the 400th anniversary of Christopher Columbus's discovery of the New World.
8. Neilson, *Exhibiting Mormonism*, 131.
9. Ibid., Neilson is quoting from the *Chicago Inter-Ocean*, 3 Sep, 1893.

Barbara Lee recalls learning as a young girl that her great-grandmother, Rosella Harrison, occasionally sang with the Tabernacle Choir and traveled to the Chicago Exposition with the Mormon choir.[10] That Rosella sometimes sang with the choir is plausible as she was an accomplished alto singer and a friend of Choir Director Evan Stephens. However, by 1893, she was significantly impaired with pulmonary disease and almost certainly did not have the stamina for an arduous schedule of practices and performances. A testament to the degree of Rosella's impairment was clear in a brief report in the Springville newspaper. The article states that George Harrison took his wife to St. Mark's Hospital in Salt Lake City for evaluation and treatment. During her hospital stay, George visited and talked to a family friend, Mrs. Edwin Lee, who thought Rosella was the best she had been for years. Mrs. Lee jovially remarked that the attendant physician ensured her that they were intending to escort Rosella "to the end of the corridor and leave her there until she walked back, thus forcing her to do something that she had not done for many years."[11]

Though she was not in the choir at the World's Fair, it is possible that Rosella was included in the one hundred supporters who accompanied the performers on their special ten-car train. If not, Rosella probably made separate arrangements to attend the performances. Seven thousand Utah residents visited the fair between May and October 1893. Many of them, including Rosella, were pioneers who walked across a thousand miles of wilderness to reach Zion. Their journey back to the Missouri River and further east to Chicago was in comfortable passenger cars, though probably not the first-class Pullman sleeper coaches provided to the choir.[12]

In March 1895, elected delegates met to frame a new Utah constitution. Springville's representative was John S. Boyer.[13] The document included provisions that banned the practice of polygamy. The new constitution also made Utah the third state to grant full suffrage to women. Utah gained statehood on January 4, 1896. Springville's reaction was typical—the news was greeted by the ringing of bells, blowing of whistles and other celebrations.[14] Two days later, democratically elected state officials were inaugurated. In November 1896, citizens of Springville, along with rest of Utah, voted in a national election for the first time.

Rank and file Mormons enthusiastically welcomed statehood, and many believed that joining the Union should have happened much earlier. A small, unelected and polygamous elite, who promised an "imminent Millennium," carried on a fruitless battle with the US government for fifty years. Historian David Bigler points out that the theocracy's eventual capitulation came less from the blows of

10. Personal communication from Barbara Lee (great-granddaughter of Rosella) of Springville, Utah, April, 2016.

11. "Local News," *Springville Independent*, 6 Dec, 1895, 6.

12. Neilson, *Exhibiting Mormonism*, 121.

13. Finley, *History of Springville*, 80.

14. Ibid.

its enemies than the arrival of a new generation of Mormons "that had adopted the democratic ideals of the American nation and wanted political reform."[15]

As a committed capitalist, George Harrison was certainly one of those who saw no need for the LDS Church's aspirations to dictate business and political affairs. At the same time he valued the Church's role in traditional religious and ecclesiastical concerns. There is no evidence that his religious faith ever wavered. He was surely presented opportunities to question his parents' beliefs as, starting at age fifteen, he spent seven formative years living with Gentiles, primarily the US Army. The remainder of his life, he comfortably worked for and around non-Mormons. Of William and Hannah's six children who survived the Martin Handcart Company, George Harrison was one of only two who did not leave the LDS Church.[16] Given the time demands of freighting and the hotel, George's participation in the Church was perhaps mostly as choir member and chorister. Nonetheless, he was active enough that a 1912 publication of prominent men in Utah described Harrison as a high priest, a twenty-year leader of the choir, and president of an elders' quorum in Springville.[17] A concrete sign of Harrison's faith was that he wore light undergarments referred to as "temple garments."[18] The apparel serves to remind church members of their commitment to live honorable lives.

Aaron Harrison made different choices—not necessarily better or worse, and possibly driven to a great extent by historical accident. George Harrison spent a week in San Bernardino and Los Angeles as part of a group of freighters who traveled the Southern Route in the 1850s and 1860s.[19] Perhaps the two brothers were able to get together and reminisce. They shared similar histories when they departed Manchester. Both worked in the glass factory as takers-in though, by 1856, Aaron was a mechanic in an iron foundry. Both were active LDS Church members and notably good singers. Aaron was highly skeptical of the handcart plan, but agreed to participate to help the family. Their paths in life diverged when they departed the disastrous Martin company under different circumstances.

George later told Howard Driggs that the malaria he contracted at the Missouri River was "the beginning of my real troubles."[20] In the short term, George's statement was true. If he had not violated family and Church authority to leave the handcart trek, George almost certainly would have died. Severe starvation led him to live with Indians and subsequently reside at Fort Laramie where he met an English cook who mentored him. Without his experience as an army cook, a

15. Bigler, *Forgotten Kingdom*, 364.

16. George's sister Olivia remained active in the Mormon Church in Springville until her death. Aaron, Mary Ann, Alice and Hannah left Utah and the Church at different times and settled in either California or Washington.

17. Frank Esshom, *Pioneers and Prominent Men of Utah* (Salt Lake City: Utah Pioneers Book Publishing Company, 1912), 457. Available online at https://archive.org/details/pioneersprominen00esshrich. "Seventies" were a local level priesthood office primarily tasked with promoting the religion.

18. Harrison, "Autobiography," 19.

19. "Pioneers Go Today, Trail Blazers Leave This Evening for Trip to the Coast," *Salt Lake Telegram*, 9 Oct 1905, 3.

20. Driggs, "Handcart Boy (First Draft)," 7.

freighting company may not have hired the young man in 1863. The freighting skills that George learned enabled him to become a trader. Trading profits yielded relative financial security that allowed him to build a restaurant and hotel where he met the drummers who made him a celebrity. Harrison probably would have lived a fulfilling life without the mosquito bite, but not the one that Howard Driggs chronicled.

The mosquito that gave George malaria also may have altered Aaron's fate. If fifteen-year-old George remained healthy, he certainly would have helped push the family handcart after the Missouri River. Aaron would have been less fatigued at Fort Laramie and, perhaps, remained with the family. We are in no position to judge Aaron's impetuous decision to join the US Army. But, it is likely that many of his contemporaries in the Mormon community viewed it as dishonorable given the dire predicament of the family. Aaron's subsequent desertion from the US Army seems defensible, but apparently caused embarrassment to generations of relatives as they tried to rewrite that history. Aaron worked as a mechanic and a farmer in San Bernardino. Visiting relatives from Utah observed that his family was doing well, "with a lovely home and all the latest in fashionable furnishings."[21] By 1900, sixty-two-year-old Aaron was living alone in Randsburg, California, a gold mining boomtown in the Mohave Desert.[22] He was working as a mechanic and was in the process of a divorce from Tryphena. While it is likely that neither regretted his choices, Aaron and George would have likely agreed that chance played a large role in both their lives.

On October 3, 1909, George Harrison learned that his brother died the day before in San Bernardino, California. George informed a Salt Lake City newspaper of the death and noted that he would be unable to attend the services. The newspaper reported, "Aaron Harrison was 78 years old. He came to Utah in 1856 with the handcart company and for many years resided in Springville."[23] Actually, George's brother was seventy-two years old, abandoned the Martin Handcart Company at Fort Laramie, and first came to Utah in 1860. Probably, the reporter mangled the article, but perhaps George revised Aaron's history.

Soon after George Harrison built his hotel in 1886, he put up a large barn on the back of his property to accommodate a livery.[24] Twenty years as a freighter gave him the skills to run the business. The livery enabled George to provide free transportation for drummers and their trunks to his hotel, which became more important when Springville's railroad tracks were moved from Main Street to 400 West Street in late 1891. Hotel customers were also able to rent carriages for local travel. An advertisement in an 1892 gazetteer shows "Thorn & Harrison

21. Hogenson, *Ursula Goddard*, 9.

22. 1900 US Federal Census, Eleventh Township, Randsburg City, Kern County, California, ED 32, sheet 6A. Available online at https://www.ancestry.com/interactive/7602/004118421_00883?pid=32610643 (subscription required). Aaron listed himself as married. On the same census, Tryphena was living in San Bernardino and declared that she was divorced.

23. "State Society" *The Salt Lake Herald-Republican*, 10 Oct 1909, 36. Available online at https://newspapers.lib.utah.edu/details?id=10449785.

24. Harrison, "History of The Harrison Hotel," 8.

George Harrison in front of his restaurant and hotel ca. 1905. The wagon on the right is probably the hotel's "hack," used to transport guests to and from the train depot. The driver is possibly George Preston Smith who married Beefsteak's daughter, Anna May, and drove the hack for many years.
Courtesy, Harold B. Lee Library, Brigham Young University,

Livery, Feed & Sale Stables" adjoining the Harrison Hotel.[25] George and his partner, Erastus Thorn, also listed themselves as dealers in "Wagons, Carriages & Agricultural Implements." Grandson Bertrand Harrison wrote that the livery stable also provided locals with buggies, a surrey, a white top, cutters, and a glass-sided hearse with ornate white fluted corners. Regarding the hearse, Bertrand added, "This of course was not intended for the use of the hotel guests."[26] Harrison's close friend, Walter Wheeler, rented the fancy white hearse for funerals for many decades.[27] The era of the horse-drawn funeral procession in Springville did not end until 1919, when the Wheeler Mortuary purchased its first motor-driven hearse.

A 1903 gazetteer lists George Harrison's livery along with two others in Springville, including one owned by George Washington Straw.[28] An inexplicable altercation between thirty-year-old Straw and sixty-three-year-old Harrison possibly developed because of business competition. Beefsteak later described the

25. *Utah Gazetteer of 1892-93* (Salt Lake City: Stenhouse and Co./Salt Lake Litho Company), 335. Available online at https://archive.org/details/utahgazetteer18900stenrich.

26. Harrison, "History of The Harrison Hotel," 8.

27. Marie Wheeler Cranmer, Helen Wheeler, and Blaine Wheeler, "History of Wheeler Mortuary," *Springville Herald*, date unknown. Copy in possession of author.

28. *Utah State Gazetteer and Business Directory*, 442.

event in court as part of an assault charge he brought against Straw.[29] On May 12, 1903, between the hours of 11 and 12 pm, Harrison heard shouting on the street outside his hotel. He stepped outside to ask "the rioters" to keep quiet as they were disturbing his customers. A voice replied, "You damned old gray beard I'll fix you!"[30] Washington Straw came out of the darkness and grabbed Beefsteak by his coat collar, while "using abusive language." Some punches were thrown, but accounts differ regarding who threw the first, or even if any punches landed. Feeling ashamed the next morning, Washington Straw visited George Harrison and asked for forgiveness, but was refused. In court, Straw denied being noisy, though he admitted to the judge that he was drinking. Two of the young man's drinking companions were unable to add any insight. At the conclusion of the evidence, the judge held the defendant guilty as charged and imposed a fine of $25. Straw gave notice of appeal.[31]

Whatever the result of the appeal, the reality was that the traditional livery business became less profitable as motorized vehicles began to appear. George was early to modernize his operation by switching from a horse drawn hack to a gas-powered bus. By 1909 the Harrison Hotel was advertised as the "Leading Hotel For Commercial Men. Free Bus Meets all Trains."[32] George continued to maintain a small livery for a number of years after buying the bus—probably because many roads outside the city limits remained impassable to automobiles.

Motorists in search of adventurous day trips became a new clientele for Beefsteak's restaurant. An article in a Salt Lake City paper shows early adopters of the horseless carriage travelling to Springville in 1907—"One of the prettiest motor trips on the surrounding map is Provoward, with dinner down at Beefsteak Harrison's. Beefsteak, by the way, is a character and enough fun in himself to make the trip worthwhile . . . There isn't a girl who has dined at Harrison's who hasn't a case on him, and a stop at the tavern of the boniface [innkeeper] is quite a feature of every week for the more enthusiastic among the motorists."[33] Two months later a report reaffirmed the restaurant's popularity—"The Sunday motor run is getting to be quite the event of the week and Beefsteak Harrison's at sleepy little Springville makes a noise like a gigantic garage every Sunday."[34] Motorcyclists also enjoyed the pilgrimage to Harrison's restaurant. A newspaper article in June 1917 solicited riders to join the Harley Davidson Motor Club for a two-hour ride from Salt Lake City to Springville for a picnic luncheon at Beefsteak's.[35]

Behind the popularity and fun of Beefsteak's restaurant was a story of mundane, hard work that was common to all small hotels. For George, the restaurant, though

29. *Springville Independent*, 28 May 1903, 4.

30. Ibid.

31. Ibid.

32. *Business Directory of Salt Lake City, Utah, 1909-1910*, 167. Available online at https://babel.hathitrust.org/cgi/pt?id=hvd.hx4j83;view=1up;seq=179.

33. *Goodwin's Weekly*, 27 Jul 1907, 11.

34. *Goodwin's Weekly*, 28 Sep 1907, 10.

35. "Motorcycle Club Will Pay a Visit to Beefsteak Man." Salt Lake Telegram, 10 Jun 1917, 15.

possibly not the hotel, seemed to be a passion more than a job. Rosella helped him greatly at the start, but weakened by bouts of pneumonia and difficult pregnancies, she moved back home after two or three years. George William, Beefsteak's oldest child, probably worked rarely in the hotel, but he later recalled a summer he spent hauling loads of firewood out of the mountains for hotel use.[36] Arvilla quit school at age eighteen because her father needed help in the restaurant and hotel.[37] She recalled "very hard work and long hours." Arvilla arose at 4 am to cook breakfast and put up lunches for the railroad men. She also cleaned hotel rooms, washed and ironed linens, and helped George cook. After two years, Arvilla married Joseph Storrs and no longer worked at the hotel.

George's other children may have contributed briefly, but only the youngest, Winfred, spent significant time in the establishment. His wife, Martha Fereday Harrison, wrote that Winn worked full time at the hotel after their marriage in 1904.[38] Winfred left the house at 8 am, returned home at 10 pm, and was paid a "small salary." After a year, he left the hotel to work as a surveyor with his brother, Lewis. Winn later returned to work with his father, but he left again after a few years for a nighttime job in Springville's sugar factory. He eventually resigned himself to working in the hotel. An advertisement in a 1913 gazetteer shows Winfred as the manager of the Harrison Hotel. Seventy-two-year-old George is listed as proprietor, and he likely limited himself to cooking and entertaining.

Martha Fereday Harrison was called upon many times to come help at the hotel. She wrote that she was never paid—"Once in a great while Daddy [George] would hand me a dollar." Winn and Martha lived with Rosella, off and on, for many years after their marriage, and George probably expected their contribution to the hotel. Martha recalled one instance when Beefsteak gave her a new quarter and said, probably teasingly, "See how long you can keep it."[39] Many young women in Springville worked in the hotel before other responsibilities interceded.

When George moved home during his last year of life, Winfred and Martha moved into the Harrison Hotel. Martha later wrote about the difficulties of the work and how little time she could spend with her children.[40] Furthermore, she noted that Winfred, who quit school after fifth grade, "wasn't cut out to manage and make a success of the hotel as Daddy Harrison had been."[41] Martha also blamed the hotel for introducing her husband to companions who were a bad influence upon him. When Winfred and Martha closed the business and sold the property to W. W. Clyde in 1940, the pink hotel was a relic.[42] Martha did not recall it with fondness—"The hotel was a monster who gobbled up our family life."[43]

---

36. "Springville Couple Note 72 Years in Marriage."
37. Stewart, "Biography of Rosella Arvilla Harrison Storrs."
38. Martha Harrison, "Autobiography," 18.
39. Ibid., 28.
40. Ibid., 30.
41. Ibid.
42. The building was razed in 1941, and a commercial structure that initially housed a JC Penney store and a Safeway store was completed in 1942.
43. Ibid.

Soon after the hotel's closure Martha divorced Winfred and moved to Salt Lake City. Martha's sister introduced her to Minerva Young who was widowed and needed a companion.[44] Martha wrote that the opportunity was too good to be true. Martha and Mrs. Young attended many Church affairs, especially in the Tabernacle where they were ushered to the best seats. They also attended events at the University of Utah. Church President Heber J. Grant and his wife were close friends of Mrs. Young. The foursome, including Martha, often had dinner together and sometimes a driver would take them for a ride. Martha enjoyed other interesting jobs before moving to Provo in 1955. She died in 1987 at age 100, and was buried next to Winfred Harrison in Springville's Historic Cemetery.

Dillon Wallace, an adventurer and writer, was riding through the west with a pack outfit in 1910 when he arrived at Beefsteak's restaurant. His journal described George Harrison as "one of the few remaining trail blazers of the desert, an early California pioneer."[45] Once the host learned that Wallace watered at some of the same "Coyote Holes" that Beefsteak visited years before, he left "Mr." off his customer's name and sang some local songs. One recalled the Black Hawk War.

"Where is Blackhawk and Chief Sanpitch?
They're having a big pow-wow;
They've gone to smoke the pipe of peace –
The Indians are ticaboo [happy] now."

"Blackhawk stole cattle from Scipio;
Was known as a wicked Ute.
He laid down his gun and his bow
When he could no longer shoot."

Wallace also made observations that offer insight into changes in Utah. South of Utah Valley, he observed that the towns he rode through could still be characterized as "pioneer," with everyone on horseback. As he passed north of Richfield, about a hundred miles south of Springville, he rarely saw a mounted man. Wagons and occasional automobiles were the means of transportation. Wallace wrote, "The spurred rider, the freighter, and the stage coach are already of the past."[46] Though no longer a pioneer village, a pastoral character still prevailed in Springville. As Wallace rode north from the town, he observed that the fruit harvest was underway, and the air was full of the perfume of ripe apples and peaches. He continued, "Utah Lake shimmered at my left. An autumnal haze lay over the valley . . . the quiet, dreamy beauty of it all was of the character that breeds in one an indescribable longing . . . a desire for something that is akin to homesickness."[47]

44. Mrs. Young's husband was US Army Brigadier General Richard W. Young, whose father was Joseph A. Young.

45. Dillon Wallace, *Saddle and Camp in the Rockies* (New York: Outing Publishing Company, 1911), 176.

46. Ibid., 164.

47. Ibid., 176.

By the time Dillon Wallace visited the Harrison Hotel in 1910, drummers were a declining proportion of the guests. Consumers in rural America were turning to new ways of obtaining the most useful and fashionable merchandise. The Sears Catalog was one of the marketing innovations that made the drummers obsolete. In 1900, when sixty percent of Americans still lived "on the farm," advances in print advertising, the creation of rural free delivery routes by the postal service, and a low postage rate on mail order publications enabled economical delivery of the 500 page catalogs.[48] Moreover, the merchandise was shipped directly to the home. The "farmer's friend" competed for business with independent retailers such as Deal Bros. & Mendenhall and H. T. Reynolds & Company. Chain stores such JC Penney and Woolworths were also proliferating.[49] The colorful drummers, who created Beefsteak's celebrity, played no role in either business model and disappeared from American life.

Though the hotel claimed much of George Harrison's time, he was busy in other activities. Beefsteak owned a farm where he raised cattle. A 1918 gazetteer that includes a list of farmers and tax assessments in Utah County suggests that George's farm was relatively large. His son's twenty acre farm was assessed at $495 while Beefsteak's farm was assessed at $5130.[50] George Harrison's great-grandson David Harrison states that the land was on Dry Creek west of Springville and bordered on its north side by 400 South, also known as State Highway 77.[51] The land was highly alkaline and better suited to grazing cattle than raising crops. George William Harrison ran cattle on the land for decades after his father's death. In the late 1950s, the Utah Highway Commission claimed most of the property for construction of Interstate 15, including an interchange for a Springville exit.

The smaller farm that Beefsteak's father, William Harrison, worked with his oxen, Prince and Albert, was very fertile, and many different crops were raised on it over the years.[52] David Harrison owns the farm, which was twelve acres at the time of William's death in 1881 and is now twenty acres. The tract continues to be cultivated, though largely surrounded by development.[53]

Beefsteak Harrison registered a cattle brand in 1899—a lazy "4H" placed on the left rear flank of a cow.[54] In addition to fattening up cattle to be served in his restaurant, George became involved in breeding. A 1901 registry of bloodlines of Shorthorn cattle shows one of his calves. On a page where other calves have names

---

48. "History of the Sears Catalogue," Sears Archives. Available online at http://www.searsarchives.com/catalogs/history.htm.

49. Spears, *100 Years on the Road*, 1.

50. *Utah State Gazetteer, 1918-1919* (Salt Lake City: R. L. Polk & Co., 1918), 552.

51. Personal communication from David Dvorak Harrison, Stateline, Nevada, Jun 2016.

52. Ibid.

53. The farm that William Harrison acquired in the late 1850s is directly east of Meadow Brook Elementary School, 748 S. 950 W.

54. C. S. Tingey, *Record of Marks and Brands for the State of Utah: Embracing All Marks and Brands Recorded to June 1st, 1901* (np, [1901]), 76. Available online at https://archive.org/details/recordofmarksbra00tingrich.

such as Red Gem, Rosebud and Anna, George proudly lists his calf as "Harrison's Beauty of Springville."[55]

In October 1891, local citizens obtained a charter for Springville's first bank. The principle stockholders were the town's largest merchandisers—Packards, Reynolds, and Deal Brothers and Mendenhall. George invested $500, which gave him one percent of the bank's shares.[56] During the Great Depression, the Springville Banking Company was one of a few banks in the country that did not require a bailout by the federal government. Today the bank operates as Central Bank, with thirteen offices in Utah County. Some family histories state that George was a director of the bank, but there is no record that he ever played a role other than investor.[57]

According to descendants, George also invested in the Springville Sugar Plant that began operations in 1899. The plant was the first in the United States to squeeze juice from beets to send by pipeline to another location to be refined into sugar. After a few years the twenty-two-mile wooden pipeline to Lehi, Utah started to leak. Within a decade of opening, the Springville plant was shut down.[58] George's most speculative venture was probably a 1911 mining claim he filed in the Eldorado Mining District in Utah County.[59] His son Lewis was one of the "locaters" for the claim.

Railroad tracks once again appeared in the middle of Springville's Main Street in 1915. The Salt Lake and Utah Railroad extended an electrically powered interurban rail line to the small town. The railroad company featured George Harrison in a promotional pamphlet that was also published in the *Salt Lake Tribune*.[60] The article stated, "At Springville, in Utah County . . . lives Beefsteak Harrison. He runs a small hotel and his name is known in every home in the state. Mentioned in New York, New Orleans or San Francisco, it is sure to bring a smile of pleasant recollection to those who believe that to eat is to live." The article went on to say that most Utah people ate one of Beefsteak Harrison's steaks, and that many motor down to his restaurant every Sunday or so. Also, "To those not fortunate enough to own a motor car, or who prefer the quicker, cleaner and more scenic electric way, or to the visitor who appreciates the good things of life, a Sunday or weekday trip to Springville will repay you."[61]

Six days later the new railroad marketed excursions to Springville's annual July 24 celebration of Utah pioneers. An estimated 10,000 people from all over Utah

55. *The American Short-horn Herd Book* 47, part 1, 326. Available online at https://babel.hathitrust.org/cgi/pt?id=coo.31924066239413;view=1up;seq=7.

56. Howard C. Maycock, "A History of Springville Banking Company, Predecessor of Central Bank and Trust Company" (np, 1985). Available at the Springville Historical Society, Springville, Utah.

57. Personal communication from Leon Lee, Springville, Utah, 2012. Lee worked at the bank for thirty years.

58. Johnson and Knight, "Historic Resources of Springville City," 8.

59. The original claim is in the possession of Barbara Lee (great-granddaughter of Harrison), Springville, Utah.

60. "A Little Journey to the Home of Beefsteak Harrison."

61. Ibid.

County attended the event.[62] Many arrived via one of fifty interurban trains that were sent to Springville that day. The reporter noted that "Beefsteak" Harrison had one of the busiest days in his history. The hotel dining room could not accommodate the large crowds and Harrison was forced to add tables on the lawn for his guests.[63]

Several decades after attaining statehood in 1896, Utah was increasingly assimilated into the nations' competitive market economy. By 1916, wrote historian Dean May, other significant signs of Americanization were a non-Mormon governor and the fact that nearly forty-five percent of Utah's 500,000 citizens were Gentiles.[64] Yet, to many Americans, the most concrete evidence of Mormon adaptation to the country's political values was participation in the nation's wars. Only two years after statehood, the Spanish American War affected Utahns. The year of 1898, wrote Springville historian Don Carlos Johnson, "was filled with military display and war alarms, and the patriotic feelings of our town folk," as young men departed for service in the war.[65] Richard Holzapfel noted that the brief war was significant for Utahns as it was the first time that a large number of the state's citizens participated in military action in common with the rest of the nation.[66] It did not go unnoticed that the number of Utah volunteers was twice that requested by the federal government. A reprise of the theme of patriotism came in 1917 with the country's entry into the First World War. Twenty-five thousand Utah citizens served in the conflict, and 665 of them died. Dean May observed, "The sacrifices to the war affirmed that Utahns were loyal and convinced many that she had integrated fully into the nation.[67]

Though young men who entered combat were the most visible sign of patriotism, entire Utah communities contributed to the eventual victory. Mary Chase Finley wrote that Springville women collected more than a thousand pounds of clothing and sewed additional garments for families in war torn areas.[68] Some women knit sweaters and mufflers for the soldiers, while others sewed hospital supplies. Backyards and vacant lots were cultivated to grow vegetables. Five hundred jars of jelly were sent to soldiers in hospitals in California. Many Springville citizens made personal sacrifices to buy "Liberty Loans" that contributed to funding the war effort.[69]

Following the war's end, Springville was part of Utah's notable contribution to feeding men, women and children who were suffering in Europe. Not long before his death in 1877, Brigham Young asked the Church's Relief Society to organize and implement a wheat storage program. He said, "I want the Sisters to have the wheat. They are the careful housewives. The men would speculate with

---

62. "Celebrate Opening of Springville Line," *Salt Lake Tribune*, 25 Jul 1915, 17.
63. Ibid.
64. May, *Utah: A People's History*, 172-3.
65. Johnson, *History of Springville*, 95.
66. Holzapfel, *History of Utah County*, 124 25.
67. Ibid.
68. Finley, *History of Springville*, 90.
69. Ibid.

it."[70] Relief Societies throughout Utah purchased wheat, grew wheat on their own fields and built their own granaries.[71] Wheat was donated to the needy in Utah and elsewhere, including survivors of the 1906 earthquake in San Francisco. In 1918, the Church reported that it granted the US government's request for all of the Relief Society's wheat to stave off famine in war torn Europe.[72] The Church's women delivered more than 200,000 bushels of wheat (12,000,000 pounds of grain) at a price set by the government. The five wards in Springville contributed 5000 bushels.[73] The Relief Society used the money received from the US government to continue charitable work.

Another global event, closely related to the war, was the outbreak of the "Spanish Flu." The lethal form of influenza, which killed 21,000,000 people worldwide in four months, first arrived in Utah in October 1918.[74] Most towns required citizens to wear gauze masks when they were outside their homes and banned all public gatherings.[75] When Church president Joseph F. Smith died in November 1918, only a handful of family members were allowed to attend the funeral. Five months later, the LDS Church's semi-annual conference was cancelled for the first time in its eighty-eight-year history.[76] Utah suffered a very high mortality rate compared to the national experience, possibly because of their large families, wrote Leonard Arrington.[77] According to Mary Chase Finley, nearly two-thirds of Springville citizens contracted the disease and many of them died.[78] Eighty-year-old Rosella Harrison died in April 1919, as the worst days of the epidemic were waning. Her death certificate lists senility, meaning general old age, and pulmonary disease as the causes of her death. Influenza possibly initiated or aggravated Rosella's demise.[79]

The deadly flu epidemic was over by October 1919, when a group that was making an automobile trek from Salt Lake City to the Grand Canyon made its first stop at the Harrison Hotel. Not long after, magazine publisher John Willy wrote about the visit with Beefsteak—"We met and dined with the veteran caterer George Harrison, known throughout this section as Beefsteak Harrison ... He is seventy–nine years old. Hale, active, and says he would rather cook than do any other kind of work."[80] Harrison served his diners a noonday meal that was a choice

70. Ibid., 91.

71. Jan, "Relief Society Wheat Project," LDS Women of God, 22 Aug 2008. Available online at www.ldswomenofgod.com/relief-society-wheat-project/.

72. Holzapfel, *History of Utah County*, 172.

73. Finley, *History of Springville*, 91.

74. Leonard J. Arrington, "The Influenza Epidemic of 1918-19 in Utah," *Utah Historical Quarterly* 58, no. 2, 165.

75. Holzapfel, *History of Utah County*, 179-80.

76. Pat Bagley, "Living History: During World War I, the Spanish flu claimed 3,000 Utah lives," *The Salt Lake Tribune*, 26 Jan 2013. Available online at http://archive.sltrib.com/story.php?ref=/sltrib/news/55659616-78/flu-utah-spanish-lake.html.csp.

77. Arrington, "Influenza Epidemic," 181.

78. Finley, *History of Springville*, 90.

79. Rosella Damon White Harrison, State of Utah—Death Certificate, #190447, filed 2 Apr 1919. Available online at https://axaemarchives.utah.gov/cgi-bin/indexesresults.cgi?RUNWHAT=IDXFILES&KEYPATH=IDX208420070155.

80. Roper, "Hotels Revisited."

Beefsteak Harrison ca. 1919-1920.
Courtesy Gerald R. Sherratt Library, Southern Utah University

of beefsteak or roast lamb accompanied by corn-on-the cob, mashed potatoes, string beans, sliced tomatoes, cantaloupe and bread and butter. Willy noted that the old gentleman is pleased when his guests come with a healthy appetite.

While the hotel and restaurant critics from Salt Lake City observed that their host was "hale and active," George was struggling with his health. Not long after the motorists departed, Harrison wrote a letter to Howard Driggs that expressed his decline—"first of all I would like to make clear to you the reason I did not serve dinner to your family the day they came to the hotel . . . It was 3:30 o'clock when they arrived. I had no help that day except a little girl 8 years old. I was so sick, I could not cut a steak to have saved my life. I have not been well since. I have been to the hospital, passed through a very critical operation, and have since buried my wife so you can see I have had some trouble, and I did not wish you to feel at all offended at me."[81]

The operation that George refers to in the letter occurred on February 15, 1919 and was related to prostate cancer that spread to his liver.[82] A statement from the Central Drug Store in Springville shows George purchasing "normal serum"

81. George "Beefsteak" Harrison to Howard R. Driggs, 28 Nov 1919, Howard R. Driggs collection, Gerald R. Sherratt Library, Southern Utah University.
82. George Harrison, State of Utah—Death Certificate, #2103953, filed 3 Feb 1921. Available online at https://archives.utah.gov/indexes/data/81448/2259285/2259285_0000919.jpg.

on two occasions after his surgery.[83] Normal serum was simply human or animal blood, and was a popular therapy for many diseases in the early twentieth century. The therapy was given orally or by injection, and, at best, caused no harm. George's drug store statement also shows that on November 15 he spent sixty-five cents on an unidentified prescription and $5.50 on cigars.[84]

After living on the third floor of the Harrison Hotel for thirty-four years, George moved back to his house. He knew that death was approaching. A census taker came to his door on January 13, 1920. George was living alone and listed his occupation as "none."[85] He probably spent more time enjoying afternoon cribbage games with his fellow quartet members—a practice they enjoyed for years.[86] George continued to serve as chorister for the Utah Indian War Veterans and, in August, led the singing at a reunion in Mount Pleasant.[87]

On February 1, 1921, George sent for the members of the Glee Club Quartet to come to his bedside at home. He asked the Wheeler brothers and Joseph Tuckett to sing his favorite song, which they did with tears in their eyes.[88] George shook hands with each of his friends and bid them goodbye. His death certificate shows that he died at 8 am the next morning. That afternoon, the *Deseret News* reported George Harrison's death, but few readers would have recognized the pioneer by his given name. The paper's front-page headline read, "Beefsteak Harrison, Utah Character is Called by Death."[89] His services two days later featured a chorus of seventy-five war veterans who rendered songs that the chorister often led them in at campfires and reunions.[90] George Harrison was buried next to Rosella, a few blocks from his house, in Springville's Historic Cemetery.

83. Copy in possession of the author.
84. Ibid.
85. 1920 US Federal Census, Springville Precinct, Springville City, ED 222, sheet 2A. Available online at https://www.ancestry.com/interactive/6061/4390822_01051/63180660 (subscription required).
86. Harrison, *History of the Harrison Hotel*, 11.
87. "Chorister of Indian War Veterans Buried."
88. Smith and Harrison, "History of George Harrison."
89. "Beefsteak Harrison, Utah Character is Called to Death," *Deseret News,* 2 Feb 1921, 1.
90. "Chorister of Indian War Veterans Buried."

Bibliography

Aird, Polly. "'You Nasty Apostates, Clear Out'; Reasons for Disaffection in the Late 1850s." *Journal of Mormon History* 30, no. 2.

———. *Mormon Convert, Mormon Defector: Scottish Immigrant in the American West, 1848-1861.* Norman, OK: The Arthur H. Clark Company, 2009.

Aird, Polly, Jeff Nichols and Will Bagley (eds.). *Playing with Shadows, Voices of Dissent in the Mormon West.* Norman, OK: The Arthur H. Clark Company, 2011.

Alexander, Thomas G. and Leonard J. Arrington. "Camp in the Sagebrush: Camp Floyd Utah, 1858-1861." *Utah Historical Quarterly* 34, no. 1.

Alford, Kenneth L and William P. MacKinnon. "What's In a Name? The Establishment of Camp Douglas," in Kenneth L. Alford, ed., *Civil War Saints.* Provo and Salt Lake City: RSC/Deseret Book, 2012.

Alleman, Glenn L. *The Legacy of the Springville Contractors.* Springville: Springville Historical Society, 2014.

Allen, Curtis R. "William Ashton: Handcart Pioneer and Five-Year Foot Soldier," 3n10. Available online at http://www.tellmystorytoo.com/pdf/handcartpioneerandfootsoldier2.pdf.

Allen, James B. and Glen Leonard. *The Story of the Latter-day Saint.* Salt Lake City: Deseret Book Company, 1976.

Alter, J. Cecil. *Jim Bridger.* Norman, OK: University of Oklahoma Press, 1962.

Altick, Richard D. *Victorian People and Ideas.* New York: W. W. Norton & Company, 1973.

The American Short-horn Herd Book 47, part 1, 326. Available online at https://babel.hathitrust.org/cgi/pt?id=coo.31924066239413;view=1up;seq=7.

Andrews, Elizabeth Wright. "Reminiscences," excerpts in Edward Martin Company, Mormon Pioneer Overland Travel database.

Available online at https://history.lds.org/overlandtravel/ sources/13352772994137629278.

Armstrong, Isobel. *Victorian Glassworlds.* New York: Oxford University Press, 2008.

"Arrival," in Edward Martin Company, Mormon Pioneer Overland Travel database. Available online at https://history.lds.org/overlandtravel/ sources/8748.

"Arrival of the Hand-Carts at Great Salt Lake City," in Edward Martin Company, Mormon Pioneer Overland Travel database. Available online at https://history.lds.org/overlandtravel/sources/8884.

Arrington, Leonard J. "Abundance From the Earth: The Beginnings of Commercial Mining in Utah." *Utah Historical Quarterly* 31, no. 3.

———. *Great Basin Kingdom, An Economic History of the Latter-Day Saints, 1830-1900.* Champaign: University of Illinois Press, 2005.

———. "The Influenza Epidemic of 1918-19 in Utah." *Utah Historical Quarterly* 58, no. 2.

Bagley, Will. "A Terror to Evil-Doers: Camp Douglas, Abraham Lincoln, and Utah's Civil War." *Utah Historical Quarterly* 80, no. 4.

———. "One Long Funeral March: A Revisionist's View of the Mormon Handcart Disasters." *Journal of Mormon History* 35, no. 1.

Bangerter, Howard K. and Cory W. Bangerter. *Tragedy and Triumph; Guide to the Rescue of the 1856 Willie and Martin Handcart Companies.* Provo: MC Printing, 2006.

Barney, Ronald O. *One Side by Himself: The Life and Times of Lewis Barney 1808-1894.* Logan: Utah State University Press, 2001.

Bell, Andrew McIlwaine. *Mosquito Soldiers, Malaria, Yellow Fever, and the Course of the American Civil War.* Baton Rouge: Louisiana State University Press, 2010.

Bigler, David L. *The Forgotten Kingdom; The Mormon Theocracy in the American West, 1847-1896.* Spokane: The Arthur H. Clark Company, 2005.

Bigler, David L. and Will Bagley. *The Mormon Rebellion: America's First Civil War, 1857-1858*. Norman, OK: University of Oklahoma Press, 2011.

Binder, William Lawrence Spicer. "Biography and journal," excerpts in Edward Martin Company (1856), Mormon Pioneer Overland Travel database. Available online at https://history.lds.org/overlandtravel/sources/44069.

"Biography of Alice Harrison (Kast) Catlin." On file at Daughters of Utah Pioneers Museum, Salt Lake City, Utah.

Bitton, Davis. "Mormon Polygamy: A Review Article." *Journal of Mormon History* 4.

Bond, John. "Handcarts West in '56," excerpts in William B. Hodgetts Company, Mormon Pioneer Overland Travel database. Available online at https://history.lds.org/overlandtravel/sources/5317.

Bone, Peter. "The Glass Industry in Manchester & Salford." *The Journal of the Glass Association* 8.

"Book A, Camp Floyd Mining District," Hickman Family Museum site, index available at http://hickmansfamily.homestead.com/campfloyd.html.

Boorstin, Daniel H. *The Americans*. New York: History Book Club, 2002 .

Brooks, Juanita. *The Mountain Meadows Massacre*. Norman, OK: University of Oklahoma Press, 1970.

Buchanan, Dorothy J. "Life on the Road; Reminiscences of a Drummer." *Utah Historical Quarterly* 34, no. 1.

Burton, Sir Richard F. *The City of Saints; Among the Mormons and Across; the Rocky Mountains to California*. Torrington, WY: The Narrative Press, 2003.

Business Directory of Salt Lake City, Utah, 1909-1910. Np, nd. Available online at https://babel.hathitrust.org/cgi/pt?id=hvd.hx4j83;view=1up;seq=179.

Camm, Elizabeth Whittear [Sermon]. "Reminiscence," in Edward Martin Company (1856), Mormon Pioneer Overland Travel database. Available online at https://history.lds.org/overlandtravel/sources/7526/.

Campbell, Eugene E. and Campbell, Bruce L. "Divorce among Mormon Polygamists: Extent and Explanations." *Utah Historical Quarterly* 46, no. 1.

Carson, Lynn R. *The Tintic War and the deaths of George and Washington Carson.* Salt Lake City: George Carson-Ann Hough Family Organization, 1979. Available online at https://familysearch.org/photos/artifacts/1921181.

Carter, D. Robert. *Founding Fort Utah: Provo's Native Inhabitants, Early Explorers, and First Year of Settlement.* Provo: Provo City Corporation, 2003.

———. *From Fort to Village; Provo. Utah, 1850-1854.* Provo: Provo City Corporation, 2008.

Carter, Lyndia McDowell. "Handcarts Across Iowa: Trial Runs for the Willie, Haven, and Martin Handcart Companies." *The Annals of Iowa* 65, nos. 2 & 3.

———. "The Mormon Handcart Companies." *Overland Journal* 13, no. 1.

Chalfant, William Y. *Cheyennes and Horse Soldiers: The 1857 Expedition and the Battle of Solomon's Fork.* Norman, OK: University of Oklahoma Press, 1989.

Chislett, John, "Narrative," in T. B. H. Stenhouse, *The Rocky Mountain Saints: A Full and Complete History of the Mormons.* New York: D. Appleton and Company, 1873.

Christy, Howard A. "Weather, Disaster, and Responsibility: An Essay on the Willie and Martin Handcart Story." *BYU Studies* 37, no. 1.

Clark, Louisa Mellor. "Autobiography of Louisa Mellor Clark," *Liverpool to Boston* (aboard the *Horizon*), Mormon Migration database. Available online at https://mormonmigration.lib.byu.edu.

———. "History of Louisa Mellor Clark," excerpts in Edward Martin Company, Mormon Pioneer Overland Travel database. Available online at https://history.lds.org/overlandtravel/sources/18557.

———. "A Record Given at Spring Lake," excerpts in Edward Martin Company, Mormon Pioneer Overland Travel database. Available online at https://history.lds.org/overlandtravel/sources/1855

Clegg, Margaret A. "Margaret A. Clegg's Statement," in Edward Martin Company, Mormon Pioneer Overland Travel database. Available online at https://history.lds.org/overlandtravel/sources/15815.

Coakley, Robert B. *The Role of Federal Military Forces in Domestic Disorders, 1789-1878.* Washington, D.C.: Center of Military History, U.S. Army, 1988.

Coleman, Daniel. "Seth Ward, Frontier Trader, 1820-1903," Missouri Valley Special Collections, available online at http://www.kchistory.org/u?/Biographies,156.

Cook, Lyndon W., ed. *Aaron Johnson Correspondence.* Orem: Center for Research of Mormon Origins, 1990.

Cornwall, Rebecca and Leonard J. Arrington. *Rescue of the 1856 Handcart Companies.* Provo: Charles Redd Center for Western Studies, 1982.

Culmer, H. L. A., ed. *Utah Directory and Gazetteer for 1868.* Salt Lake City: J. C. Graham & Co.

Culmer, Henry L. A., ed. *Utah Directory and Gazetteer for 1879-80.* Salt Lake City: J. C. Graham & Co., 1879. Available online at https://archive.org/stream/utahdirectorygaz00culmrich#page/n5/mode/2up.

Curtis, Edward S., *The North American Indian*, vol. 3, The University Press, Cambridge, Massachusetts, 1908. Available online at curtis.library.northwestern.edu.

Davis, Sam Post, ed. *The History of Nevada*, Volume I (Reno/Los Angeles: The Elms Publishing Co., 1913), 158. Available online at https://archive.org/stream/historyofnevada01davirich.

Defa, Dennis R. "The Goshute Indians of Utah," in *A History of Utah's Native Americans*, Utah History to Go. Available online at http://historytogo.utah.gov/people/ethnic_cultures/the_history_of_utahs_american_indians/chapter3.html.

DeMallie, Raymond J., "Sioux Until 1850," in R. J. DeMallie, ed. *Handbook of North American Indians: Plains*, vol. 13, part 2. Washington D. C.: Government Printing Office, 2001.

Di Certo, Joseph J. *The Saga of the Pony Express.* Missoula, MT: Mountain Press Publishing Company, 2002.

Dickens, Charles. *Hard Times*. New York: Signet Classics, 2008.

Driggs, Howard R. "Beefsteak was a Handcart Boy." *Millennial Star* 120, no. 7.

————. *George, the Handcart Boy*, Southern Utah University Press, 2012.

————. "Handcart Boy," *The Children's Friend*, Jul 1944-Jan 1945.

————. "Handcart Boy (First Draft)," box 17, folder 9, p. 4, Howard R. Driggs collection, Gerald R. Sherratt Library, Southern Utah University.

————. Handwritten notes of interview with George (Beefsteak) Harrison," Howard R. Driggs collection, box 17, folder 9, Gerald Sherratt Library, Southern Utah University.

————. "Theirs Was the Handcart Way to Zion," *The Instructor* 91 (July 1956).

Dunn, Richard J. "Dickens and the Mormons." *BYU Studies* 8, no. 3.

"Eastbound To Wahsatch; Union Pacific's Route Through Weber and Echo Canyons," UtahRails.net. Available online at http://utahrails.net/articles/weber-echo.php.

1891 History of Harrison County Iowa, Find a Grave website, Deborah Jane Bushnell Blair Chapman available online at https://www.findagrave.com/cgi-bin/fg.cgi?page=gr&GRid=87364164.

Esshom, Frank. *Pioneers and Prominent Men of Utah*. Salt Lake City: Utah Pioneers Book Publishing Company, 1912. Available online at https://archive.org/details/pioneersprominen00esshrich.

Fales, Susan L. "Artisans, Millhands, and Laborers: The Mormons of Leeds and Their Nonconformist Neighbors," in Richard L. Jensen and Malcolm R. Thorp, eds., _Mormons in Early Victorian Britain. Salt Lake City: University of Utah Press, 1989.

Farmer, Jared. *On Zion's Mount; Mormons, Indians, and the American Landscape*. Cambridge: Harvard University Press, 2008.

Faux, Steven F. "Faint Footsteps of 1856-57 Retraced: The Location of the Iowa Mormon Handcart Route," *The Annals of Iowa*, 65, no. 2.

Finley, Mary J. Chase. *A History of Springville*. Springville, UT: Art City Publishing, 1992.

"Fox, a Champion Puller," William R. Palmer Collection, Gerald R. Sherratt Library, Southern Utah University.

Fradkin, Philip L. *Stagecoach: Wells Fargo and the American West*. New York: Free Press, 2002.

Furniss, Norman F. *The Mormon Conflict, 1850-1859*. New Haven, CT: Yale University Press, 1966.

Gallup, Luke William. "Luke William Gallup, Reminiscences and Diary 1842 May – 1891 March," p. 196, MS 8402, found online at LDS Church History Library, Salt Lake City. Available online at https://dcms.lds.org/delivery/DeliveryManagerServlet?dps_pid=IE1754642.

Gowans, Fred R. and Eugene E. Campbell. *Fort Bridger: Island in the Wilderness*. Provo, UT: Brigham Young University Press, 1975.

Grant, Jedediah M. "Discourse," *Deseret News* [Weekly], 12 Nov. 1856, in Edward Martin Company, Mormon Pioneer Overland Travel database. Available online at https://history.lds.org/overlandtravel/sources/8827.

Griggs, Karen Ann. "Handcarts Going East." *Journal of Mormon History* 35, no. 2.

Hafen, Leroy R. *The Overland Mail, 1849-1869*. Norman, OK: University of Oklahoma Press, 2004.

Hafen, LeRoy R. and Ann W. Hafen. *Mormon Resistance*. Lincoln, NE: Bison Books, 2005.

——— . *Handcarts to Zion*. Lincoln, NE: Bison Books, 1992

Hamilton, Henry. "Journal of Henry Hamilton," *Liverpool to Boston* (aboard the *Horizon*), Mormon Migration database. Available online at https://mormonmigration.lib.byu.edu.

Hammond, Otis G., ed. *The Utah Expedition, 1857-1858; Letters of Jesse A. Gove, 10th Inf., U.S.A.* Concord, NH: New Hampshire Historical Society, 1928.

Hanks, Ephraim. "Ephraim K. Hanks' Narrative." Edward Martin Company, Mormon Pioneer Overland Travel database. Available online at https://history.lds.org/overlandtravel/sources/97569.

Harris, Jan G. "Mormons in Victorian Manchester." *BYU Studies* 27, no. 1.

Harrison, Aaron. "Membership of The Church of Jesus Christ of Latter-day Saints, 1830-1848," Ancestry database. Available online at http://ancstry.me/2mnmGd0 (subscription required).

———— .Register of Enlistments, United States Army, NARA microfilm 233, roll 25, (1856 series) line 311.

Harrison, Ada Bissell, "Biography of Hannah Ellis Harrison," Camp Aaron Johnson, DUP of Utah County, Springville, Utah.

Harrison, Bertrand F. "The History of The Harrison Hotel, Springville Utah." Special Collections, Harold B. Lee Library, Brigham Young University, Provo, UT.

Harrison, Bertrand Kent, "Remembrances of the Harrison Hotel of Springville, Utah," August, 2004. Copy in possession of author.

Harrison, George. "Commissioner of Indian War Records, Indian War Service Affidavits, 1909-1919," Series 2217, box 2, folder 2, Utah State Archives. Available online at http://images.archives.utah.gov/cdm/compoundobject/collection/2217/id/3583/rec/1.

———— . George "Beefsteak" Harrison to Howard R. Driggs, 28 Nov 1919, Howard R. Driggs collection, box 17, fld 9, Gerald R. Sherratt Library, Southern Utah University.

———— . "The Story of the Vented Brand," Howard R. Driggs collection, box 17, fld 9, Gerald R. Sherratt Library, Southern Utah University.

Harrison, George William. "Autobiography" 1951. Original in possession of author.

Harrison, Martha Fereday. "Autobiography" (ca. 1980). On file at Springville Pioneer Museum, Springville, Utah.

Harrison, Myrtle. "Harrison Hotel," in Kate B. Carter, comp., *Heart Throbs of the West*, vol. 5. Salt Lake City: Daughters of Utah Pioneers, 1944.

Harrison, William. "Utah, Veterans with Federal Service Buried in Utah, Territorial to 1966." FamilySearch database. Available online at https://familysearch.org/ark:/61903/3:1:S3HT-69D7-RS?mode=g&cc=1542862.

———. "Utah Wills and Probate Records, 1800-1945." Probate Estate Files, Case No. 249-267. Ancestry database. Available online at http://ancstry.me/2mCEOV4.

Hartley, William G. "'Down and Back' Wagon Trains: Bringing the Saints to Utah in 1861." *The Ensign* (Sep 1985). Available online at https://www.lds.org/ensign/1985/09/.

———. "Mormons and Early Iowa History (1838 to 1858): Eight Distinct Connections." *Annals of Iowa* 59, no. 3.

———. "The Place of Mormon Handcart Companies in America's Westward Migration Story." *Annals of Iowa* 65, nos. 2 & 3.

Haven, Jesse. "Haven, Jesse, to Brigham Young, October 9, 1856, Fort Laramie," in Edward Martin Company, Mormon Pioneer Overland database. Available online at https://history.lds.org/overlandtravel/sources/86089.

———. "Journals, 1852-1892, vols. 4-5.," excerpts in Edward Martin Company (1856), Mormon Pioneer Overland Travel database. Available online at https://history.lds.org/overlandtravel/sources/5319/.

Hedges, Charles, comp. *Speeches of Benjamin Harrison, twenty-third president of the United States; a complete collection of his public addresses from February, 1888, to February, 1892.* New York: United States Book Company, 1892. Available online at https://archive.org/details/speechesofbenjam00harrrich.

Henry, Guy V. *Military Record of Civilian Appointments in the United States Army,* vol. 1. New York: D. Van Nostrand, 1873. Available online at https://archive.org/details/cu31924092906134.

"History of Milan Packard, Utah," Online Utah.com. Available online at http://www.onlineutah.com/packard_milan_history.shtml.

"History of the Sears Catalogue," Sears Archives. Available online at http://www.searsarchives.com/catalogs/history.htm.

Hogenson, Shirley Carson, comp. *Tryphena Ursula Goddard—Second Wife of William Duff Carson, Her Ancestors and Progenitors*. Salt Lake City: The George Carson and Anna Hough Family Organization, 1981.

Hollander, Stanley. "Nineteenth Century Anti-Drummer Legislation in the United States." *The Business History Review* 38, no. 4.

Holzapfel, Richard Neitzel. *A History of Utah County*. Salt Lake City: Utah State Historical Society, 1999.

Honey, Mark E. "A Dockside View of Ellsworth, When Lumber was King," *The Ellsworth American*. No longer available online.

Horizon ship register, roster of Edward Martin company. *Liverpool to Boston* (aboard the *Horizon*). Mormon Migration database. Available online at https://mormonmigration.lib.byu.edu.

Hubbard, George U. "Abraham Lincoln As Seen By The Mormons." *Utah Historical Quarterly* 31, no. 2.

Huff, Emma N., comp. *Memories That Live, Utah County Centennial History*. Np: Daughters of Utah Pioneers of Utah County, 1947.

Hyde, George. *Red Cloud's Folk, A History of the Oglala Sioux Indians*. Norman: OK, Oklahoma University Press, 1987.

———. *Spotted Tail's Folk: A History of the Brule Sioux*. Norman, OK: University of Oklahoma Press, 1987.

Isaac A. Canfield Emigrating Company, Journal, 1862 July-Oct., Isaac A. Canfield Company, 1862, Mormon Pioneer Overland Travel database. Available online at https://history.lds.org/overlandtravel/sources/4937.

Jan. "Relief Society Wheat Project," LDS Women of God, 22 Aug 2008. Available online at www.ldswomenofgod.com/relief-society-wheat-project/.

Jaques, John. "[Diary]," excerpts in Edward Martin Company, Mormon Pioneer Overland Travel database. Available online at https://history.lds.org/overlandtravel/sources/7540.

———— . "Life History of John Jaques," *Liverpool to Boston* (aboard the *Horizon*). Mormon Migration database. Available online at https:// mormonmigration.lib.byu.edu.

Jensen, Richard L. "Names of Persons and Sureties Indebted to the Perpetual Emigrating Fund Company, 1850 to 1877." *Mormon Historical Studies* 1, no. 2.

Johnson, Alan P. *Aaron Johnson; Faithful Steward.* Salt Lake City: Publisher's Press, 1991.

Johnson, Don Carlos. *History of Springville.* Springville: Art City Publishing, 2003.

Johnson, Kent D. and Nelson W. Knight. "Historic Resources of Springville City." National Register of Historic Places, Multiple Property Documentation Form, National Park Service, 1997. Available online at https://npgallery.nps.gov/pdfhost/docs/NRHP/Text/64500673. pdf.

Jones, Albert. "Address, 4 Oct. 1906, in Handcart Veterans Association, Scrapbook, 1906-1914," excerpts in Edward Martin Company (1856), Mormon Pioneer Overland Travel database. Available online at https://history.lds.org/overlandtravel/sources/20745/.

———— . "Autobiography," excerpts in Edward Martin Company, Mormon Pioneer Overland Travel database. Available online at https://history. lds.org/overlandtravel/sources/7543.

Jones, Daniel W. *40 Years Among the Indians.* Springville: Council Press, 2004.

Jones, Samuel S. "[Reminiscences]," excerpts in Edward Martin company, Mormon Pioneer Overland Travel database. Available online at https://history.lds.org/overlandtravel/sources/15475.

Jorgenson, Lynne Watkins. "The Mormon Handcart Disaster: The London Participants." *Journal of Mormon History* 21, no. 2.

Keys, David. "Revealed: Industrial Revolution was powered by child slaves," *The Independent*, Aug. 1, 2010. Available online at http://www.independent. co.uk/news/uk/home-news/revealed-industrial-revolution-was-powered-by-child-slaves-2041227.html.

Kingford, Elizabeth Horrocks Jackson. "[Reminiscences]," excerpts in Edward Martin Company, Mormon Pioneer Overland Travel database. Available online at https://history.lds.org/overlandtravel/sources/7550.

Larson, Gustive O. *The Americanization of Utah for Statehood*. San Marino, CA: The Huntington Library, Publishers Press, 1971.

———. "The Mormon Reformation." *Utah Historical Quarterly* 26, no. 1.

———. *Prelude to the Kingdom*. Boston: Marshall Jones Company, 1947.

"Latest from Utah. Death of an Eminent Mormon Saint. Hand-Cart Trains in a Wretched Condition," *New York Semi-Weekly Tribune*, 27 Feb. 1857, in Edward Martin Company, Mormon Pioneer Overland Travel database. Available online at https://history.lds.org/overlandtravel/sources/15915.

LDS Church, "Peace and Violence among 19th-Century Latter-day Saints," Gospel Topics Essays, available online at www.lds.org/topics/peace-and-violence-among-19th-century-latter-day-saints.

LeCheminant, Wilford Hill. "A Crisis Averted? General Harney and the Change in Command of the Utah Expedition." *Utah Historical Quarterly* 51, no. 1.

Lively, Robert L. Jr. "Some Sociological Reflections on the Nineteenth-Century British Mission," in Richard L. Jensen and Malcolm R. Thorp, eds. *Mormons in Early Victorian Britain*. Salt Lake City: University of Utah Press, 1989.

Long, Bill. "Drummers, Canvassers, Knockers, et. al.," archived at http://archive.is/KdZBx (original article no longer available).

Lyman, Edward Leo. *The Overland Journey From Utah to California*. Reno: University of Nevada Press, 2004.

Lyman, Paul D. *The Willie Handcart Company*. Provo: BYU Studies, 2006.

MacKinnon, William P. *At Sword's Point, Part 1, A Documentary History of the Utah War to 1858*. Norman, OK: The Arthur H. Clark Company, 2008.

———. "Utah's Civil War(s): Linkages and Connections." *Utah Historical Quarterly* 80, no. 4.

Madsen, Betty M. and Brigham D. Madsen. *North to Montana; Jehus, Bullwhackers, and Mule Skinners on the Montana Trail.* Logan, UT: Utah State University Press, 1998.

Madsen, Brigham D. *Glory Hunter: A Biography of Patrick Edward Connor.* Salt Lake City: University of Utah Press, 1990.

Madsen, Brigham D. *The Northern Shoshoni.* Caldwell, ID: The Caxton Printers, Ltd., 1980.

Matsumura, Takao. *The Labour Aristocracy Revisited; The Victorian Flint Glass Makers, 1850-1880.* Manchester, UK: Manchester University Press, 1983.

Mattes, Merrill J. "Fort Laramie, Guardian of the Oregon Trail." *Annals of Wyoming* 17, no. 1.

———. "The Sutler's Store at Fort Laramie." *Annals of Wyoming* 18, no. 2.

May, Dean L. "Rites of Passage: The Gathering as Cultural Credo." *Journal of Mormon History* 29, no. 1.

———. *Utah: A People's History.* Salt Lake City: University of Utah Press, 1987.

Maycock, Howard C. "A History of Springville Banking Company, Predecessor of Central Bank and Trust Company." Np, 1985. Available at the Springville Historical Society, Springville, Utah.

McBride, Heber Robert. "Autobiography of Heber Robert McBride," *Liverpool to Boston* (aboard the *Horizon*), Mormon Migration database. Available online at https://mormonmigration.lib.byu.edu.

McChristian, Douglas C. *Fort Laramie, Military Bastion of the High Plains.* Norman, OK: The Arthur H. Clark Company, 2008.

Metcalf, Warren "A Precarious Balance: The Northern Utes and the Black Hawk War." *Utah Historical Quarterly* 57, no. 1.

Moorman, Donald R. with Gene Sessions. *Camp Floyd and the Mormons: The Utah War.* Salt Lake City: The University of Utah Press, 1992.

"Mormon Emigrant Companies." Available online at http://user.xmission.com/~nelsonb/ship_list.htm.

"Mormon Temple Endowment," Temples of the Church of Jesus Christ of Latter-day Saints, available online at http://www.ldschurchtemples.com/mormon/endowment/.

National Register of Historic Places Inventory – Nomination form for Wood-Harrison House, 310 South 300 West, Springville, Utah, 1982. Available online at https://npgallery.nps.gov/pdfhost/docs/NRHP/Text/83003198.pdf.

Neilson, Reid L. *Exhibiting Mormonism: The Latter-day Saints and the 1893 Chicago World's Fair*. New York: Oxford University Press, 2011.

Nielson, Roger B. *Roll Call at Old Camp Floyd*. Springville, UT: by the author, 2006.

———. *Utah's Black Hawk War Veterans*. Springville, UT: by the author, 2009.

"Old Ordnance Survey Maps." Ancoats (North), published in 1848. Ancoats, published in 1849. Reproductions of these maps are published by Alan Godfrey Maps, Leadgate, Consett, DH8 7PW, alangodfreymaps.co.uk.

"On the Road, 1885-1897," The American Menu. Available online at http://www.theamericanmenu.com/2011/03/on-road.html.

Openshaw, Samuel. "Autobiography of Samuel Openshaw," *Liverpool to Boston* (aboard the *Horizon*), Mormon Migration database. Available online at https://mormonmigration.lib.byu.edu.

"Original Land Titles in Utah Territory." Utah Department of Administrative Services, Division of Archives and Records Service. Available online at http://archives.utah.gov/research/guides/land-original-title.htm.

Orton, Chad M. "The Martin Handcart Company at the Sweetwater: Another Look." *BYU Studies* 45, no. 3.

Palmer, William R. "Early Day Trading with the Nevada Mining Camps." *Utah Historical Quarterly* 26, no. 4.

Parshall, Ardis E. "'Pursue, Retake & Punish': The 1857 Santa Clara Ambush." *Utah Historical Quarterly* 73, no. 1.

"Peregrine White," Pilgrim Hall Museum, Plymouth, Massachusetts. Available online at http://www.pilgrimhallmuseum.org/peregrine_white.htm.

Peterson, John Alton, *Utah's Black Hawk War*. Salt Lake City: University of Utah Press, 1998.

Peterson, Paul H. "The Mormon Reformation of 1856-1857." *Journal of Mormon History* 15.

Petree, Sandra Ailey, ed., *Recollections of Past Days; The Autobiography of Patience Loader Rozsa Archer*. Logan: Utah State University Press, 2006.

Pfeiffer, David A. "Bridging the Mississippi: The Railroads and Steamboats Clash at the Rock Island Bridge." *Prologue Magazine* 36, no. 2.

Poll, Richard D. "The Move South." *BYU Studies* 29. no. 4.

Reese, James. "James Reese to Bro. Taylor, 29 July 1856." Company Unknown (1856), Mormon Pioneer Overland Travel database. Available online at https://history.lds.org/overlandtravel/sources/8716.

Reeve, W. Paul. *Making Space on the Western Frontier; Mormons, Miners and Southern Paiutes*. Urbana: University of Illinois Press, 2006.

———. *Religion of a Different Color: Race and the Mormon Struggle for Whiteness*. New York: Oxford University Press, 2015.

"Remarks," *Deseret News* [Weekly], 10 Dec. 1856, in Edward Martin Company, Mormon Pioneer Overland Travel database. Available online at https://history.lds.org/overlandtravel/sources/8543.

Review of "George, the Handcart Boy," *The Instructor* 87, no. 11, 338-39. Available online at https://archive.org/stream/instructor8711dese.

Richards, Franklin D. and Daniel Spencer, "Journey from Florence to G. S. L. City," in Edward Martin Company, Mormon Pioneer Overland Travel database. Available online at https://history.lds.org/overlandtravel/sources/8762.

Rogerson, Josiah. "Autobiographical Sketch of Josiah Rogerson," *Liverpool to Boston* (aboard the *Horizon*), Mormon Migration database. Available online at https://mormonmigration.lib.byu.edu.

Roland, Charles P. *Albert Sidney Johnston, Soldier of Three Republics.* Lexington: KY, University Press of Kentucky, 2001.

Roper, Roger V. "Hotels Revisited, Retracing a 1919 Utah Road Trip." *Utah Preservation* 2. Available online at https://collections.lib.utah.edu/details?id=418888&q=*&page=1&rows=200&fd=title_t%2Csetname_s%2Ctype_t&sort=&gallery=&facet_setname_s=dha_hpp.

Sanborn Fire Insurance Map of Springville, Utah, 1890.. Digitized by the J. Willard Marriott Library, University of Utah. Available online at https://collections.lib.utah.edu/details?id=320874.

Sessions, Gene A. *Mormon Thunder: A Documentary History of Jedediah Morgan Grant.* Salt Lake City: Greg Kofford Books, 2008.

Settle, Raymond W. and Mary Lund. *Saddles & Spurs; The Pony Express Saga.* Lincoln, NE: University of Nebraska Press, 1955.

Smith, Don H. "Leadership, Planning and Management of the 1856 Mormon Handcart Emigration." *Annals of Iowa* 65, nos. 2 & 3.

Smith, Mae Harrison and Ada Bissell Harrison. "George 'Beefsteak' Harrison," in Kate B. Carter, comp., *Treasures of Pioneer History*, vol. 2. Salt Lake City: Daughters of Utah Pioneers, 1953.

Smith, May Harrison, "History of Rosella Damon White Harrison." Aaron Johnson Camp, Daughters of Utah Pioneers of Utah County, Springville, Utah.

Southwell, John William Southwell. "Autobiography of John William Southwell," in *Liverpool to Boston* (aboard the *Horizon*), Mormon Migration database. Available online at https://mormonmigration.lib.byu.edu.

Spears, Timothy B. *100 Years on the Road: The Traveling Salesman in American Culture.* New Haven, CT: Yale University Press, 1995.

Statistical Report on Sickness and Mortality in the Army of the United States, January 1855 to January 1869. Washington, D. C.: George W. Bowman, 1860.

Stegner, Wallace. *The Gathering of Zion, The Story of the Mormon Trail*. Lincoln, NE: University of Nebraska Press, 1992.

———. *Mormon Country*. Lincoln, NE: University of Nebraska Press, 2003.

Stewart, Myrl Storrs. "Biography of Hannah Ellis Harrison," July 1957, Daughters of the Utah Pioneers Camp 49, South Company, Weber County.

———. "Biography of Rosella Arvilla Harrison Storrs," Daughters of the Utah Pioneers Museum, Salt Lake City, Utah.

———. "Biography of Rosella Damon White Harrison." Daughters of the Utah Pioneers Camp 49, Weber County, Utah.

———. "Biography of William Harrison," July 1957, Daughters of the Utah Pioneers Camp 49, South Company, Weber County.

"The Story of the Pony Express and the Paiute War/High Danger in the Desert," WesternHistory. No longer available online.

Stowers, Robert and John M. Ellis, eds. "Charles A. Scott's Diary of the Utah Expedition, 1857-1861." *Utah History Quarterly* 28, no. 2.

Swanson, Clifford L. *The Sixth United States Infantry, 1855 to Reconstruction*. Jefferson, NC: McFarland & Company, Inc., 2001.

Taylor, John. "*The Mormon* on Handcart Emigration, John Taylor, December 1, 1855" in Sandra Ailey Petree, ed., *Recollections of Past Days; The Autobiography of Patience Loader Rozsa Archer*. Logan: Utah State University Press, 2006.

Taylor, Philip A. M. "Why Did the British Mormons Emigrate," *Utah Historical Quarterly* 22, no. 3.

"The Thiede's and Allied Families of North Dakota: Information about Thomas M. Blakely," Gencalogy.com. Available online at http://www.gencalogy.com/ftm/t/h/i/Kenneth-Thiede/WEBSITE-0001/UHP-0040.html.

Thompson, E. P. *The Making of the English Working Class*. New York: Vintage Books, 1966.

Tingey, C. S. *Record of Marks and Brands for the State of Utah: Embracing All Marks and Brands Recorded to June 1st, 1901*. Np, [1901]). Available online at https://archive.org/details/recordofmarksbra00tingrich.

Tullidge, Edward W. *Tullidge's Quarterly Magazine* 3 (1883), 246. Available online at https://archive.org/details/tullidge1.

Turner, John G. *Brigham Young, Pioneer Prophet*. The Belknap Press of the Harvard University Press, 2012.

Twain, Mark. *Roughing It*. Oakland: University of California Press, 1995.

Unruh, John D. *The Plains Across*. Urbana and Chicago: University of Illinois Press, 1993.

Utah and Pleasant Valley Railroad section of "Utah Railroads" from *Our Pioneer Heritage*, vol. 10 (Salt Lake City: Daughters of the Utah Pioneers, 1967), 137-192. Available online at UtahRails.net, http://utahrails.net/utahrails/utah-railroads-dup.php

Utah Gazetteer of 1892-93. Salt Lake City: Stenhouse and Co./Salt Lake Litho Company. Available online at https://archive.org/details/utahgazetteer18900stenrich.

Utah State Gazetteer and Business Directory, 1903-1904, vol. 2. Salt Lake City: R. L. Polk and Co., 1903. Available online at https://babel.hathitrust.org/cgi/pt?id=njp.32101074870112;view=1up;seq=33.

Utah State Gazetteer, 1918-1919. Salt Lake City: R. L. Polk & Co., 1918.

Varley, James F. *Brigham and the Brigadier*. Tucson: Westernlore Press, 1989.

Volf, William. "Mormon Polygamy in the Nineteenth Century: The Practice of the Principle in Reality." *Nebraska Anthropologist* 15. Available online at http://digitalcommons.unl.edu/nebanthro/126.

Walker, Ronald W. "Buchanan, Popular Sovereignty, and the Mormons: The Election of 1856." *Utah Historical Quarterly* 81, no. 2.

———. "Toward a Reconstruction of Mormon and Indian Relations, 1847-1877." *BYU Studies* 29, no. 4.

Wallace, Dillon. *Saddle and Camp in the Rockies.* New York: Outing Publishing Company, 1911.

Weight, Fredrick. "A Short History of the Life Of Fredrick Weight By Himself," available online at http://weightfamily.net/FamHist/Pioneers/weight/

Wheeler, Mary L. "Biography of David Wheeler." Feb. 3, 1930. Aaron Johnson Camp, Daughters of Utah Pioneers of Utah County, Springville, Utah.

White, Everett. Everett White (Romney, VA) to Rosella Damon White Russell, 16 Nov 1861. Original in possession of Barbara Lee, Springville, Utah.

———. Everett White (Sister's Ferry, GA) letter to Rosella Damon White, January 30, 1865. Original in possession of Barbara Lee, Springville, Utah.

White, Thomas and Samuel White. *Ancestral Chronological Record of the William White Family from 1607 to 1895.* Concord, NH: Republican Press Association, 1895. Available online at https://archive.org/details/ancestralchrono00whitgoog.

Whitney, Orson Ferguson. *Popular History of Utah.* Salt Lake City: George Q. Cannon & Sons, 1904. Available online at https://archive.org/details/popularhistoryof00byuwhit.

Woodger, Mary Jane. "Abraham Lincoln and the Mormons," in Kenneth L. Alford, ed., *Civil War Saints.* Provo and Salt Lake City: RSC/Deseret Book, 2012.

Woods, Fred. "Iowa City Bound: Mormon Migration by Sail and Rail, 1856-1857." *Annals of Iowa* 65, nos. 2 & 3.

Young, Brigham. "Present and Former Persecutions of the Saints," October 8, 1857, in *Journal of Discourses*, vol. 5. London: Asa Calkin, 1858. Available online at http://scriptures.byu.edu/.